YOUTH WITHOUT WORK

THREE COUNTRIES APPROACH THE PROBLEM

Report by Shirley Williams
and Other Experts

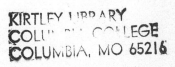
ORGANISATION FOR ECONOMIC CO-OPERATION AND DEVELOPMENT

The Organisation for Economic Co-operation and Development (OECD) was set up under a Convention signed in Paris on 14th December 1960, which provides that the OECD
shall promote policies designed:
— to achieve the highest sustainable economic growth and employment and a rising
    standard of living in Member countries, while maintaining financial stability, and
    thus to contribute to the development of the world economy;
— to contribute to sound economic expansion in Member as well as non-member
    countries in the process of economic development;
— to contribute to the expansion of world trade on a multilateral, non-discriminatory
    basis in accordance with international obligations.
The Members of OECD are Australia, Austria, Belgium, Canada, Denmark, Finland,
France, the Federal Republic of Germany, Greece, Iceland, Ireland, Italy, Japan, Lux-
embourg, the Netherlands, New Zealand, Norway, Portugal, Spain, Sweden, Switzerland,
Turkey, the United Kingdom and the United States.

THE OPINION EXPRESSED AND ARGUMENTS EMPLOYED
IN THIS PUBLICATION ARE THE RESPONSIBILITY OF THE AUTHORS AND
DO NOT NECESSARILY REPRESENT THOSE OF THE OECD

Publié en français sous le titre :

LES JEUNES SANS EMPLOI
Trois stratégies

*
* *

ALSO AVAILABLE

YOUTH UNEMPLOYMENT - Vol. I
A Report on the High Level Conference - 15th-16th December 1977
(October 1978)
(81 78 04 1) ISBN 92-64-11815-2
140 pp. .... US$10.00 £4.90 F40,00

YOUTH UNEMPLOYMENT - Vol. II
Inventory of measures concerning the employment and unemployment
of young people
(October 1978)
(81 78 02 1) ISBN 92-64-11806-3
184 pp. .... US$8.50 £4.20 F34,00

YOUTH UNEMPLOYMENT.
The Causes and Consequences (March 1981)
(81 80 05 1) ISBN 92-64-12137-4
136 pp. ....US$8.00 £3.20 F32,00

Prices charged at the OECD Publications Office.

THE OECD CATALOGUE OF PUBLICATIONS and supplements will be sent free of charge
on request addressed either to OECD Publications Office,
2, rue André-Pascal, 75775 PARIS CEDEX 16, or to the OECD Sales Agent in your country.

CONTENTS

Part Four

A REVIEW OF YOUTH EMPLOYMENT POLICIES IN THE UNITED STATES

Part Five

SUMMARY RECORD OF THE REVIEW MEETING

PREFACE

The OECD programme on youth employment was established following the High Level Conference on Youth Unemployment held at the Organisation's headquarters in Paris in December 1977. The programme of work has included research, evaluation and description of many facets of youth labour market problems: the creation of jobs, the transition from school to work, the role of education and training, the malfunctioning of the labour market, and the question of minimum wages - to mention but a few.

This publication is the result of another part of the programme. In order to better understand national policies and problems, a series of examinations of policies in selected countries has been undertaken. This report presents the results of the first three national policy reviews of Denmark, the Federal Republic of Germany and the United States of America.

The reviews have been undertaken by groups of distinguished independent examiners. The composition of each review team reflects a mix of political and administrative experience in the field of education and labour market policy, together with academic labour market expertise. Each review has been chaired by The Rt. Hon. Mrs. Shirley Williams, P.C., formerly Secretary of State for Education and Science in the United Kingdom.

This report brings together their studies, which were considered at a special meeting held at the Organisation's headquarters in Paris on 4-5 December 1980. The meeting was chaired on the opening day by Mr. Gene Fitzgerald, then the Irish Minister of Labour and the Public Service (and latterly the Irish Minister of Finance) and on the second day by Mr. Svend Auken, the Danish Minister of Labour.

The first part of the volume consists of a report by Mrs. Williams in which she presents her own conclusions from the exercise on the broader social and economic issues as they relate to problems of youth employment and unemployment. This is followed by the three country reviews prepared by the review teams. The views expressed in Mrs. Williams' report and in the country reviews are those of their authors and do not commit either the Organisation or the national authorities concerned in any way. The final section is a brief résumé of the proceedings of the December 1980 meeting.

Part One

THE BROADER ECONOMIC AND SOCIAL QUESTIONS
AS THEY RELATE TO YOUTH UNEMPLOYMENT

A Report presented to the OECD Meeting
on Youth Employment Policies

by

The Rt. Hon. Mrs. Shirley Williams, P.C.

Throughout the 1960s unemployment in Western Europe rarely exceeded 5 per cent, and in most countries most of the time remained below 3 per cent. After 1975, fuelled by unemployment, the recession increased rapidly. By the end of the 1970s, the United States, the United Kingdom and France were all experiencing unemployment rates of 6 per cent or more, with much higher rates among young people and in the economically depressed regions. A whole armoury of measures was used by governments to try to keep unemployment down: regional investment incentives, public works programmes and factories built in advance of requirements, to mention only three. For the most volatile group, young men and women in the first few years after leaving school, special measures have been adopted.

The outlook, however, is bleak. What are the prospects for full employment? The first half of the 1980s offers a discouraging combination of low or nil growth, and a still increasing working population. In the United States, France and Britain, the gross national product will be constant or negative in 1981. The effect on unemployment will be mitigated by low productivity. Germany has the obverse phenomenon — a continued rise in productivity, which can only be translated into more jobs if markets for German products expand very quickly too. The OECD estimated in July 1979 that an average growth rate of 35 per cent per annum would be necessary to maintain the then existing rates of employment. Because of further oil price increases and the deepening of recession by the end of 1979 the OECD's growth estimates for 1980 were down to 0.5 per cent, and the prospects for 1981 and 1982 look no better. Forecasts of general unemployment show an upward spiral. Even more disturbing are the estimates for youth unemployment, expected by OECD in 1981 to exceed 16 per cent in Britain and France and 15 per cent in the United States. Such levels recall the Great Depression. Nor are they the highest. In Italy and Spain, one young person in four is already out of work; among American young blacks, one in three.

The poor prospects for employment in the 1980s are compounded by two other developments. High interest rates, the outcome of tight monetary policies directed against inflation, discourage capital investment. Firms in all the OECD countries observing the weakness of markets also have cut back on investment plans.

The other development is also a consequence of policies to curb inflation. Public expenditure has been reined back in most Western countries, sometimes as a direct outcome of government policies, sometimes because of action by legislators reflecting grassroots feeling among taxpayers. In the United States, for instance, many state legislators have imposed limits on spending, or enjoined balanced budgets. Under the new Administration federal public expenditure seems likely to decline as well. In short, as private consumption falls neither investment nor public expenditure is likely to compensate for that decline. The new recession, coming on the heels of the old, may be long and profound.

Unemployment by no means affects all workers equally. It is misleading to think of the workforce as homogeneous; it is more and more segmented. Young people between 16 and 24 suffer disproportionately when the economy slows down, and youth unemployment typically is two or three times higher than adult unemployment. The exceptions are Germany, Austria and Switzerland, all countries that have adapted the medieval system of apprenticeship to modern conditions. Among young people, the least educated, and especially the least educated girls, are the hardest hit. It is almost impossible for them, as for ethnic minority youngsters without skills, to get acceptable jobs. Unqualified young people tend to move from one dead-end or unsatisfactory job to another, rarely spending more than six months in any one job, drifting in and out of work and in and out of the labour market. This rather aimless in-and-out pattern is much more usual than long unbroken periods of unemployment, the fate of a relatively small minority.

Some young people are not much damaged by the experience of repeated short periods out of work. Others, like the minority of long-term unemployed who are young, lose confidence and finally abandon themselves to apathy, making a living out of odd jobs, whatever their families can spare and intermittent unemployment insurance or welfare payments. Being out of work confirms the low opinion such youngsters have of their own abilities, and seems to them to justify the modesty of their aspirations. Creating self-confidence has to be a main objective of any young employment policy.

Better educated boys and girls do stand a reasonable chance of a job in most OECD countries, but graduates may have to lower their sights. As in the United States and Canada, graduates in Western Europe are now competing for jobs as technicians, technologists, foremen, health ancillary workers and skilled workers with those holding vocational qualifications. In Germany, boys and girls qualified to enter university have entered an apprenticeship first. In Italy and Spain, many graduates can find no work at all. These young people, usually the sons and daughters of professional middle-class parents, are raw material for social unrest, more so than the unqualified unemployed, for their expectations are much higher and their anger at being unwanted consequently greater.

Before turning to what governments have done, and can do, about unemployment, one more comment on the labour market may be illuminating.

11

In the last twenty years, the position of people who already possess a job has been strengthened in all sorts of ways. Laws have been passed to underpin job security, for instance by making it difficult to dismiss employees once taken on, and by requiring long notice of redundancy or a consultative procedure before redundancies are declared. In addition, the financial penalties of dismissing an employee are considerable, at any rate in the industrialised European countries where provision exists for redundancy pay and transfer of pension rights. Collective bargaining often ensures additional severance pay, silver or bronze handshakes. In some industries, dismissed employees are entitled to have their incomes made up to 85 per cent or 90 per cent of their earnings when in work. Such laws and practices are well-intentioned and valuable. But, by putting a premium on job-holding, and by making the decision to employ an extra person much more like a capital investment, they discourage the recruitment of new entrants to the labour force. Indeed, employers themselves may actively encourage turnover among their young workers, to avoid acquiring a whole range of legal obligations towards them.

Young people's employment is discouraged too by heavy non-wage costs, such as national insurance or social security constributions paid by the employer, training costs, holiday pay and pensions. In the 1950s, young people's wages were lower in relation to adult wages than they are today, and non-wage costs were very much less. Young people are more expensive on both counts than they were; if they are also believed to be less reliable, less productive and more trouble than older workers, including married women, the difference in cost no longer tips the balance in their favour.

Governments since 1973 have been torn between policies to stimulate growth and employment, and policies to curb inflation. But there is no longer a simple choice to be made, since inflation can co-exist with high unemployment, partly because of institutional rigidities in advanced economies. Characteristically, governments have leaned towards anti-inflationary measures until unemployment rose so high it became a political threat. Then they have relaxed monetary control, run budget deficits and even encouraged public investment and public works. It is not the purpose of this report to comment on governments' macro-economic policies, though unquestionably those policies have more influence on employment than the educational, training and labour market policies set out below. A successful international initiative to recycle the surpluses of the oil producers to create effective demand in the Third World would lower interest rates and start a new era of economic growth. But the economic and political climate does not favour such radical ideas, nor is such Keynesianism fashionable in intellectual circles. Ours is a dour and stony time.

Worried about inflationary pressures, governments have therefore
looked to structural measures to modify unemployment, directed in
particular at unemployment among young people. Each country has built
on existing foundations. The United States expanded public works programmes in 1977, creating thousands of additional jobs, and also tried
various incentives to keep young people at school after 16, including
financing part-time jobs and summer jobs for those enrolled in, and
attending high schools. Germany expanded her traditional dual system
of vocational education and apprenticeship. In 1976, the Training
Places Promotion Act proposed to levy firms if insufficient additional
training places were offered to absorb the rising number of young
people looking for them. The law has never been activated, because
German firms offered 625,000 training places in 1979, 145,000 more
than in 1975. The United Kingdom in 1978 pioneered a youth guarantee
for 16- to 18-year-olds, under which anyone still unemployed at
Easter after leaving school the previous summer would get a place on
a work experience scheme or on a short industrial course. In the
first full year, 1979-80, 210,000 young people were found places on
this Youth Opportunities Programme. Denmark subsidises jobs in both
private and public sectors for persons who have been unemployed for
over three months.

DEMOGRAPHY

Before looking in more detail at what is being done in various
OECD countries about youth unemployment, and at what policies have
proved themselves enough to justify wider adoption, let me add a few
considerations about the longer-term future. In most OECD countries
the number and proportion of young people will fall by the mid-1980s.
In the United States, for instance, the number of young people aged
14 to 24 rose from just over 27.3 million in 1960 to just over 45
million in 1980. It will decline to about 35 million in 1990. Demographic swings are greater in the United States than in most of
Western Europe, but in Western Europe also the number of young people
between 14 and 24 will soon sharply decline. There is also some
reason to believe that the rate of labour force participation among
married women may be levelling out after a very rapid rise in the
United States, the Scandinavian countries and the United Kingdom. In
Denmark, for instance, the figure has recently slowed after a steady
rise. In the United States, Sweden and the United Kingdom, where the
growth has been phenomenal, it is difficult to believe it can continue
at such a rate. On the other hand, there is plenty of potential for
increased female participation in the labour markets of Italy and
Germany, where obviously more women are employed in the unpaid economy

of domestic work. Germany's employment record would be less impressive
if these women were in the employment market.

LABOUR SUPPLY

Certain policies followed by governments have decreased the supply
of people seeking work in the past three years. These include:

a) Early retirement: schemes to permit men and women in
   work to retire before normal retirement age, usually on
   the basis of a partial pension or a reduced unemployment
   benefit. There is normally a lower age limit below which
   the scheme is not available. The Danish scheme in its
   first year, 1979-80, removed 50,000 workers from the labour
   market, the German scheme 300,000 between 1973 and 1977.
   Early retirement, if made compulsory, can produce a back-
   lash, however. In the United States proposals to reduce
   the retirement age led to a powerful lobby of the elderly
   sweeping the existing retirement ages away - a triumph
   for what was called "grey power".

b) Repatriation of foreign workers: Between 1973 and 1977
   some 650,000 foreign workers left Germany when their
   contracts ended. Recruitment of new foreign workers was
   suspended in November 1973. Some foreign workers have
   returned to their countries of origin from France and the
   United Kingdom, but the drop has not been comparable
   since few were employed under contract. The United States,
   on the other hand, has large inflows, now mainly of
   illegal immigrants, especially from Mexico and Latin America.

c) Shorter hours: There has been a trend towards shorter
   hours of work. For instance, in Germany hours of work
   are falling at the rate of about one per cent a year. But
   small reductions in hours do little to create extra jobs:
   they are usually offset by increasing productivity. Trade
   unions are attracted by 35- or even 30-hour weeks at wage
   rates high enough to produce the same weekly pay. Such
   proposals, however, are more relevant to better working
   conditions than to reducing unemployment.

d) Compensation for short-time working: such as the German
   Kurzarbeit scheme, or the Temporary Short-Time Working
   Compensation Scheme in the United Kingdom, which do actually
   save jobs. Firms are helped through periods of market
   weakness or, sometimes, crises related to a particular
   industry. In Germany, two-thirds of the wages lost
   through short-time working are made up from government

and EEC funds. At the depth of the 1973 to 1975
recession a maximum of 773,000 German workers were
maintained in work by this scheme, equivalent to
175,000 full-time jobs.

Several of the policies mentioned above that influence the supply
of labour have a once-for-all effect, like the repatriation of foreign
workers, or an initial effect that is considerably greater than in
subsequent years, like early retirement. The labour force in Germany
fell by over a million between 1973 and 1977 largely offsetting the
loss of 1.7 million jobs in the same period. Much of that fall was
due to once-for-all measures that cannot be repeated.

JOB CREATION

The United States has been remarkably successful in creating new
jobs. Between 1975 and 1979 twelve million new jobs were created in
both the public and private sectors, 90 per cent of them in the tertiary sector with an emphasis on information-related services. Many,
indeed most, of the jobs in the private sector were in firms with
under 20 employees. The decentralised US banking structure seems much
better at providing risk capital for small or innovative firms than
the more formal European banks. Job creation by government in the
United States has been mainly through public works, and has been a
feature of US counter-cyclical employment policy since the 1930s.
Public service job creation is however hampered by very strict rules
and regulations intended to prevent substitution. In those areas of
the United States that are traditionally high wage areas these restrictions limit the efficiency of public works schemes.

European governments are much more ready to subsidise temporary
or permanent jobs in the private sector than the United States is.
Apart from its Employment Projects, which again are really public works
schemes, Denmark pays employment subsidies for the long-term unemployed
for up to a year. Germany subsidises training places in private industry for handicapped and disadvantaged young people who cannot be
easily placed, and the United Kingdom government has subsidised additional apprenticeships and sandwich places in industry. There is
scope for increasing public works and subsidised employment projects
as emergency measures for reducing youth unemployment. The Youth
Conservation Corps in the United States and the Community Industry
Scheme and Work Experience Programmes in the United Kingdom's Manpower
Services Commission provide examples, ranging from afforestation and
the clearing of rivers and canals to improving derelict neighbourhoods
or insulating existing housing stocks. Such projects, however, especially when directed at unemployed young people, should include a training

15

element, and should not be so short that the young person is given no adequate grounding for permanent employment. The "make work" schemes of the inter-war depression are not an acceptable model. The combination of work experience with training is the key to helping young people to get jobs.

EDUCATION, TRAINING AND THE TRANSITION TO WORK

The Dual System

The most elaborate transition from school to work in any OECD country occurs in Germany and her largely German-speaking neighbours, Austria and Switzerland, where the traditional dual system of vocational education and apprenticeship has been brought up to date. The dual system has been used in Germany both as a means of improving the knowledge and skills of the workforce, and as a buffer against teenage unemployment. Young Germans must by law attend vocational schools for a minimum of eight hours a week after they leave school and until they reach the age of 18. The overwhelming majority of school-leavers, over 90 per cent, also enter into an apprenticeship, which is an individual contract with an employer intended to provide on-the-job training in a given occupation. The young person has to qualify by taking a series of tests and examinations. The regulations for each trade or industry are administered and regularly updated by the Federal Institute of Vocational Education, on which employers and trade unions are represented, as well as the Land and federal governments.

The system has its weaknesses. In some crafts and in some enterprises the quality of training is unimpressive, and monitoring is sketchy. Training allowances - apprentices do not get wages - are established in a collective bargaining process, and vary a good deal, traditional female occupations receiving the lowest rates. Furthermore, many apprentices qualify in occupations for which there is no demand.

The central tenet of the apprenticeship system, however, is that a young man or woman trained for any occupation is better placed than one who is not trained at all. He or she will know something about how the economy works, will have acquired good working practices and will have the benefit of a solid vocational foundation. Not only will the qualified apprentice be a more attractive employee, he or she will also be more better equipped to work independently and to share in decision-making through Works Councils and the other representative institutions of industrial democracy.

In 1976 a basic full-time vocational year, the Berufsgrundjahr was introduced, both to meet the need for additional places and to broaden the occupational training of school-leavers. It has been controversial, largely because it is controlled by the education authorities, the Laender, and not by the employers. But it has given the German system extra capacity to cope with rising numbers of young people, and the ability to place those who do not get apprenticeships in private firms.

Germany has consistently held youth unemployment down to 5 per cent or less. When, in 1973, youth unemployment became a serious problem in all OECD countries, it was Germany that came up with the most effective response, challenging employers to increase the number of apprenticeships on offer against a legal power by the federal government to create the places needed itself. The policy was rein-forced by providing places in the Berufsgrundjahr, which took 67,000 young people in 1979, and related full-time courses directed at children with physical handicaps or low educational attainments. As for adaptation to the new technologies, the content of vocational and training courses is regularly reviewed to ensure it is up to date. Recently the metal trades moved over to a new form of apprenticeship, the co-operative year, interspersing blocks of vocational education with blocks of on-the-job training, and broadening each apprentice's experience of different metal-working skills. The government has also recognised the need for retraining people already at work. In 1980 the federal government offered 500 million Deutschmarks to subsidise "in-house" training and retraining of existing employees in new pro-cesses, a proposal that was immediately taken up by German enterprises. Largely because of this eagerness to maintain and improve "human capital", Germany has attracted investment in processes requiring skilled labour. A virtuous circle has been established in which the presence of skilled people acts as an engine for growth, and the growth in turn demands more skilled people. Part of the answer to the problem of unemployment, and particularly of youth unemployment, lies here.

It would be difficult and expensive, however, for other countries to adopt the German system of nearly universal apprenticeships for school-leavers, a system with a long tradition. Nor is Germany the only OECD country in which education and work are interwoven. In an opposite sense, they are interwoven in the United States, where work-ing one's way through school and college is a long-standing tradition. The difference is that in the United States the work element is a means of achieving education. In Germany the education is a means of getting work. Not surprisingly, therefore, the educational element in the dual system is vocational in Germany, general in the United States. One fortunate by-product for the United States is that the

world of education, even of higher education, is much less divorced
from the world of work than in European countries. The ivory towers
of academe, we said in our Review of Youth Employment Policies in the
United States (Part IV), are not so hermetically sealed. Where the
American system falls down, however, is with the high school dropouts and the school-tired youngsters. There is no structural transition from school to work at 16 or even 18. Training opportunities
are very sketchy, and apprenticeships are a form of adult training,
largely for men in their 20s and 30s. Many disadvantaged young people,
especially inner city blacks and those without prosperous families
behind them, simply sink in the choppy waters of the youth labour
market, drifting from one dead-end job to another, or into apathy and
crime.

The Transition

In countries endowed with neither kind of dual system recent
initiatives like the British Youth Opportunities Programme or the
Danish EIFU vocational preparation courses have already shown the
value of an ordered transition from school to work. Efforts are made
to combine social skills - how to dress, how to talk to employers and
customers, how to answer the telephone or write a letter - with some
simple vocational training and with work experience. The unemployed
youngster emerges better equipped to get a job, more confident, and
with some idea of what work involves.

Such short transitional courses should not only be offered to
unemployed school-leavers but to all who leave school before completing
their full secondary education. Wherever possible, such courses
should be conducted partly on work premises, so that boys and girls
experience what the world of work is like.

Ideally, children should have their first experience of work
before they leave school, at the age of 14 or 15. In Germany, most
Laender now offer children three weeks' work experience, preceded by
appropriate preparation in school and followed by a comparison of
experiences. Similar courses are available in Britain, Denmark and
elsewhere, though not on the same scale. In all these countries,
however, children studying in the Gymnasia are rarely offered work
experience, which seems unimaginative; for even if these more academic children enter the universities and then the professions, some
knowledge of the industrial world is immensely important to them.

Work experience at school complements a structural transition
and vice-versa. The existing transitional courses however are too
short to offer much more than a chance to sample what the working world
is like, and the training is too scrappy to constitute a foundation
for skill training. Two other developments fill the gap between the
transition course and the full 3- or 4-year apprenticeship.

The Vocational Year

The first of these has already been mentioned, the full-time
vocational year, offered as an alternative to continuing with full-time
schooling. The German Berufsgrundjahr, the Danish EFG and the British
Engineering Training Board foundation year, normally taken in colleges
of further education, are examples. All attempt to widen vocational
education by teaching the student about a cluster of related occupations, or a range of skills within a broad area, for example engineering. They are, in the jargon, polyvalent courses. As such, they are
intended to be a foundation for a range of apprenticeships; they also
overcome the problem of training for too narrow a skill, or for one
that becomes obsolescent or no longer in demand. Variations on the
vocational year include the co-operative year in Germany, which re-
sembles the British sandwich course - periods of several weeks at
work followed by periods of several weeks in school or college.

Given the rate of technical change, the foundation year looks
attractive. It keeps young people off the labour market, provides
them with training, yet allows them to enter the adult world of work.
The co-operative year in particular offers new motivation to the
'school-tired' young person.

Traineeships

The second development is the traineeship system, based on a
British experiment called 'unified vocational preparation'. These
are induction courses of six months or so providing the trainee with
a broad introduction to a particular industry; they have been adopted
particularly by the distributive industry and the plastics industry
for jobs requiring limited skills. Traineeships, which again combine
vocational training with work experience, can vary in length according
to the occupation. They do not have to be as long, and expensive, as
the traditional craft apprenticeship. Yet they do offer boys and
girls a useful grounding in a trade.

What I would hope to see is a period of work experience for all
school children in the fourth or fifth forms; a choice between
staying on at school or entering a full-time vocational education
year or a co-operative year at 15 or 16; and then a range of transitional courses from short introductory courses to traineeships or
apprenticeships after that, depending on the occupation finally chosen.
All such courses, like the foundation year, should include material
to make young people familiar with the new technologies, what they are
and what their potential may be. Educational material could be
complemented by radio and television programmes showing young people
what job opportunities the new technologies are creating, and what
qualifications are needed for them, and where they can be acquired.

Apprenticeships

These changes would in turn entail a reform of the traditional apprenticeship system, which in most European countries is rather rigidly tied to beginning at 16 or 17. Apprenticeships should be open to any young person up to the age of 18. Their duration should be linked to the achievement of certain standards of knowledge and performance and not to the passage of time. The content of apprenticeships needs to be regularly reviewed and brought up to date, and the quality of training should be monitored by inspectors independent of the social partners; the social partners should, however, be involved in establishing the syllabuses and the examinations, as in Germany. Skill training courses ought to be open to adults as well, but adults will obviously need to be paid a minimum adult wage or its equivalent.

Allowances

Young people will be reluctant to stay on in full-time education if they thereby lose earnings from work or an apprentice's pay. So financial remuneration should be broadly equivalent for those entering training or staying on at school. Young people should choose the most appropriate form of further education for each person individually, whether it is staying on at school, an apprenticeship or a traineeship. These allowances up to the age of 18 should be enough for basic subsistence, with some flexibility to allow for the extra costs of travelling to work, tools, etc. To keep the cost down it could at least initially be related to family income. Employers might contribute to the apprentice's allowance, but in the first year the basic allowance should come from public funds. The net cost would not be high since the young person might well otherwise be unemployed. These proposals would go a long way to deal with the 'mismatch' between jobs available or likely to be created, and people with no skills or no longer relevant skills. They would also encourage productivity and hence competitivity. But they are essentially structural. Given the resistance of governments to stimulating demand, what can be done about the excess of people seeking jobs, even if mismatch is dealt with?

What follows assumes that high unemployment among young people is not a passing phenomenon, to cure itself as the population bulge passes. The assumption may be wrong. Governments have reacted to increases in unemployment since the war with remedial measures of a temporary kind - public works, short training courses, subsidised jobs and so on. I assume rather that the coming of new technologies, many of them net savers of labour, the demand for paid employment among women, and the reduced rates of growth present us with a permanent problem, one that shorter hours cannot solve. Obviously, hours can be cut to the point where young people in fact hold only

20

part-time jobs. But unless compulsion is used, some young people will
then have two jobs while others have none. Governments need to explore
all possible methods of offering at least the option of employment.

MAKING BETTER USE OF PEOPLE

It is in looking afresh at the use of people as compared to
capital, energy and raw materials that we may find a route back to
full employment. For what matters in measuring the efficient use of
resources is not just the productivity of labour, but the productivity
of all the factors combined - labour, capital, land, energy, raw
materials and knowledge. In the past decade land and raw materials
have become more expensive in both absolute and relative terms.
Energy costs - as we know - have gone up faster than the general rate
of inflation and much faster than earnings. Therefore, a fresh
assessment of the mixture of factors of production is required, and
that fresh assessment must break with traditional attitudes.

Over a wide area, labour can be substituted for capital without
significantly raising overall costs of production, although this
generally requires the application of different technologies. In
some cases, costs of production may even be reduced by substituting
labour for capital. But during past decades all of us adopted the
habit - and we were long justified in doing so - of thinking in terms
of saving labour. On this account many managers trained in our
countries' universities and colleges simply do not know how to organise
substantial labour forces, so they use machinery instead. Further
significant evidence of this conditioning process can be seen in the
way highly capital-intensive processes have been introduced and used
in Third World countries by Western-trained experts despite the
availability of large local labour reserves prepared to work for low
wages. An arresting case is quoted by the British economist, Sir
Andrew Shonfield, in his book, Attack on Poverty, when he describes
the contrast between the building of two dams, one in India and the
other in China. The Indian dam was built by sophisticated imported
machinery and employed only a handful of workers, under the watchful
eyes of a hungry, unemployed local population. In China, it was the
local people who built the dam, moving hundreds of tons of earth in
wheelbarrows and baskets, and being paid a living wage to do it.

Alternative mixes of factors of production aiming at the best
result for society as a whole have been little studied, no doubt
because labour productivity has usually been used as a convenient
shorthand measure of efficiency. But here and there some provocative
findings have emerged. A report submitted by a group of independent
experts to the Social Affairs Directorate of the EEC Commission in

July 1976 concluded that "the time now seems ripe to question the general preference given to investment aids at the expense of employment subsidies." The group pointed out that between 1950 and 1971 gross fixed capital formation increased as a proportion of GNP in every Member State of the Common Market. Yet studies in some countries, particularly in France, showed a decline in value added per unit of capital employed over the same period. Ill-judged or inefficient investment adds to inflation. The experts questioned the purposes of investment projects: "Have they not been directed more towards the productivity of labour (and the displacing of jobs) than towards the total productivity of the factors of production?" Answering their own question, they proposed that investment for expansion be distinguished from investment for rationalisation, which can destroy more jobs than it saves.

Labour and capital are not the only factors of production that can be substituted for one another. Labour can also be substituted for land or raw materials. The rehabilitation of existing houses and neighbourhoods is thus more labour-intensive than pulling them down and rebuilding them by industrialised methods, and also makes fewer demands on land. Agriculture provides an even better example. Intensively farmed land, such as gardens, smallholdings, allotments and fish farms, has a very high yield per acre and a low labour productivity compared to extensively farmed land. If land is scarce and labour is plentiful, agricultural methods can be changed to allow for this new balance. Modern agriculture is energy-intensive, but it need not be. Methods of organic farming make for fewer demands on fuel and fertilizer and greater demand for labour.

Inputs of labour and prime fuel are also to some extent interchangeable. District heating schemes supplying electricity for both lighting and heating that use low-grade fuels and domestic rubbish are more labour-intensive than big generating stations. To conserve energy, such highly labour-intensive methods as insulating both newly built houses and the existing housing stock and other buildings may be needed. Well-insulated buildings require more initial labour in construction than standard buildings, but produce a very high return on the extra cost, which can be amortized within a few years. Producing more power to heat poorly insulated houses is expensive in terms of energy but not labour costs. Long-life products such as consumer durables, including motor cars, need very little additional input of raw materials or energy compared to short-life products, but require more careful design and better workmanship. Maintaining and repairing them makes greater demands on labour than scrapping and replacing them. The marketing of goods can also use more labour and less raw material: for instance, home delivery or good after-sales service can be as effective selling methods as attractive packaging.

POLICY IMPLICATIONS

What action can governments take to promote positive development in these areas? Employment would be encouraged by changes in the tax system to make it more fiscally neutral: it is a matter of the balance between taxes and allowances affecting the relative cost of labour, capital and other factors. In a growing economy, the capital available to each worker is normally increased in order to enable him to produce a higher added value. But, as the group of experts said in their European Commission report: "the granting of interest rate subsidies, tax relief in respect of depreciation, and investment aids, regional or others, lowers the cost of using capital. Furthermore, the use of wages as the base for social security contributions and certain parafiscal charges leads to changes in the parameters within which the employer makes his calculations and tends to accelerate the substitution of capital for labour."

Governments might also take action in regard to non-wage costs of labour, which continue to grow as social security contributions are increased and as occupational pensions and company health schemes are more widely introduced. In some circumstances these non-wage labour costs could be a significant disincentive to additional recruitment. On top of that, the cost of training the worker is an additional expense which cannot easily be depreciated or written off like capital investment. A serious attempt to restore full employment, therefore, would involve a review of tax incentives and tax allowances for capital investment, at least distinguishing between capital investment that produces a net growth of jobs and capital investment which destroys jobs. It should be possible to write off the cost of training and retraining against revenues for tax purposes - as a human capital allowance. (In Germany, a large part of the cost to an enterprise of training can be offset against revenues for the purposes of determining profits tax. Taken together with the value of production by apprentices, it is estimated that between one fourth and one half of training costs are not borne by the employer.)

Governments intent on restoring full employment would have to consider shifting social security and health costs from payroll taxes to general tax revenues, or meeting them by a levy on turnover rather than on wages and salaries alone. Another proposal worth exploring is waiving the employer's national insurance payments for a period when he recruits an additional young person, as is done in Southern Italy and under the "Pacte national pour l'emploi" in France.

Encouraging employment growth by favouring labour-intensive forms of production rather than capital intensive routes should be pursued through a policy of encouraging small and medium-sized firms.

The case for aiding small enterprises

A change of attitude towards small and medium-sized enterprises could have a considerable impact on unemployment, as they are usually more labour-intensive than big firms (the whole net increase in jobs in the United States since 1967 - 15 million of them - has, for example, been achieved thanks to small firms). Communication between managers and workers is easier and more informal in a small enterprise; the human problems are on a scale that can be dealt with by readily available management and shop steward skills. But in a big company the difficulties of communicating with and organising large numbers of people are often acute. Great size requires exceptional management ability, which may be extremely hard to come by. The problems of managing human beings multiply at every intervening stage of communication between those who make the decisions and those who carry them out, or between those who should consult and those who have to be consulted. This is one reason why large firms are inclined to substitute capital for labour. In the last decade, they have provided few of the additional new jobs, and in the United States their workforces have actually declined.

There are implications in these ideas for government policy, both for central government and for local government. Taking a closer look at the example of the United States, one of the few countries which has been remarkably successful in creating new jobs, mainly, as noted, in small firms, it will be observed that its banking and financial structure seems more ready to lend risk capital to small businesses than is the case in Europe. This raises the question whether the banks, possibly backed by a government guarantee, could not make more money available to small firms, and what agencies are needed to encourage them. Denmark has recently persuaded pension funds and insurance companies to invest in risk capital of small and medium businesses at favourable interest rates. Can other steps be taken? Is the tax climate, for example, harsher in most countries for small businesses than for large?

A vital and relatively inexpensive way of helping small businesses and local and community enterprises would be to provide them - through appropriate government departments or local authorities - with the expertise they can rarely afford to help them get off the ground (such as the advice of accountants, tax advisers or marketing experts). Certain firms are offering the help of one or more of their own senior managers to enable new enterprises, both private and public, to be launched and kept afloat. In the United Kingdom, Shell and British Steel - and in the United States, IBM - have been involved in either hiving off small innovative companies or in backing workshops and labour-intensive businesses able to offer jobs to redundant workers. British Steel (Industries) supported one such venture in Scotland,

24

Clyde Workshops, which has now created several hundred permanent jobs at an average cost of under £1,000 a job - less than a tenth of what it costs the United Kingdom government to create jobs in the regions.

Small firms may also need help with marketing and with training costs. Co-operative marketing has been an important factor in improving the income of horticulturists and small farmers. Big retailers or manufacturers willing to buy in from a host of small sub-contractors can sustain large numbers of jobs. Examples are Japan's car industry and Marks and Spencer - the British retail chain. Publicly-owned corporations could do much more to help sustain small sub-contractors if they were encouraged by governments to do so, for small-scale enterprise is also showing signs of vitality in the public sector. The Highlands and Islands Board in Scotland has launched a number of community co-operatives in its remote rural areas based on a matching grant of a pound for every pound raised locally. The co-operatives range from knitwear to plant hire and fish farming. In Watts, California, a non-profit-making, community-based company has created several hundred jobs. In Denmark, several community projects have produced goods which could now be more commercially marketed. Local enterprise trusts in certain English cities have supported teams of young people undertaking repair and maintenance work with finance for tools and equipment and with expert help in drawing up budgets, keeping books and rendering accounts.

In concluding, I wish to emphasise two important points. First, re-examining our assumptions about the use of labour would have repercussions for management, engineering and design courses in our universities as well. The responsibilties of enterprises to the local community and to their employees would be emphasised. Management of people would be a much larger part of the courses. Engineers and designers would learn to think more about the makers and users of their products. They would minimise the need for energy and they would avoid wasting raw materials, even though the design might be less simple and might need longer to make.

Second, I should add that my fellow examiners and I have often found that institutional rigidities and traditional attitudes militate against the opportunities for young people to be employed, such as by insisting that apprenticeships must start at age 16; resisting recognition of vocational qualifications; refusing to allow vocational preparation in schools; disdain towards industry; insistence on the full adult wage at 18; antipathy towards employing young people, especially those from ethnic minorities; refusal to train girls outside traditional female occupations; we have encountered all these and many more. Full employment may indeed be unattainable, but the truth is that we have only just begun to try.

Part Two

<u>A REVIEW OF YOUTH EMPLOYMENT POLICIES</u>
<u>IN DENMARK</u>

THE OECD EXAMINERS

The Rt. Hon. Mrs. Shirley Williams, P.C.
Chairman

- Senior Research Fellow at the Policy Studies Institute
  (formerly Secretary of State for Education and Science),
  the United Kingdom.

The Hon. Robert Andras, P.C.

- Senior Vice-President, the Teck Corporation (formerly
  President of the Treasury Board and President of the
  Board of Economic Development Ministers), Canada.

Professor Robert Leroy

- Professor of Economics at the Catholic University of
  Louvain and Director of the Unité Economie et Société,
  Institut des Sciences Economiques, Belgium.

INTRODUCTION

The turbulent 1970s have brought with them new problems, especially for the young as they enter the world of work. Consequently, in recent years much of the OECD concern in the field of manpower education and training has been directed to tackling the human, social and economic problems represented by youth unemployment, believing that they are not only a challenge to our social values and economic institutions but also to our political will and foresight.

The importance attached by Member countries to the problems of youth unemployment is reflected in the current OECD work programme of which this exercise is a part. The invitation of the Danish authorities to the OECD to undertake a review of Denmark's special measures to tackle youth unemployment was deliberately timed to coincide with a major re-appraisal of policy as the Danish authorities, like many others, felt the need to introduce more long-term and structured programmes than those that were introduced in the wake of early increases in youth unemployment in 1975 and 1976.

Our report is derived from a number of sources of information:

a) The background report prepared by the Danish Ministry of Labour;(1)

b) Statements from the consultative committee of the Ministry of Labour and the contact committees of the Ministry of Education;

c) A number of research reports from independent research institutes in Denmark;

d) Meetings with national representatives of the Ministry of Labour, the Ministry of Education and discussions with the Danish Economic Secretariat;

e) Meetings with a wide range of interested groups including employers, labour unions, researchers, youth organisations and representatives of women's groups;

f) Meetings with members and officials of counties and municipalities involved in the implementation of the

---

1) The latest date for which data were available to be used in this report was September 1980.

programme, as well as representatives of the national
associations which represent the county and local
authorities at the national level;

g) Field visits to a number of projects and discussions
   with programme operators;

h) Some discussion with young people themselves.

Our team visited Denmark for an intensive programme which lasted
one week in October 1979. Although Denmark is a small country, its
systems are not simpler to understand, nor its programmes easier to
evaluate, than those of much larger countries. Further, our visit
coincided with the Danish General Election and consequently the review
team members confronted some reticence and uncertainty about what the
future held.

The review has largely been conducted at a policy level, with
all the advantages and limitations which stem from such an approach.
This report does not involve original research or new data collection.
The Danish approach has been an integrated one, recognising the importance both of educational and of manpower measures. Our review
has therefore considered both the existing educational provision for
young people in the last years of school and beyond the statutory
period as well as the programmes provided under the Special Employment
Plan Number 2 adopted by the Folketing (Danish Parliament) in
September 1977. There is one omission we should mention. We have
said nothing about the special educational and labour market problems
of second-generation migrants, although we are aware that Yugoslav,
Turkish and Pakistani nationals account for some one-half of one per
cent of the Danish labour force. During our visit to Denmark, their
problems were not discussed.

We had both official consultations and informal conversations
with a wide spectrum of concerned people during our visit. Our
itinerary took us to town and country on the main island of Sjelland,
as well as to the mainland. We salute the dedication of the many
individuals and organisations whose hard work and generosity at both
the professional and the personal level made us feel welcome and
privileged guests in Denmark. We gratefully acknowledge the continuing
support we received from both the Ministry of Labour and the Ministry
of Education which greatly facilitated our task.

I

THE ECONOMIC AND SOCIAL SETTING

We begin by setting out the economic and social context within
which any consideration of Danish youth employment policies has to
take place.

The Broad Setting

Denmark is a small country with a population of 5 million people
occupying some 43,000 square kilometres of northern Europe between
the North Sea and the Baltic. It comprises the Jutland Peninsula and
no fewer than 406 islands, excluding Greenland and the Faroe Islands.
Communications are nonetheless very good. Denmark has few natural
resources and virtually no energy base. By pioneering modern agriculture, however, and by subsequently diversifying the economy, it
has reached an advanced level of both economic and social development.
Whilst its gross domestic product is small in relation to the two
other countries forming part of this exercise (e.g. 2.6 per cent of
that of the United States and 8.7 per cent of that of Germany in
1978), it ranks second amongst the countries of the OECD area on a
per capita income basis (a per capita income in 1978 of 10,950 US $)
placing it 13 per cent ahead of the United States and 5 per cent
ahead of Germany. The standard of living has thus reached a very
high level. Most Danes today experience a strong sense of material
comfort and in other Scandinavian countries the Danes have a repu-
tation of being care-free spenders. Allied to this economic success
is a remarkable programme of social and educational provision, making
Denmark one of the most developed and envied welfare states within
the OECD countries.

This has not always been so. The Danish economy and way of
life has been gradually transformed since the middle of the nineteenth
century. The pace of economic change quickened in the aftermath of
the world-wide breakdown of international trade during the Great
Depression. Though still vitally important for export trade, the
role of agriculture in the economy has declined significantly (from
9 per cent to 6 per cent of GDP during the 10 years up to 1978). By
contrast, there has been a steady expansion in the manufacturing and
tertiary sectors. Perhaps most important, very considerable expansion

31

has taken place in the public sector, reflected in the substantial increase in total government consumption, investment and transfer payments which represented 46.4 per cent of GNP in 1974-76 compared with 35.5 per cent in 1967-69.(1) Crucial to the economic stability of the Danish economy has been Denmark's particular adeptness at developing export industries, especially those involving high-level technology in the industrial and agricultural domain. In 1979 the export of goods and services accounted for 29 per cent of Denmark's GDP (factor cost),(2) a vital ingredient of economic survival for a country with so few natural resources and so dependent on imported energy sources.

The remarkable leap forward in national wealth has had a profound impact on individual aspirations and community expectations, indeed on the very essence of the Danish character. In the nineteenth century, following severe military defeat, the Danes accepted the reality of no longer being a European middle power. They concentrated instead on developing their homeland identity, producing, in the process, an unusually close-knit society. A liking for informality does not denote any lack of order or efficiency. On the contrary, life in all its aspects is unobtrusively well organised - the outcome of experience over several generations in seeking pragmatic solutions to problems and in achieving social harmony. Nor did the Second World War break this process.

Social class differences exist but are little commented upon. Much of the nation's wealth has been used to build a welfare state, of which most Danes are intensely proud. It has, however, recently run into problems. Danes tend to think in terms of collective responsibility when caring for their people; in consequence, social public expenditure is among the highest in the OECD world. Taxation is not only accordingly high, but vigorously progressive.

Perhaps paradoxically, alongside this highly developed welfare state there exists a strong free market ethic within the private and productive sectors. The Danish private economy is characterised by very little government involvement, and a strong resistance to "state interference". A similar situation prevails in the labour market, where wage rates and working conditions are regulated by highly organised trade unions and employers who jealously guard their control over it. This "private market" tradition has, however, not been without its problems, not only for incomes policies but also for attempts by the Danish authorities to introduce subsidy measures to encourage the employment of young people. We shall say more about this later in our report.

A further paradox is that whilst the Danes have accepted a collectivist approach to tackling social problems they, perhaps in

---

1) OECD, Public Expenditure Trends, Paris, 1978; as revised.
2) OECD, Economic Survey: Denmark, Paris, July 1980.

32

line with their independent characters, have in recent years increasingly decentralised decision-making and programme operation;
this has involved an increasing role for the municipal and county
authorities. Examples of this decentralisation are the Youth Employment Programmes run under Employment Plan Number 2, where not only
are these local authorities the principal operators of programmes,
but are also responsible for raising part of the revenue to finance
them. We shall comment later on the institutional and organisational
issues involved in youth employment programmes, but at times there
seemed to us to be so many actors on the stage that there was a
danger of expending too much effort in co-ordinating the actors,
rather than in tackling youth unemployment.

The Recent Economic and Labour Market Developments

The factor of paramount importance for Danish economic policy
has been the external balance of payments. From 1968 to 1979 the
Danish economy was in deficit every year. A large part of Danish
economic policy has been directed to redressing this trade imbalance.
Remarkably, however, the country has been able and willing to finance
its current deficit through capital imports. Since 1976 the growth
of the Danish economy has generally been very sluggish. GDP expanded
by 1.8 per cent in 1977 and 1.3 per cent in 1978.(1) After increasing
in 1979 (especially following the June oil package) to produce GDP
growth of 3.5 per cent the Danish economy is expected to decline by
0.5 per cent in 1980 and forecast to grow by 1.5 per cent in 1981.(2)

Demographic Movements and Participation Patterns

The youth population between 15 and 19 will begin to decline
after 1982 but the population between 20 and 24 years of age will
continue to rise until 1988. The whole cohort between 15-24 will
begin to fall after 1984 and will fall sharply between 1988 and 1992;
it will then be at a level significantly lower than that prevailing
in 1980. The projected forecasts for labour force participation yield
a somewhat different picture, with the estimated rate of labour force
participation for 15-19-year-olds falling from 42 per cent in 1980 to
a projected 39.5 per cent in 1992, largely on the expectation of increased participation in the education system. Labour force participation for the 20-24 age group is expected to remain at approximately 82.5 per cent for the period up to 1992. Tables 1 and 2 set
out the figures in greater detail. It should also be stressed that
youth activity rates differ considerably between males and females.
Some 48 per cent of boys (15-19) participated in the labour market

---

1) OECD Economic Surveys: Denmark, op.cit.
2) OECD, Economic Outlook, 28, Paris, December 1980, p. 113.

in 1978, compared with only 36 per cent of girls. Whilst the gap is
narrower for the 20-24 age group, a differential remains, with male
participation rates running at 85 per cent compared to female participation rates of 81 per cent.   Youth unemployment, affecting some
16.3 per cent of the full-time insured under-20-years-old group and
18.7 per cent of the full-time insured 20-24-years-old group in 1979
is not distributed evenly by age, by geographic region, by sex or by
level of educational attainment.

Table 1

FORECASTS FOR 1980, 1982, 1984, 1988 AND 1992
OF THE TOTAL POPULATION BY AGE AND SEX

Year	Age	Male	Female	All
1980	15-19	198,900	190,000	388,900
	20-24	189,500	180,000	369,500
1982	15-19	210,100	200,200	410,300
	20-24	188,900	180,700	369,600
1984	15-19	208,800	198,300	407,100
	20-24	193,500	185,900	379,400
1988	15-19	187,000	177,700	364,700
	20-24	211,500	202,300	413,800
1992	15-19	180,600	173,300	353,900
	20-24	189,400	180,400	369,800

Source: Danish Ministry of Labour Official Statistics

Table 2

FORECASTS FOR 1980, 1982, 1984, 1988 AND 1992
OF THE LABOUR FORCE BY AGE AND SEX

Year	Age	Male	Female	All
1980	15-19	93,900	69,500	163,400
	20-24	157,500	145,800	303,300
1982	15-19	99,200	74,200	173,400
	20-24	156,800	148,600	305,400
1984	15-19	97,800	71,900	169,700
	20-24	160,400	153,000	313,400
1988	15-19	86,100	61,700	147,800
	20-24	175,400	166,300	341,700
1992	15-19	82,300	57,500	139,800
	20-24	157,000	148,500	305,500

Source: Danish Ministry of Labour Official Statistics

Despite slow growth of output, labour market conditions improved
somewhat in late 1978, largely due to a significant increase in public sector employment and the special employment measures. As in
previous years, the number employed or seeking work rose by between

34

1.5 and 2 per cent (approximately 40,000 people) or roughly twice as
fast as the rise in the working age population. Almost 75 per cent
of the growth of the labour force was accounted for by the rising
female participation rate, which reached approximately 60 per cent in
1978. This compares to 54 per cent in 1973. In 1978 the male labour
force advanced roughly in line with demographic trends, participation
rates for men rising over the period 1973-1978 by only 0.5 percentage
point; it actually declined slightly during the 1960s. Between 1973
and 1978 total employment is estimated to have increased between 0.5 -
1 per cent; slightly less if adjustment is made for part-time work.
This development can be attributed to the rising trend in public sector employment, and, since 1977, to the range of special employment
measures introduced to tackle unemployment. Between October 1978 and
October 1979 the pattern appears to have changed to some degree in
the labour force surveys revealing a net decrease in the labour force
of 18,284. This is accounted for by a net reduction of the male
labour force of 28,630 counteracted by a net increase of female
participation of 10,346.(1) Further total employment in this period
increased by some 20,794 principally accounted for by growth in the
public sector.(2)

Against this economic and employment background there has been
a dramatic increase in both youth and general unemployment since 1973.
Denmark was remarkably successful at achieving full employment in the
1960s and 1970s with, for example, an effective rate of unemployment
of only 0.9 per cent in 1973, and an average rate of unemployment of
under 2 per cent for the years 1968-1975. Since that date, however,
unemployment has risen dramatically, increasing to an overall estimated unemployment rate of 6.2 per cent in 1979. Table 3 sets out
the development of unemployment. The most recent OECD forecast suggests a total unemployment rate of 8 per cent by end 1981 compared
with around 6 per cent for 1979.(3)

With the rise in general unemployment came an even more substantial rise in youth unemployment. General unemployment peaked in 1978
and has shown some improvement since then, which reflects the extent
of measures introduced to reduce it and the relatively poor productivity performance of the non-agricultural private sector in recent
years. Almost one half of the unemployed in 1978 were women. Their
share of total unemployment also rose, continuing the trend seen since
1973. In 1973 women accounted for 22 per cent of the insured labour
force, while their share of unemployment was 20 per cent. In 1979
the corresponding shares were 42 and 52 per cent respectively.

1) The fall in the male labour force was principally accounted for by
   the early retirement scheme discussed later in this report.
2) Supplementary Statistical Information supplied by the Danish
   Ministry of Labour, 29 September 1980.
3) OECD, Economic Outlook, 28, op.cit.

Table 3

THE DEVELOPMENT OF UNEMPLOYMENT: 1973-1979

	1973	1974	1975	1976	1977	1978	1979
Total unemployment rate (a)	0.9	2.1	5.2	5.3	6.5	7.3	6.2*
Youth unemployment rate (b)							
- Under 20 years of age	2.6	3.7	16.3	15.2	14.7	15.8	16.3
- 20-24	3.4	3.9	16.2	15.7	15.5	18.4	18.7

* Estimate.
a) The number of registered unemployed proportional to the number of persons in the labour force.
b) The number of full-time insured unemployed persons proportional to the number of full-time insured persons.
Source: Statistical information supplied by the Danish Ministry of Labour, 29 September 1980.

Structural changes

Within the span of three decades the Danish economy has been transformed. This has involved a shift of resources away from the primary sector. One measure of the size of change is the decline in the importance of agriculture. In 1950 agriculture contributed 19 per cent of GNP, by 1960 it had fallen to 14 per cent and by 1978 it represented 6 per cent. In 1950, total employment in agriculture was 400,000. By 1963 it had fallen to 240,000; by 1970 it was down to 160,000. During the period 1960-1970 employment in the secondary and tertiary sectors rose by some 434,000, drawing largely on the outflow from primary industries like agriculture and domestic service as well as from the pool of unemployment, which had averaged around 10 per cent in the 1950s. More recently, the public sector has been the main source of new jobs. Labour surveys show that the share of public employment in total employment was 16 per cent in 1967, 22 per cent in 1972 and 28 per cent in 1978. The 1978 percentage, however, includes a significant number of jobs provided under special employment measures.

During the past decade or so the Danish labour market has witnessed substantial changes in female participation, which increased 33.3 per cent between 1967 and 1979, whilst during the same period the female population of working age (15-74) rose only 7.4 per cent. In absolute numbers this represents an increase from 862,000 in 1967 to 1,149,000 in 1979.(1) By 1979 44 per cent of the labour force(2)

1) "Statistical News" 1968/15, 1970/72, 1975/19 and A 1979/11.
2) Note this is a larger figure than the insured labour force, figures for which are quoted elsewhere in this report. Relatively fewer women than men active in the labour force are insured against unemployment.

36

was female compared to 37 per cent in 1967. Whilst there has been
a substantial increase in participation, and progress in achieving
effective rates of equal pay in this period (an absolute improvement
of 11 percentage points between 1968 and 1977), there remains a
highly sex-segmented labour market in Denmark. We shall say more
about this in Chapter III.

The Danish Education System

The Danes have invested heavily in their education system with
expenditure running at 7.9 per cent of GNP in 1979. Despite their
collectivist approach to many areas of social policy, the Danes have
maintained a substantial plurality within their education system.
In Denmark education is compulsory for children between 7 and 15
years of age, and this education is provided generally in a common
school (the Folkeskole). In the 9th and 10th form (15 and 16 years
of age) young people have their first opportunity to choose between
staying in the formal education system and entering the world of work.

The Primary Cycle (Compulsory Schooling)

The Danish folkeskole is equivalent to the elementary and junior
secondary (i.e. compulsory) school in most OECD countries. Seven
years of schooling was made compulsory for all children as far back
as the early nineteenth century. During the 1960s social demand for
schooling increased, so that when, in the early 1970s, schooling was
made mandatory for a period of nine years, this was merely legislative affirmation of a de facto situation. Recently, a demand to move
towards twelve years of compulsory education for all has been expressed
by some student groups and a couple of the smaller left-wing political parties; this is a minority view, most interested organisations
and individuals being advocates of comprehensive but not compulsory
education and training provision for 16-19-year-olds. The folkeskole
already provides a 10th grade and consideration is being given to
offering the equivalent of 11th and 12th grade programmes attuned to
the needs of those who desire them, but these would be provided outside of the folkeskole framework (primarily within the gymnasium or
in the basic vocational training system).

The most striking development in the folkeskole sector over
recent years has been the progressive deferment of selection and
streaming into different ability and aptitude groupings and in many
schools their virtual abandonment. Annual examinations have largely
ceased, with a view to assisting each pupil to progress at his or her
own most appropriate pace. Thus, all pupils now progress automatically from grade to grade. For similar reasons, the curriculum has
been broadened considerably. The former segregation of grades 8 to
10 into a preparatory division for the final public examination (the

"realeksamen") and a general division for the non-academically
inclined has been abolished. Students may still opt for either of
two levels of study in the final years, one of which is in preparation for the gymnasium. This is a flexible option with parental
preference (after due counselling by school staff) being the final
arbiter. But individual school districts may decide not to divide
classes at all.

The Second Cycle

On completion of the 9 to 10 year primary cycle, young people
may continue their study or training in a variety of ways. If they
are interested in entering a university, a teacher training institution, or a business or commercial college, they may proceed to a
gymnasium or follow what is known as a higher preparatory course (HF);
they may commence basic vocational training (EFG) or join the apprenticeship scheme; or they may participate in some form of further education - evening classes or, if they have not already done so, enrol
in a continuation school; if they are 18 years of age or older they
may attend a folk high school.

In Denmark there appears to be some lack of fit between what the
compulsory period provides (some 55 per cent of age cohorts proceeded
to the 10th year in the folkeskole in 1979 but some 85 per cent were
in receipt of full-time education or training) and what is expected
of the increasing proportion (now over one-third) who proceed to the
gymnasium. A majority of young people who seek more education after
the folkeskole, and their numbers and proportion have increased
enormously, tend to favour gymnasia studies. Correspondingly, the
proportion, if not the absolute number, of all young people who want
a form of study aimed at direct preparation for jobs in trade and
industry is decreasing. Some critics argue that the advantage of an
extended general education is more than offset by postponing decisions
about future careers. Further, the choice is itself affected by the
availability of gymnasium places which local authorities are obliged
to provide in numbers sufficient to meet demand, and the scarcity of
places in vocational schools, which are centrally financed and need
not meet the level of demand for such places.

At the entry to the gymnasium, whose syllabuses and modes of
organisation are laid down by the Ministry, students choose between
two strands of study - "science" and "modern". In the first year most
subjects are common to both strands. After that the two strands are
further split into sub-groupings. While the curriculum is broad by
international standards, the units selected from it become increasingly
specialised. Gymnasium education finishes with the written and oral
"studentereksamen". This is the main vehicle for entry to university.

Until a few years ago the gymnasium was the only means for continuing higher education after the folkeskole. Since 1967, however,
a higher preparatory course (HF) normally attached to a gymnasium has
been offered. The credential for this course is the higher preparatory examination; candidates must attain the age of 18 years before
they present themselves. While gymnasium education is of 3 years'
duration, HF lasts for only two years. HF subject coverage is basically the same as that of the gymnasium, although the course is intended for those who wish to finish the twelve-year cycle of education
but do not necessarily wish to proceed onto academic higher education.
Although there are no strands in HF, a distinction is made between
core subjects and optional subjects.

At the upper secondary level, then, Denmark faces a classic set
of issues. The gymnasium now takes in a much larger and more heterogeneous section of the post-primary level age group, as both community
expectations and parental aspirations spiral upwards. It is highly
problematic whether a curriculum fundamentally designed for university
matriculation is suitable for all the students who now wish to study
in the gymnasium. Questions arise about the kinds of curriculum that
will best suit all needs, the best arrangements for providing young
people with useful and marketable qualifications, the extent to which
the education system contributes to broader patterns of living and
working, and what all this means for the first cycle of education and
for the relationship between the folkeskole and the gymnasium.

As in other countries, those most vulnerable to unemployment are
young people who left school at, or soon after, the compulsory school
leaving age and those who were discharged from the folkeskole. Girls
are at a greater disadvantage than boys. There is a tendency, also
noted in other OECD countries, for employers to raise the minimum
education qualification level for jobs that remain unchanged in nature
and so to reject applicants with lower qualifications whom previously
they would have accepted. In other words, everyone requires more
formal education just to keep the same place in the queue of job
seekers.

The authorities have taken particular pains to try to quantify
and categorise the number of disadvantaged young people, for whom
they have coined the phrase "the residual group" or "restgruppen".
The Ministry of Education estimated in 1973 that it numbered a fairly
constant 20,000 (almost 30 per cent of the cohort of school leavers).
Of these, some 3,000 young men and 7,000 young women have adequate
educational qualifications to qualify for entry into the further
education and training courses which have selective entry. The needs
of the 10,000 or so school leavers who are without such qualifications
cannot easily be met by the traditional education and training
arrangements. Some of them attend EFG courses, which in 1979 had a

total of 31,000 participants. The EFG courses are vocational training courses, lasting one year in a vocational school, and normally leading on to some kind of apprenticeship. There is no screening for young people starting EFG courses and these courses may not always be appropriate for disadvantaged children. The main impediments to assisting them are that they are poorly motivated or do not see the relevance of schooling to their needs and interests. New ways must therefore be found to arouse their enthusiasm and develop their potential.

It is recognised that many useful but essentially palliative measures have been introduced to tackle the employment-related problems of the young. However, we believe the need now is for a long-term strategy based on co-ordinated labour and educational policies at the national and local level. We note that it is the view of a majority of the members of the Central Council of Education that Denmark should move fairly rapidly towards the adoption of a comprehensive but non-compulsory three-year system of education and training for the 16-19-year-old group, characterised by freedom of choice for the student and a pluralistic system of institutions.

Individual Local Initiatives

Recognising that the situation necessarily varies from one locality to another, the government has also encouraged the establishment of local or regional committees representing local authorities, employment offices, vocational schools and labour organisations. A considerable number of initiatives have therefore been taken by and at the regional or local level under the auspices of these committees.

II

THE PROBLEMS OF YOUTH IN THE LABOUR MARKET

During our visit we were struck by the fact that those who were interviewed rarely mentioned the overall context within which youth unemployment occurs, i.e. the general labour market situation and the state of the economy. Unless asked, the people we spoke to scarcely mentioned the overall picture, whether they were people in charge of local projects, national youth organisations, pressure groups, unions, managements or employers. They did not see youth unemployment in the context of general unemployment, nor as perhaps reflecting an overall deficiency of demand.

An unwillingness to consider whether youth unemployment might reflect general economic conditions could rule out radical approaches to the problem, such as work-sharing or fiscal and economic incentives to intensify the use of labour as against other factors of production (capital, energy, raw materials, land). It may also be only through macro-economic policies that disparities in regional unemployment or discrimination against women workers can be effectively tackled. Measures directed at the transition from school to work, or at structural unemployment, certainly have their place. But they are no substitute for general economic policies intended to restore full employment, and may even raise false hopes if too much is expected of them.

One complication of comparative employment studies is that statistical practices differ between OECD countries. Some countries use statistical methods that maximise the officially registered numbers unemployed. Other countries leave some young people out of account, because they are not entitled to benefit or because they are looking for a training place. The vagaries of national insurance systems make a fair comparison of youth unemployment between countries especially difficult. Denmark is among the group of countries whose estimates of unemployment maximise its extent. Danish unemployment benefits are high and readily accessible, which encourages people to register as unemployed. Furthermore, unemployment is assessed on an hourly basis, so that part-time workers seeking full-time work are included.

41

The International Context

Given the sluggish growth rate of GDP in the OECD area over the past three years, it is not surprising that youth unemployment (1) has worsened since 1976. For the area as a whole (excluding Turkey) the youth unemployment rate was estimated at 11.3 per cent in 1979 compared to 10.4 per cent in 1976. Since the total unemployment rate in the OECD area (excluding Turkey) declined slightly over the same period from 5.4 to 5.1 per cent, this means that the youth share in total unemployment in the OECD area increased from 44 per cent in 1976 to 47 per cent in 1979. The severity of youth unemployment differs widely between countries but the problem in Denmark despite some recent improvements remains very serious. An internationally comparable estimate for youth unemployment for Denmark in 1979 was not yet available at the time when this report was prepared. However, the overall youth unemployment rate in 1978 was 13.9 per cent compared to 13.0 per cent in 1976.(2) Some improvement was reported in 1979, part of which is probably accounted for by the youth employment measures which were introduced by the Danish authorities.

In January 1980 the number of full-time insured jobless (3) young people (15-24) was 40,800 (16.1 per cent) compared with 43,800 (18 per cent) in January 1979 and 42,600 (17.8 per cent) in January 1978. This relatively stable position followed after a continuous rise from 6,000 young unemployed (3.9 per cent) in January 1974, i.e. a four-fold percentage increase. But these statistics do not give a complete picture of the unemployment problem for young people, as only 70-80 per cent of them are members of unemployment benefit funds. Danish statistical estimates for January 1979 reported a youth unemployment total of 56,212, some 28 per cent higher than the reported figure for youth unemployment among members of the insured labour force. This estimate includes the part-time insured and the non-insured unemployed.

The Age Factor

The age distribution of youth unemployment in Denmark is especially striking. Registered unemployment rates for the 18-25-year-old age group are much higher than for those under 18 years of age. The average rate of unemployment for under-18-year-olds was 4.2 per cent in 1979 (an average number of 1128) compared with a rate of 12.1 per cent for 18-19-year-olds (an average number of 8743).

---

1) The term "youth" generally refers to the 15-24 age group. There are some exceptions to this, e.g. in Norway, Sweden, the United Kingdom and the United States where the data refer to the 16-24 age group, and in Italy and Spain, where the data refer to the 14-24 age group. For further details see OECD, Youth Unemployment: The Causes and Consequences, Paris, 1980.
2) Youth Unemployment: Causes and Consequences, Ibid.
3) Young people under 18 were given the right to join an unemployment benefit fund in 1975.

42

and 13.3 per cent for the 20-24-year-old age group (absolute average number of 35,202).(1)   Table 4 gives the absolute distribution of unemployment (full-time equivalents) for 1979. A number of factors account for these differences. First, the level of school participation among 15-17-year-olds is still rising and in consequence there are fewer young people in this age group looking for work. Second, wages for young people under 18 years of age are much lower than for those over 18, and this has significantly affected youth unemployment rates. The average wage of a young person under 18 in 1979 was D.Kr.19.35 per hour compared with a guaranteed minimum wage of D.Kr.35.75 per hour for a young person 18 years of age or over (excluding apprentices). Juvenile wages are therefore approximately 50-70 per cent of the guaranteed minimum wage for those 18 years of age and above. This sudden jump in wages at the 18th birthday accounts for a significant part of the change in employers' attitudes to young people over 18 and seems to be strongly reflected in unemployment rates. The review team were informed on many occasions of young people being dismissed from employment on their 18th birthday and also of the existence of a special labour market (which could well be regarded as a secondary labour market) for those under 18 years of age. We shall say more about this later in our report.

Table 4

NUMBER OF UNEMPLOYED BY AGE AND SEX 1979
(CONVERTED INTO FULL-TIME EQUIVALENTS)

Age	Men	(1)	Women	(2)	Total	(3)
-18	453	(3%)	675	(2%)	1,128	(2%)
18-19	2,929	(17%)	5,814	(21%)	8,743	(19%)
20-24	13,737	(80%)	21,465	(77%)	35,202	(78%)
Total	17,119	100%	27,954	100%	45,073	100%

Source: Danish Statistical Yearbook, 1980.

Employment Differences between the Sexes

Unemployment among young Danes is also unevenly distributed by sex, with young girls and women experiencing higher levels of unemployment at all ages despite the fact that their level of labour force participation is significantly lower than that of men. The 1979 unemployment figures reveal the following pattern (see Table 5). This shows a rate of unemployment some 69 per cent higher for girls aged

1) Danish Statistical Yearbook, 1980. These figures are full-time equivalent estimates and therefore understate the number of young people who are affected by unemployment.

15-19 than for boys and a rate some 66 per cent higher for those aged
20-24. This compares with a female unemployment rate some 42 per cent
higher for primary age workers between 25-59.(1)

Table 5

UNEMPLOYMENT RATE: 1979 AVERAGE

Age	Males	Females
15-19	7.7	13.0
20-24	10.1	16.8
25-59	7.2	10.2

Source: Danish Statistical Yearbook, 1980.

We have already commented in Chapter I on the way labour markets
in Denmark are segmented by sex, and we have indicated in this chapter
some segmentation by age. Before proceeding we must, however, stress
that the vocational training and apprenticeship systems also show
markedly different participation patterns between young men and women.
In October 1976 approximately one-third of pupils in basic vocational
training (including EFG courses) were women, as were 20 per cent of all
apprentices. However, in the same year, intake into the traditional
apprenticeship system was approximately twice as large (by number of
participants) as into the basic vocational training system (EFG).
What is even more striking is the distribution of men and women within
different areas of training. In October 1976, only 0.3 per cent, or
64, women were apprentices in the iron and metal industries (the
largest section of the apprenticeship system); the remaining 21,750
(99.7 per cent) were males.(2) Conversely, at the same time women
accounted for 70.3 per cent of apprentices in the service trades and
57.8 per cent in the commercial and clerical fields. Table 6 sets
out the position in greater detail.

The Regional Distribution of Unemployment

The upsurge in unemployment which occurred from 1973 onwards was
not evenly distributed across the whole country. The trend seems to
be towards the traditionally weaker regions experiencing a smaller
rise in unemployment than those regions which normally have the lowest
unemployment rate, which is substantially higher than the national
average. On the other hand, the regions which normally have favourable

1) Danish Statistical Yearbook, 1980, Ibid.
2) Danish Ministry of Education Statistics quoted in Sex Roles in
   Education, Danish Equality Committee, 1978.

Table 6

POPULATION OF APPRENTICES AND PUPILS AT BASIC
VOCATIONAL TRAINING COURSES, DISTRIBUTED
ACCORDING TO SEX AND MAIN AREA
(1 October 1976)

Main Area	Apprentices				Pupils			
	Men	Women	Total	Women in % of total	Men	Women	Total	Women in % of total
Iron and metal industries	21,750	64	21,814	0.3	3,894	46	3,940	1.2
Building and construction area	10,643	299	10,942	2.7	2,113	126	2,239	5.6
Food and beverage industries	2,655	406	3,061	13.3	395	640	1,035	61.8
Graphic industries	920	136	1,056	12.9	583	393	976	40.3
Service trades	491	1,162	1,653	70.3	251	756	1,007	75.1
Agricultural field	15	2	17	11.8	108	31	139	22.3
Commercial and clerical field	7,103	9,716	16,819	57.8	1,421	3,046	4,468	68.2
of which:								
Retail trade	3,540	4,147	7,687	54.0	–	–	–	–
Clerical work	3,563	5,569	9,132	61.0	–	–	–	–
Total	43,577	11,785	55,362	21.3	8,765	5,038	13,803	36.5

Note: Participation in the basic EFG year is included under the
        heading "Pupils".
Source: Statistical material, Danish Ministry of Education, quoted in
        Sex Roles in Education, Danish Equality Committee, 1978.

employment conditions – e.g. Funen and East Jutland – have registered
a slightly higher increase and now suffer an unemployment rate which
is above the national average. No breakdown of youth unemployment
figures by region is available but it is thought that ratios of youth
to general unemployment (2.4 in 1973, 2.9 in 1976 and 2.0 in 1978)
apply in most regions. Table 7 sets out the regional distribution of
unemployment for all insured workers for 1973-1979.

Unemployment and Educational Attainment

     Unemployment is closely correlated with levels of educational
attainment, not only in Denmark but also in most OECD countries.
Table 8 indicates how unemployment in Denmark is most heavily concentrated on those who only received 7 or 8 years of education, and declines consistently as the level of educational participation and

Table 7

UNEMPLOYMENT AMONGST INSURED EMPLOYEES
DISTRIBUTED ACROSS REGIONS

Region	Unemployment ratio						
	1973	1974	1975	1976	1977	1978	1979
Copenhagen	2.3	4.1	8.8	8.7	9.9	10.4	7.8
Sealand	2.6	6.1	12.6	10.4	11.6	12.7	8.0
Laaland-Falster	3.5	6.3	11.7	10.5	13.7	15.0	8.0
Bornholm	3.9	5.5	10.3	8.3	9.9	13.2	9.8
Funen	2.7	6.1	13.1	11.0	13.2	15.3	10.7
South Jutland	2.2	3.7	9.4	7.3	8.5	10.8	8.0
East Jutland	2.5	5.8	13.2	9.4	11.7	13.4	9.8
West Jutland	2.9	5.9	11.4	7.5	10.0	11.9	9.9
North Jutland	5.8	8.9	15.7	12.7	16.4	17.6	12.6
Whole country	2.9	5.5	11.4	9.5	11.3	12.4	9.2

Note: Average of the month-end survey, which is why the sums
        deviate from the annual ratios stated elsewhere, which are
        averages of the weekly surveys.
Source: Ministry of Labour, "The Statistical and Economic Adviser",
        1979; and Danish Statistical Yearbook, 1980.

Table 8

UNEMPLOYMENT RATES FOR PERSONS AGED 15-24 BY
LEVEL OF EDUCATION AND SEX, 1978 (in percentages)

	Males	Females	All
A. Not attending school	13.8	18.5	16.1
1. Solely a school education			
7-8 class	19.6	31.2	23.7
9-10 class	17.5	24.3	21.3
lower secondary school exam.	14.3	16.6	15.9
upper secondary school exam.	15.8	14.9	15.3
2. Vocational education			
Apprentices	9.7	11.6	10.5
Further vocational education and training	1.1	9.3	10.0
B. Attending school	2.3	4.3	2.9
1. School education incl.			
upper secondary schools, higher preparatory courses, etc.	17.3	18.4	17.7
2. Vocational education			
Apprentices	0.7	2.2	1.2
Further vocational education and training	4.1	8.7	5.5
All	10.3	16.1	13.0

Source: Statistiske Efterretninger A-1979-I.

attainment increases. In 1978 the two extremes were an unemployment rate of 23.7 per cent for 15-24-year-olds with 7-8 years of education and of 10 per cent for graduates of further vocational education and training courses. The figures also reveal that, for the less well-qualified, unemployment rates are much higher for women than for men whilst for the more qualified (and those who have had a longer participation in education) the rates of unemployment are much more similar.

Who Suffers Most?

We have indicated a pattern of unemployment biased towards certain geographical areas, disproportionately female, higher for those over 18 years of age, and concentrated on those with lower levels of educational attainment. The experience of short-term unemployment, however, seems to be widely and rather randomly dispersed; the earlier longitudinal research of the Danish National Institute for Social Research indicates that at any one time more than one-third of young people have been unemployed. The Institute estimates that in the deteriorating labour market situation which has developed since that research, approximately half the population of young Danes will have to cope with unemployment at some time or other. The research, however, shows that whilst the incidence of unemployment seems rather randomly distributed, the question of who suffers most certainly is not. Their findings indicate that the long-term unemployed, and those with repeated experiences of unemployment, are highly correlated to those with no general educational competence and/or no occupational education. This latter group, known in Danish as the "restgruppen" - or residual group - are identified by the following characteristics and experiences:

- There are almost twice as many girls as boys (25-30 per cent of girls and 15-20 per cent of boys).
- Many of the boys and some of the girls have had an unsuccessful time at school. Many are unmotivated by traditional and theoretical education and regard themselves as "educational failures".
- Few of the men under 21 years of age, but many of the women (approximately one-third) had parental responsibilities.
- Many have suffered the effects of some other social disadvantage at home.
- Over one-third started vocational education, but have given up.

The pattern which emerges for this "residual group" is therefore broadly characterised by the following: the young person's experience of school has not been successful; the labour market pattern is one of leaving school and then doing unskilled work, or dropping out of

47

vocational education followed by unemployment, or withdrawing from
the labour market (sometimes to become housewives). This seems to be
followed by intervals of unemployment and a pattern of in and out of
work. Frequently, the social situation is characterised by these
young people living separately from their parents - more often than
not with a partner, and often also with a child or children.

Possible Explanations of the Problem

The review team considered a number of possible explanations of
youth unemployment in Denmark along the traditional lines of demand-
deficient unemployment, transitional unemployment and structural unemployment. Within these three broad definitions set out below,
special emphasis was placed on the macro-economic situation and its
consequences for youth.

Definitions

These three situations are characterised in the following way:

i) Demand-Deficient Unemployment

Where young people are unable to find work because of
lack of aggregate demand for goods and services in the
economy as a whole, or in particular regions.

ii) Transitional Unemployment

Where young people are unable to find work because they
cannot compete effectively with other groups of workers
or because of the structure of wage rates for young
people and relative differentials between them and other
groups of workers. Also included under this heading is
that unemployment which results when young people, new
to the labour market, try out a variety of jobs in order
to find out which sort interests them most, and unemployment owing to insufficient vocational and professional
skills.

iii) Structural Unemployment

Where young people, because of inadequate or limited
education or because of social disadvantage, are unable
to find work. This includes the particular problems of
unemployment based on sex or other social discrimination.

During our discussions in Denmark considerable emphasis was
placed on the problems of transitional and structural unemployment
but very little mention was made of demand-deficient unemployment.

At times, there seemed an almost univeral acceptance that the problem was exclusively of a transitional and structural nature. We can but disagree.

General Demand Deficiency

As we have noted earlier, for the years between 1970 and 1973 Denmark achieved remarkable success in maintaining full employment, at times being in a position of significant labour scarcity. In 1973 unemployment among insured workers was 2.4 per cent, equivalent to a figure of 0.9 per cent for the total labour force. This highly favourable employment situation was suddenly changed at the time of the world-wide downturn in trade which followed the first repercussions of the oil price increase of that year. In the period 1974-1978 Danish production stagnated and the growth of GNP was limited to 1.7 per cent in real terms. Unemployment increased substantially, especially among young people. We therefore feel that the deficiency of demand in the Danish economy is an important element in explaining the youth unemployment problem. Whilst there are undoubted structural elements affecting youth employment, the review team consider that during periods of general demand deficiency structural problems simply emphasise the underlying trend. We do, however, recognise that whilst the sharp downturn in the Danish economy and the increase in unemployment coincided with the first oil-price shock, the early decline in labour demand in Denmark is not wholly attributable to the international recession. The effect of the recession seems to have coincided with considerable domestic structural changes, viz. declining employment in the building sector and a slower rate of expansion in the public sector.

Whilst unemployment stabilised in 1978, and there was some improvement in 1979, the growth in domestic demand and output, whilst significant in 1979, does not appear to have been sustained into 1980. The improvement in the youth employment situation as in the general employment situation appears to be largely attributable to a growth in public sector employment; the impressive results of the Danish early retirement scheme which accounts for the equivalent of a 42,500 reduction in the level of unemployment,(1) and the fall in the labour force perhaps partly induced by the job offer scheme for the long-term unemployed. The improvement in the labour market situation in 1979 does not appear to come principally from general economic upturn. Therefore measures introduced to tackle youth unemployment should take

---

1) 50,000 people opted for the scheme in 1979. Of the 50,000, 60 per cent or 30,000 were employed, while the rest came directly from unemployment. It has been estimated that out of the 30,000 jobs becoming available due to the early retirement scheme about 75 per cent were subsequently filled.

special account of the overall level of demand in the Danish economy.
Given what we have previously said about the Danish balance of payments
and the vital importance of export industries, a clear long-term objective might be to bring demand management, industrial and labour
market measures together in a strategy to tackle youth unemployment
by training many more people for export-related industries, trades and
professions or for those that save imports, such as energy-conservation
measures.

Transitional Unemployment

The Danish authorities have invested substantially in measures
to ease the transition from school to work, in particular the EIFU
courses of basic vocational preparation and orientation which provide
a 10-week programme in the classroom and at the workplace, introducing
young people to the world of work and providing some job-tasting opportunities, as well as a number of work and education measures introduced under the Special Employment Plan. Despite these measures for
easing the transition from school to work there is considerable evidence of transitional unemployment, in particular as it relates to
the wage structure for those 18 years of age and older.

The effective free market for wages of young people under 18
years of age and the sharp and steep rise in minimum wages after the
eighteenth birthday both encourage a secondary labour market for the
under-eighteen-year-olds and produces an unfavourable attitude to
young people over eighteen from employers. The review team received
numerous reports which indicated that, whilst unemployment rates were
much lower for the under-eighteen-year-old group, the sort of employment they found was often highly unstable and did not always represent
a useful or positive introduction to the labour market. The fact that
many in this group found themselves unemployed after their eighteenth
birthday, despite the fact that they had work experience, suggests
that the cause was the increase in their cost of employment from
eighteen years onwards, a cost that may not be reflected in compen-
sating increases in productivity. The labour market for these young
people appears to be an unregulated (and often ununionised) wilderness.
The fact that regulation is introduced for those over the age of 18
does not resolve the problem; rather, it compounds it. We shall say
more about how the problem may be tackled later in this report, but
it undoubtedly requires changes in the structure and extent of training provision, an extension of labour market regulation for young
workers under 18 years of age and a more gradual move to the full
adult wage.

The review team are further concerned that the existing structure
of incentives to employers to provide sufficient training places,
especially for the least qualified, may be inadequate. The special

subsidies to employers, to hire and train young workers, account for
only a small percentage of expenditure and participation under the
Employment Plan. Indeed, the Danish Background Report indicates that
only 7 per cent of participants under the Employment Plan were covered
by subsidy measures accounting for just 2 per cent of the budget in
1978 and 5 per cent of participants and 3 per cent of the budget in
1979. A condition of successfully operating subsidy programmes is
that they should be acceptable to the social partners; indeed, we
understand that it has been the lack of support from the social partners which accounts for the low operating level of this programme.
We shall say more about this later in the report, but it seems essential that an acceptable framework of incentives to employers to hire
and to train less qualified young people be introduced.

Provision of labour market information, counselling/guidance services and placement services could be strengthened. As in most OECD
countries, there is some evidence that young people change jobs quite
rapidly and that their approach to work is somewhat more casual than
that of older workers. In times of high unemployment, this puts young
people at a considerable disadvantage in the labour market. Further,
we have noticed that the guidance and counselling services have a
strong social basis, often recruiting their professional staffs from
a social-work or teaching background. It is important that a strong
labour market orientation be introduced into such services and that
greater provision for work experience and work observation be introduced into the statutory education system.

Finally, we should like to comment on one aspect of the transition
as it relates to young women. Despite the efforts made by the Danish
authorities, it seems that sex discrimination is still alive and well
in Denmark, young women being concentrated in public sector employment
and in clerical and related areas. Both areas are vulnerable to increased unemployment, the first through pressure on public sector
budgets and the latter through the impact of technological change and
automation. Special attention needs to be given to emphasising non-
traditional employment options. Preparation for this must take place
early in school life and be reflected in curriculum choices made by
girls. The Danish authorities may also like to consider introducing
a system of incentives to employers to attract young women to non-
traditional apprenticeship areas in order to try and redress the
balance in apprenticeship provision indicated in Table 6.

Structural Unemployment

The structural problem of unemployment has at least three aspects
which the review team thought especially important, i.e. the problems
of the "restgruppen" or "residual group", the extent of unemployment
and labour market discrimination experienced by young women, and the

much wider question of the structure of the Danish economy and, particularly, how manpower policy can be related to industrial policy.

Whilst youth unemployment is traditionally higher than general unemployment in most, but not all, OECD countries, the problem of the unqualified, and often socially disadvantaged, is likely to increase most significantly in times of high unemployment. This is the most marginal of all groups in the labour market and whilst a structural phenomenon in itself, it is acutely sensitive to demand pressures. Many of the historic gains of this group in the Danish labour market derive from the exceptional level of growth in employment experienced in the 1960s and early 1970s, i.e. they benefited from Denmark's successful macro-economic performance in those years. Despite the very impressive social Welfare State and the enormous investments in education which have been made in Denmark, the disadvantaged group persists. We would, however, wish to record our impression that the equivalent groups in many other OECD countries appear to be disadvantaged to a greater absolute degree. Perhaps this owes at least something to the impressive investments in the Welfare State made by the Danish authorities over many years.

The problems of this group go much wider than issues of manpower policy. Many of the influences which combine to put young people into this group are the cumulative results of a cycle of disadvantage often starting from a very early age in the home. We have already said something about regularising the labour market for young workers under 18 years of age. Many of the members of this group leave school at the earliest opportunity. The fact that they enter the most unsatisfactory part of the Danish labour market only compounds social disadvantage and educational failure. Whilst measures to extend regulation in the labour market will help, as will expanding training facilities, we are conscious that this group have rejected traditional education and want to work. Two particular approaches might be considered: first, an effective structure of recurrent education and training aimed at this group in later life - say from 20 years of age onwards. This may well be a more effective response than the movement which we have noticed to have all 16-19-year-olds in full-time education and training. Second, the approach to tackling the problems of this group is as important as the programmes themselves. We saw in Denmark impressive models of a successful approach to this group, especially in the Vejle projects in Jutland. Emphasis on the all-round development of young people and emphasis on independence and initiative, rather than the reinforcement of dependence, are critically important. Within this context, a strong emphasis on learning-by-doing provides an effective basis for tackling the problems of this group.

In conclusion, we should add a few words of caution. In the main, these are not unemployable young people – they are those most vulnerable to the harsh economic climate we find ourselves facing at the moment. Unless we make effective provision for them, the danger remains that we will extend their cycle of disadvantage and they will never be able to make the transition into the primary labour market. We should therefore avoid the danger of mounting programmes to tackle imaginary problems; the overriding need of these young people is for work, with relevant education and training as an integral part; it is not the other way round.

We have commented in the section about transitional unemployment on the sex distribution of participation in the vocational education and apprenticeship system. There are also two structural elements of the problem which need to be taken into account when considering the reasons for disproportionately high levels of female youth unemployment; first, labour market segmentation and, second, equal pay.

As is illustrated in Table 9, women are typically employed in the service sector, whereas men dominate primary and secondary industries. This distribution may be influenced by women choosing or being offered jobs similar to the functions they undertake at home. Women usually are employed in jobs requiring a lower level of skill than men.

A person's level of education is one of the decisive factors in the kind of occupation he or she may undertake, especially when he or she first enters the labour market. Yet as far as school is concerned, there is no substantial difference between the educational attainment of boys and girls. The difference between the proportion in individual occupational groups is much more pronounced.

A presumption that the distribution by sex of educational attainment would be reflected in the distribution by occupation must be rejected on the basis of inquiries made by the Danish National Institute of Social Research. The proportion which received no vocational training is much bigger for women than for men. In groups receiving a short vocational education, women are predominant, while men more often get long-term vocational education and enter apprenticeships. This vocational training pattern helps explain both the higher rate of unemployment among women and the fact that men, to a much higher degree than women, have subordinates. Changing the structure of incentives to encourage employers to hire young women in non-traditional areas might be a useful way of improving their opportunities.

We would like to comment on the question of equal pay. Denmark has been one of the most successful countries in the OECD in achieving equal pay. Average female earnings were 85 per cent of average equivalent male earnings in 1977, only exceeded by France at 86 per

Table 9

NUMBERS EMPLOYED BY OCCUPATIONAL GROUPS AND SEX (1) 1950-1978

(in percentage)

	1950	1980	1967			1974			1976			1979		
			Men	Women	Total	Men	Women	Total	Men	Women	Total	Men	Women	Total
Agriculture, fishing, etc.	26	18	16	9	13	12	6	9	11	6	9	10	5	8
Manufacturing industries, etc.	27	30	32	22	29	32	17	26	31	16	25	31	14	24
Building and construction	7	7	13	1	9	12	2	8	13	1	8	13	2	8
Administrative, managerial and professional services, etc.(2)	9	13	12	29	18	17	44	28	17	46	29	19	50	23
Other services (3)	29	29	26	38	30	26	31	28	27	30	28	26	27	27
Respondents not stating any industry or occupation, conscripts	2	3	1	1	1	1	0	1	1	1	1	1	2	1
Total	100	100	100	100	100	100	100	100	100	100	100	100	100	100
Total in absolute figures (thousands)	1,920	2,066	1,478	863	2,341	1,413	977	2,390	1,423	1,001	2,424	1,439	1,090	2,529

1) Survey of the distribution by sex is only available from 1967.
2) Public administration, police and armed forces, education, libraries, health services, social institutions, other professional services.
3) Distributive trades, transport and communication, miscellaneous services.

Source: "The Living Conditions in Denmark", The Danish National Institute of Social Research and the Danish National Bureau of Statistics, 1976: material from "The Statistical and Economic Adviser", the Ministry of Labour and "Statistical News" 1968/75, "Statistical News" A 1980/18.

cent and Sweden at 87 per cent.(1) However, the "price" of this
considerable progress towards equal pay may be higher rates of unemployment for women. The point we wish to emphasise is that whilst
discrimination is alive and well, the nearer a country moves towards
effective rates of equal pay, the greater the impact of discrimination
by employers becomes. Particularly vulnerable in these circumstances
will be the young, because of their very newness in the labour market.

Finally, we wish to comment on the relationships between manpower policy and industrial and economic policy. We have commented in
Chapter I on the structure of the Danish economy in which the total
labour force in the productive sector is under 40 per cent. If the
Danish economy is to get back to full employment once again, it is
important that growth in the productive, as opposed to the public
(service) sector, be its main sustenance. In this regard, it is
important, especially in regions most seriously affected by unemployment, such as Jutland, that there should be an effective interface
between manpower policy and industrial policy.

---

1) OECD, Equal Opportunities for Women, Paris, 1979.

III

PRESENT PROGRAMMES TO TACKLE YOUTH UNEMPLOYMENT

The administration of manpower policy in Denmark is not significantly dissimilar to that found in most developed OECD countries.
The Ministry of Labour is responsible for policy areas such as the
public employment service, training of skilled and unskilled workers,
vocational guidance and a substantial number of the special measures
introduced under Employment Plan No. 2. The Ministry of Education is
responsible for vocational education and apprenticeship training, and
the Ministry of Commerce for regional development policy.

Within the scope of this report, we have looked at the following
programmes and services:

Ministry of Education:

  i) Apprenticeship
 ii) Basic Vocational Training (EFG)
iii) Extraordinary Traineeships and Apprenticeships) Employment
                                                     Plan
 iv) Continuation schools
  v) Courses for the Young Unemployed in Youth   )
     Schools   ) Employment
 vi) Contact and Information Services for Young   )   Plan
     People   )

Ministry of Labour:

  i) Employment projects   )
 ii) Vocational preparation courses (EIFU courses)   ) Employment
iii) Subsidies for the Employment of Young People   )   Plan

Joint Scheme:

  i) The proposal for a youth guarantee for young
     people.

In this chapter we outline the size and nature of the programmes
we have seen. In Chapter IV we present our evaluation of them.

Employment Plan No. 2

Most of the direct efforts to tackle youth unemployment are funded through Employment Plan No. 2, adopted by the Folketing in September 1977 and covering the period 1978-1980 (three years). This programme consists of energy conservation investments, measures to stimulate industrial production, youth employment programmes and provision for increased public sector employment. The total cost of these measures is D.Kr. 10 billion (1978 prices). Of this sum D.Kr. 1,500 million (just over half of one per cent of Danish GNP in 1978) is for youth employment measures. These youth employment measures are jointly run by the Ministry of Education and the Ministry of Labour and are intended for the age group under 25 years of age. Table 10 sets out the absolute and percentage participation in these measures by age, by sex and as a percentage of the primary labour force.

The local and county authorities are the main operators of the youth programmes provided under the Plan. Act 488 of 14 September 1977 (which authorises the programmes) provides that local and county authorities must each allocate at least D.Kr. 40 and D.Kr. 20 per inhabitant, per year, to help finance these extraordinary measures to tackle youth unemployment. Thus at least 60 per cent of the total cost of these measures was intended to be met through locally-raised revenue. Actually local and county authorities have spent more than they were required to by law; in 1979 locally raised revenue was D.Kr. 65 and D.Kr. 38 per inhabitant. Because of such large locally-raised contributions the national contributions have been reduced to some 30 per cent of total expenditure.

Arising from the report of the Working Party on Youth Unemployment appointed by the Danish Government in 1974, a Central Committee on Youth Unemployment was created in 1975. This Committee was succeeded by the Consultative Committee on Unemployment at the time of the introduction of Employment Plan No. 2 and consists of representatives of the Ministry of Labour, the Ministry of Education, the Directorate of Employment, the Secretariat for Vocational Training and the associations of local authorities. It is charged with the dual task of monitoring trends in youth unemployment and co-ordinating measures to tackle it. In addition to this, there exist a number of specialist advisory committees; five in the Ministry of Education and one in the Ministry of Labour. Finally, there are the local Labour Market Boards, comprising the social partners, the local authorities and representatives from the local labour market agency in each particular area. Their role is advisory.

Apprenticeship

The employer and worker organisations have, by law, a decisive influence in the training of apprentices. There is a Central

Table 10

PARTICIPATION IN EXTRAORDINARY EDUCATION AND EMPLOYMENT MEASURES
BY YOUNG PEOPLE 15-24, 1 JANUARY 1978 - 31 DECEMBER 1979

Programme	Men			Women			Total	% (1)
	Under 18 %	18-24 %	Absolute Number	Under 18 %	18-24 %	Absolute Number		
I Employment Projects	11	89	5,500	9	91	7,500	13,400	2.9
II Subsidies to Employers	30	70	1,000	12	88	800	1,800	0.4
III EIFU Courses	42	58	1,541	24	76	5,884	7,425	1.6
IV Additional Apprenticeship and Traineeship with Private Employers	50	50	4,060	21	79	2,570	7,130(2)	1.5
V Traineeships and Apprenticeships in Public Offices and Administration	16	84	185	8	92	483	776(3)	0.2
VI Partial Payment of Student Fees at Folk High School	52	48	205	37	63	305	510	0.1
VII Other Educational Activity offered by local authorities	29	71	230	22	78	350	580	0.1
Sub-Total I - VII	30	70	13,120	16	84	17,890	31,620	6.8
VIII Courses offered by County Authorities (estimate)							900	0.2
IX Continued payment of Unemployment Benefit during Participation at High School							1,750	0.4
X Courses at Commercial and Technical Schools (State financed)							600	0.1
XI Courses for long-term unemployed							800	0.2
Grand Total							35,670	7.7

1) Percentage of primary labour force aged 15-24 covered by these measures. The primary labour force comprises persons who have vocational work as their main occupation and other young people who have or are seeking permanent full- or part-time employment. Conscripts are included.

2) Includes 500 participants sex not specified.
3) Includes 100 participants sex not specified.

Source: Derived from Danish Background Report to the OECD Review of Youth Employment Programmes and Policies.

Apprenticeship Council and a network of joint committees for various trades, all of which are representative of employers and employees. The Ministry of Education administers the law but it is the joint committees which effectively determine what occupations are suitable for training, what practical and theoretical training is given, entry conditions and terms of apprenticeship, including wages.

At present there exist two apprenticeship training systems in Denmark. The old traditional apprenticeship system normally lasts for a period of three to three-and-a-half years, and is subject to signed indentures between the employer, the apprentice and his parents or guardians which may be broken by either part at any time and for any reason within the first three months following signature. There are two basic models for this system; one covering apprenticeship training in trade and industry and the other covering apprenticeship in commerce and clerical employment. Traditional apprenticeships in trade and industry are principally based on the employers' premises where the majority of training is expected to be provided, although there are usually four periods of college-based education. Approximately 80-85 per cent of the apprenticeship period is spent on the employer's premises under his supervision. At the end of the period apprentices are accredited as skilled workers if they pass the Journeyman's Test which is set by the Journeyman's Commission (composed of employers and employees) and judged by inspecting master craftsmen.

Within the commercial and clerical fields apprenticeships under the traditional system are usually $2\frac{1}{2}$-3 years long, and are similarly regulated by signed indentures. Again the majority of training takes place on the employer's premises although between 720-800 hours of college-based education is included. Certification is by written examination.

The EFG System

In the late 1960s there was a substantial decline in the intake of apprentices and corresponding shortfalls in the overall level of technical training, especially in those areas growing as a result of capital investment and new technology. This trend, as well as criticism of the highly specialised nature of much apprenticeship training, led to the creation of the basic vocational training system (EFG) in 1969, as the basis of a new apprenticeship system (hereafter referred to as the EFG system).

The EFG system consists of a 12-month basic period of training provided in a technical or commercial school. This first year aims to provide a much broader basis of education and training than that which exists under the traditional apprenticeship system. It is organised in eight main fields, each student choosing one broad area for his or her EFG training. These fields are:

Building and Construction

The Graphic Trades

Commerce and Clerical

Iron and Metal Work

Agriculture

Land Conveyance

Food Industry

Service Trades

In addition to specialised studies in his or her particular field, each student follows a programme of common education in subjects such as Danish, foreign languages, mathematics, sociology, business studies and sport.

This first basic year is unpaid in contrast to the first year in the traditional apprenticeship system. Following completion of the basic year apprentices move on to a sandwiched $2\frac{1}{2}$-3-year indentured apprenticeship with employers. Table 6, Chapter II, gives some indication of the distribution of places on the two schemes in October 1976 and Table 11 shows the intake pattern between the two systems over the period 1939-1979. It is, however, important to point out that successful completion of the first basic year in the EFG system does not guarantee a place as an indentured apprentice with an employer. There is in fact a marked shortfall of places for successful graduates of the basic year: some 26,000 successfully completed the course in 1979 but only 21,000 found places to continue their apprenticeship.

Table 11

INTAKE INTO EFG AND TRADITIONAL APPRENTICESHIP SYSTEMS

Year	Intake of basic vocational training students EFG system	Intake of apprentices traditional system		
		Commerce and clerical work	Crafts and industry	Total
1939	–	3,700	7,200	10,900
1945	–	4,300	8,400	12,700
1950	–	6,400	12,500	18,900
1955	–	8,000	13,000	21,000
1960	–	12,900	20,200	33.100
1965	–	16,200	21,700	37,400
1970	200	11,200	16,800	28,000
1975	6,400	5,500	9,500	15,000
1976	9,000	8,200	12,800	21,000
1977	13,000	7,800	12,500	20,300
1978	27,000	6,700	12,000	18,700
1979	31,000	5,000	11,000	16,000

Source: Danish Ministry of Education. These figures include participants on extraordinary apprenticeships operated under the Employment Plan.

Extraordinary Apprenticeship and Training

In addition to the two apprenticeship systems described above, there are additional places financed under the Employment Plan. These are provided:

i) directly by the Ministry of Education;

ii) by the local and county authorities in their own administration;

iii) by the local and county authorities in other public services;

iv) by subsidy from county authorities (and Copenhagen) to private employers.

In 1979 approximately 7,900 places were provided as follows:

a) Within State Offices and Institutions
(100 per cent subsidy):   435

b) Within county offices and institutions
(100 per cent subsidy):   99

c) Within local authority offices and institutions
(100 per cent subsidy):   242

d) Within private firms (subsidy D.Kr.10 per hour
up to a maximum of D.Kr.15,000):   7,130

Whilst some 42 per cent of participants were women, they were concentrated in apprenticeships in the public sector; 61 per cent of apprenticeships in the private sector were for men. Apart from the subsidy element, the organisation, supervision and legal regime are the same as in the two apprenticeship systems.

Continuation Schools

Continuation schools are provided as ordinary but alternative residential education opportunities for 14-18-year-olds. Their traditional purpose was to offer young people an opportunity to return to education at a time when the school leaving age was fourteen. The schools used to offer short courses (about five months) for young people who had been out in employment for one or more years. However, in light of the extension of compulsory schooling in 1972, the schools have responded by offering 8-10-month courses, parallel to a normal year at a folkeskole, which can be taken in the last two years of compulsory schooling. This has had the effect of increasing enrolment. Continuation schools are of many types and styles, some having a high proportion of pupils with educational or emotional problems. During the past few years the continuation schools have increasingly contributed to the special counter youth unemployment measures. Given that they serve the 14-18-year-old group and that they have widespread opportunities to introduce practical activities into their educational programmes, they have been seen as natural operators of special programmes. Despite this they remain an integral part of the Danish education system.

Courses at Youth Schools

Youth schools used to be an additional avenue of education to that provided in primary and lower secondary schools. Traditionally, they have catered for those 14-18-year-olds who have few marketable skills. They are run by the municipalities and attendance at them is not always full-time. Their original intention was to provide leisure activities for children who had dropped out of school. However, now they provide a wide range of special courses. In 1978 some 400 young people were receiving grants under Employment Plan No. 2 to attend courses at such schools. Youth schools are characterised by few rules and regulations and may be regarded as the Danish equivalent of free schools in the United States.

With financial support from the Employment Plan some 65 per cent of Denmark's 277 local authorities have established extended school guidance services.(1) These services, an extension of the existing education system's vocational guidance service, keep in touch with school leavers, providing advice and counselling during the transition into the labour market.

Employment Projects

Employment Projects are essentially public sector job creation programmes (public relief works) for the young, which provide additional local and community services. Some are involved in the provision of new services or maintenance, repair and recycling activities. Young unemployed people under 25 years of age may participate on a project for up to 26 weeks and in return receive a wage which averaged D.Kr. 36.60 per hour in 1979. In 1979 some 14,200 young people participated in one of these projects.

The State pays a subsidy of approximately 80 per cent of the wage costs and the local, or county, authority meets the remainder of wage costs and any supervision, planning and material costs which exceed the provisions made in central government allowances. Only 18 per cent of all participants in Employment Projects were enrolled on projects which had a fully integrated training element. The average length of participation was 17 weeks (with no significant difference between men and women) in 1979. Employment projects are operated by local and county authorities which may, and often do, sub-contract, with independent or private institutions such as church or youth groups to run projects.

Vocational Preparation Courses (EIFU courses)

The aim of EIFU courses is to provide locally planned basic vocational preparation which takes account of the types of work

---

1) On a basis of 239 returned reports from local authorities.

available in the local economy. The schemes are supervised by the
Directorate of Adult Vocational Education and implemented by the local
training college responsible for the training of unskilled workers.
Recruitment to the scheme is undertaken by the local labour exchange.
Originally introduced under the Vocational Training and Retraining
Act (June 1971) for workers between 18-25-years of age, the law was
amended to allow participation by 15-18-year-olds in 1976.

EIFU courses aim to give young unemployed people an introduction
to several trades and skills as a way of familiarising them with the
labour market, as well as providing broader information about training
and employment opportunities. They provide a course period of 6-8
weeks and normally a trainee service period of practical experience
of 4 weeks. The practical experience takes place in an area related
to the course instruction.

In 1979 EIFU courses were provided for some 7,450 young people,
80 per cent of whom had had 10 years or less of full-time education
and 85 per cent of whom had had no previous vocational education.
Participants were generally younger in EIFU courses (i.e. 20 years
and below) and a significant number (26 per cent) progressed to other
schemes provided by the Employment Plan (compared with 42 per cent in
1978). Some 33 per cent proceeded to employment (compared with 24
per cent in 1978) and 7 per cent were unemployed at the end of their
course (compared with 23 per cent in 1978).

Subsidies for the Employment of Young People

Employment subsidies provided under the Plan are targeted to
those who have been unemployed for three months or more (the minimum
eligibility requirement). Normally, subsidies are paid for a period
of up to six months, but in the case of a young person unemployed for
12 months or more within the previous 15 months, the subsidy may be
paid for up to 12 months.

The subsidy (in 1978) was D.Kr.10 per hour but from February 1979
it was increased to D.Kr.16 per hour for the first thirteen weeks of
subsidy, reducing to D.Kr.11 for the remaining period of subsidisation.
For young people under 18 years of age the subsidy is D.Kr.11 per
hour for all the subsidies period.

The local authority, following consideration by the local labour
market board, makes the final decision on each case; however, participating firms must be able to show that their employees are willing
to co-operate with the programme.

Whilst the scheme only accounts for 5 per cent of all participants in special employment programmes (1979) and 3 per cent of the
total budget, the majority had no previous vocational education and
had often experienced quite long periods of unemployment. In 1978
some 85 per cent of the participants were either in employment (71 per

cent), apprenticeship (8 per cent) or education (6 per cent) at the end of their period of subsidy; in 1979 some 75 per cent were either in employment or education and training at the end of the subsidy period.

The Youth Guarantee

The Youth Guarantee was not in operation at the time of our visit but it was a major new policy proposal discussed with us on several occasions during our visit to Denmark. The proposal, as we understand it, is to organise sufficient measures in such a way as to provide all young unemployed people with a positive and constructive alternative to unemployment. Whilst the proposal was still at a discussion stage (and very loosely defined) we shall comment on it later in this report, as it appears to us to represent a major extension of policy in the field of youth unemployment. We understand that subsequent to our visit, in September 1980, a youth guarantee pilot scheme has been started.

IV

THE OPERATION OF DANISH YOUTH EMPLOYMENT PROGRAMMES:
SOME COMMENTS

We have indicated the extent and type of the programmes that we were able to see and to discuss in Chapter III. In this chapter we offer some of our observations on the programmes that we have seen and discussed.

The Apprenticeship System and Basic Vocational Training (EFG)

Denmark now has two parallel systems of apprenticeship, both under the aegis of the Ministry of Education: a) the long-established apprenticeship system controlled by a rigorous Apprenticeship Act; b) a broadly conceived and still much disputed system, commonly known and hereinafter referred to as EFG.(1) Whatever the initial trials and tribulations of EFG, it is an imaginative departure. Training under EFG covers a period of three to four years. All students spend their first year in a vocational school pursuing a core curriculum in one of eight clusters of subjects collectively embracing the whole range of jobs in trade and industry. This reflects the growing international tendency to develop "transferable skills" rather than to restrict the student to preparation for one specific job. Thereafter, there is a gradual delineation of the occupational career to be chosen. The overriding intention is to defer career choices by leaving open the possibility of a change of direction until the student is really clear about where he wants to go. After the initial year, the student spends a large part of his time in paid employment outside school but the feature of EFG that above all distinguishes it from traditional apprenticeship training is the amount of time devoted to general education.

EFG began as an experiment in 1969 with very limited capacity — 200 in 1970, rising to 6,400 in 1975 — and the demand for places in this period exceeded the supply. Since then, the capacity has grown rapidly until in 1978 some 27,000 students were in the basic vocational year of EFG. Today, the number of places available exceeds the demand in some of the first year units and in some geographical areas. It is

1) A fuller description of this scheme was given in Chapter III.

important to ask why. There appear to be at least three reasons,
besides the obvious one that the rate of expansion of services has
been too great: a lack of financial support for students during the
first basic year, as distinct from the wages paid to young apprentices
in the first year of traditional apprenticeship; the difficulty experienced by many students in finding a training placement with an
employer after the basic year (some 5,000 failed to do so in 1979);
and no guarantee of a job on completion of the course.

The issue of financial support during the first year may well be
crucial. The majority of those taking EFG courses come from lower income groups where the urge to earn as rapidly as possible is a paramount concern. One solution would be to provide student grants from
public sources to make EFG as attractive financially as apprenticeship
training. But this raises the question of equity across the whole age
cohort still in some type of formal education. The most satisfactory
answer is to make student grants available to boys and girls in full-
time education or training from the age at which education ceases to
be compulsory. Such a scheme would cover both the first basic year
of EFG and the optional school years after the ninth grade. If it
were to be related to the income of the young person's family, it would
not necessarily be very expensive. Without such grants – or where, as
in Denmark, apprentices are remunerated but those in the EFG system or
staying on at school are not, the whole pattern of opportunity and
choice becomes distorted, especially for less well-off young people.

Placement for on-the-job training after the basic year is proving
to be a grave problem for many EFG students because the scheme does
not call for an indenture to a master tradesman at the beginning.
There is a need for major reform which we discuss later, but financial
inducements to employers to provide places and a further extension of
the extraordinary apprenticeship measures could be implemented quickly.
We wish, however, to note how impressive and up to date the plant and
equipment in the technical school we visited were, and the enthusiasm
of the staff with whom we had the opportunity to discuss their functions
and problems. By international standards, it seemed to us that the
technical institutions in Denmark are very well equipped and serviced.
Apart from the problem of financial support for students in their first
year of study, it is not from lack of finance that the EFG system is
suffering.

A further problem with the apprenticeship systems, both the old
and the new, is the way in which they reinforce labour market segmentation. We have set out in Chapter II the sex distribution of participation within these schemes. If there is to be a gradual move
towards providing allowances for the first year's participation in the
EFG scheme, priority could be given to boys and girls who undertake
courses for areas of employment not traditionally associated with their

own sex. Further, the State might offer incentives to employers to provide openings after the basic year to young women. Such an approach would need to be supplemented by practical advice and counselling to young people and their employers undertaking and providing apprenticeship in non-traditional areas. In this regard, we would suggest that the Danish authorities review the evaluation of the experimental measures to encourage female apprentices in traditionally male occupations which have been undertaken in Germany.

We noted a number of rigidities within the new Danish apprenticeship system. One which especially concerned us was the effective age ceiling on participation in apprenticeship. In Denmark, the vast majority enter apprenticeship after the completion of the tenth year of education. Indeed, in some apprenticeship occupations, entry after 18 years of age is effectively not possible. Such restriction makes it extremely difficult for a worker to upgrade his or her skills at a later age, especially given the rigid lines of demarcation enforced in skilled crafts by the Danish trade unions. Given that the distribution of unemployment is so biased towards the over-18-year-old group, and even more to the 20-24-year-old group, the Danish authorities should consider introducing a second route of entry into apprenticeship for young people between 20 and 24 years of age. Such an arrangement might well form the basis of a programme for recurrent education and training for young adult workers. We feel that a programme of "second opportunities" is vital, given the fact that it is virtually impossible for a semi-skilled worker to upgrade himself through on-the-job experience as might be the case in the United Kingdom or North America.

We are concerned that the EFG system does not take account of the likely level of demand for skilled workers in 3-4 years' time. Further, it appears to us that it is inflexible to the extent of being unable to take quick action to overcome skill shortages in times of economic growth or change because the availability of places within enterprises is outside the control of either government or any joint body of the social partners, a problem made more serious by the rigid demarcation of craft and skilled employment. The attitudes of Danish trade unions and employers in this regard cannot go without criticism. It appears that there is an unspoken agreement between the two parties to control intake into the EFG programme, in such a way as to provide maximum security for skilled workers in work, even at the expense of skill shortages, unemployment among the unskilled, and the consequent costs for the national economy. Despite the traditions of control of the labour market by the social partners and a non-interventionist approach to industrial and economic issues by the Danish government, the review team feel that the relative strength of the social partners and of the government (representing the general public interest) needs to be redressed in favour of the public interest. In this

regard, the Ministries of Education and Labour should consider establishing minimum quotas for apprenticeship intake for each sector of
the Danish economy with a provision for instituting training levies
on those sectors and those firms not reaching the required target.
We would suggest that the approach to tackling this problem should
first concern itself with training in the major export-related industries.

Before concluding this section on apprenticeship, we should like
to comment on the problems of small firms. Several small industrialists
reported to us their dissatisfaction with the new EFG scheme which
took away apprentices from the enterprise for much longer periods of
time than the previous system and also resulted in their waiting longer
before a young person is able to contribute to the output of the
enterprise. In our view these are very real problems and we would
recommend that the structure of incentives to employers to train should
take account of the particular constraints within which small firms
operate. In particular, we would suggest that Group-Training Associations grouping small employers together for apprenticeship training –
with indenture contracts between the Association and the apprentices
rather than with an individual firm – might be encouraged. Such an
approach would also provide a wider range of work experience for the
apprentice than a single small firm is able to provide.

Employment Projects

The Employment Projects which we saw – the carpentry and textile
workshop in Copenhagen and the fish farming and agriculture project
in Vejle – were impressive examples of a combination of practical work
and related education and training. However, their approaches to
tackling the educational needs of young people were quite different.
The Copenhagen project favoured a highly structured and supervised
approach, whilst the Vejle project was concerned to encourage young
people to learn for and about themselves through self-exploration.

Whilst the Employment Projects have been especially successful
in recruiting young people from the so-called "restgruppen", we are
concerned that in 1979 only 18 per cent of participants in these projects received any training integrated into the course. This particularly worries us because the target group they are trying to serve
is particularly vulnerable in the labour market. It is perhaps inevitable, in face of the pressures to mount programmes as quickly as
possible to "do something about youth unemployment", that the quality
of programme slips from what was originally intended. It is, however,
important that an integrated approach to work and education be
developed within all these programmes. In this regard, greater control needs to be exercised by both the Ministry of Labour and the
Ministry of Education in approving and re-approving projects. Further,

there is a need for a team of specialist advisors to help integrate
training into programmes as well as to extend effective sources of
information about the best practices as between different Employment
Projects.(1)

The quality of direction and supervision of these projects
should be the subject of constant attention. Whilst criticisms were
not made of the projects we saw, the review team received numerous
reports of inadequate direction and supervision on other projects.
Young people are quick to become cynical. Often unemployed for considerable periods and from socially disadvantaged backgrounds, they
require positive leadership, real and not illusory work, and a visible
opportunity for self-improvement. In this regard, the Danish authorities might, in the light of continuing high and projected levels of
youth unemployment, consider whether there should not be a career
development plan for the staff involved in operating programmes such
as this.

Whilst Employment Projects have been successful in recruiting
young women, and participation in this programme is roughly in line
with the sex distribution of unemployment, there is a danger of re-
inforcing labour market segmentation. Encouraging participation by
women in areas of work with which they are not traditionally associated
is an important objective; but in programmes such as this, dealing
with the disadvantaged, it is not the most important problem to tackle,
which inevitably is how to place young people in permanent employment.
There is a danger in establishing so many objectives for programmes
dealing with this group that none are effectively achieved. Employment Projects could, however, be used as "taster" experiences of work
in non-traditional areas before young people move into apprenticeships.

The maximum length of participation on an Employment Project is
26 weeks and the average length 3-4 months. Whilst many young people
do progress to full-time employment, there is a need for a longer
period of participation by the most disadvantaged participants. A
finer distinction should be drawn between those unemployed for reasons
of general demand deficiency and those unemployed by virtue of long-
standing social and educational disadvantages.

We should like to comment on the question of the sale of the output produced in the Employment Projects. Both the carpentry and textile projects in Copenhagen and the fish farming and agriculture project in Vejle were producing commercially saleable output. The review
team were, however, informed that the regulations which covered these

---

1) This might be modelled on the United Kingdom's Her Majesty's
Inspectorate of Education which is a group of highly qualified
advisers, professionally independent of the civil service and
answerable only to the Secretary of State for Education.

programmes prohibited the commercial sale of their output. In our
discussions with both employers and trade unions, we discovered no
general opposition to the output being marketed commercially. We
would strongly recommend that, wherever possible, Employment Projects
be encouraged to sell their output and to move towards commercial
viability for two reasons:

i) If Projects can become partially or wholly commercially
viable, they both reduce demands on the public purse and
add to the permanent industrial and commercial infrastructure.

ii) Such projects are a much more realistic introduction to
the world of work than programmes so unlike the real
world that confidence in them is eroded.

Courses of Vocational Preparation (EIFU courses)

The EIFU courses (courses of basic vocational preparation) which
we saw appeared both well and efficiently managed. We would, however,
wish to make three particular points:

i) First, the balance of these courses (six weeks' classroom instruction and four weeks' practical experience)
may be the wrong way round. We have noted earlier in
this report that the unemployed are disproportionately
drawn from the "restgruppen". These are the very same
young people who have not enjoyed especially successful
school experiences and have favoured leaving the education system for work at the earliest possible date. It
is important that young people's wishes and attitudes be
taken into account. A stronger emphasis on practical
experience might well help in this regard. Further, not
all of these courses manage to provide an element of
practical experience. It may well be that some system of
inducement to employers to provide sufficient places is
necessary; in any event, the central purpose of these
courses cannot be achieved unless the practical experience
element is assured.

ii) Second, we are concerned about the length of these
courses. A maximum duration of ten weeks in total seems
to us to be too short a period in which to achieve the
objectives for which they have been established. If, on
the other hand, the EIFU courses are intended only as a
"filter", then the ten-week period is probably too long.
It might be preferable for EIFU courses to commence with
a programme of practical work experience and then to be
followed by a period of classroom instruction. Ideally

the course should then lead to a further period of
practical work and perhaps the offer of subsidised employment. In this way, a progression into the normal labour
market might be facilitated and higher rates of post-
programme placement achieved. In this regard, we note
that post-programme placement rates for the EIFU were
lower than for other programmes in 1978 but have made
some improvements in 1979.

iii) Third, we are concerned about the pattern of entry into
EIFU courses. We note that some young people proceed
to Employment Projects and then to the first year of
apprenticeship (usually the EFG system). There is therefore some duplication; young people might be better
served by moving straight into apprenticeship. We feel
that clearer definitions of the target group and the
purpose of the programme are required.

Subsidies for the Employment of Young People in the Private Sector

The attitude of employers and trade unions towards improving the
level of youth employment through the wage subsidies offered by the
local authorities to employers who recruit the young unemployed is in
our view less than encouraging. The initial failure of this scheme
stems directly from the attitude of the Danish Employers' Federation
and the Danish Trade Unions, in particular their failure to find
mutually acceptable terms to operate the scheme. We fully understand
that employers will want to protect their prerogative over hiring
practices, and that unions will want to extend industrial democracy
and to safeguard against abuses of a scheme such as this, which could
create a "cheap labour force". But whilst the new agreement of
February 1979 seems to have resolved some of these issues, the operating level of the programme fell considerably in 1979 (from its 1978
level) and appears to us to be much lower than its full potential.
This may stem from a less than enthusiastic attitude on the part of
the social partners; the fact is that young people have to pay the
price for these attitudes. This is not an isolated example; it is
a reflection of the closely guarded control over the labour market
enjoyed by the social partners in Denmark, a subject we shall say
more about later in the report.

The Danish authorities have gone some way to distinguish between
different groups of the unemployed, by providing larger or longer
subsidy periods for those who have been out of work for 12 months or
more within the previous 15 months. We recognise that one reason for
this is to bring the long-term unemployed back into entitlement for
unemployment benefits. Nevertheless, we find this a sensible provision and would wish to see a similar approach used to tackle the

problems of labour market sex discrimination. The subsidy scheme could be arranged in such a way as to pay higher subsidies to employers recruiting young women in areas of employment with which they are not traditionally associated whilst maintaining the general level of subsidy as it is at the moment. Unless this happens, the subsidy scheme will continue to support and indeed reinforce the existing patterns of segmentation in the labour market. We note in particular that the existing scheme has not promoted any change in the traditional pattern of employment of young women. In this regard, we would strongly recommend that the Employment Service encourages firms participating in the programme to recruit young people on a non-discriminatory basis. Here, the Equal Opportunity Advisers proposed by the Danish Women's Equality Committee could play a useful role in educating both the Employment Service and employers.

The Continuation Schools

We were impressed by the Continuation School System and the continuation school that we visited. The system of continuation schools represents a remarkable example of the plurality of the Danish education system and plays an important role in the development of cultural and social values. We would, however, wish to make the following points: first, the schools may do a disservice to their students if they fail to point them in a positive direction at the end of their participation. For this reason, we would endorse the trend for these schools to devote more attention to the future employment needs of students, although this is a question of degree rather than of a fundamental change of direction. Second, in the light of the high cost of this part of the education system, we would recommend careful longitudinal follow-ups of the histories of continuation school graduates in regard to health, employment and general well-being to see how effective, in comparison with participation in other areas of education, the system is.

Youth Schools

The Youth School that we visited in Jutland appeared to us to so lack structure that young people attending courses there could be at risk of having their previous poor experiences with the education system converted into cynicism. This may well be an exaggeration but we would be interested to know if the Danish authorities believe that such an open-ended approach as existed in this school is the only way of meeting the needs of the educationally disillusioned. We found the youth school in marked contrast to the Vejle project which, whilst also pursuing a similarly open-ended approach to education, was characterised by a sense of purpose and participation. We would, however, comment that provision for part-time courses made available through youth schools (with corresponding part-time grants for the young unemployed) is an important aspect of provision.

Contact and Information Services and Vocational Preparation in Schools

In the view of the review team, the best strategy to tackle youth problems in the labour market is a preventive one. This means that preparation within the folkeskole for working life must be improved. Three major elements need to be taken into account; the curriculum, the attitudes of administrative and teaching staff, and guidance and counselling.

The curriculum in the last years of the primary school has recently been broadened to include a larger element concerned with preparation for working life and to soften the distinction between general and vocational education. Vocational studies as such, now an optional subject during the 8th to 10th years, is expressly designed to facilitate the transition to employment. Work experience is allowed for, periods of one to two weeks being spent at a workplace on two separate occasions during the final years. These curricular innovations could go far to arouse the interest and enhance the life and social skills of previously unmotivated students. It is our impression that the curriculum for many students is not yet sufficiently related to work and life after school and this problem is exacerbated by increasing numbers wishing to attend the gymnasia and heightened competition for entry into university.

On the question of the attitudes of professional staff we gained the impression from various meetings that, despite the desire of the Ministry of Education to strengthen the relationship between education and employment, the great majority of administrators and teachers are not concerned with preparation for working life except in a very diffuse sense. Nor are they sufficiently persuaded that significant learning takes place in many settings apart from the school. This is understandable, given the background and experience of most educational administrators and teachers, but it is hardly to be defended. Specific efforts are required to heighten their awareness of the practical, pedagogic and organisational implications of the concept by such routes as exchanges or secondments between professional educators and industry and services.

The authorities fully recognise that in order to make a sensible personal choice among the multiplicity of options available at the end of compulsory schooling, young men or women must be able to obtain reliable advice. To this end they have recently taken measures to improve guidance and counselling facilities within the schools and through the public employment services. The authorities also recognise that choices should not be irreversible and that it should therefore be possible to transfer from one type of programme to another. But our impression is that in practice it is far from easy to make a transfer.

Under the terms of the new Primary and Lower Secondary Education Act (1976), educational and career guidance is a mandatory part of the curriculum in the 7th to 9th years. The Upper Secondary Act (1977) requires that guidance will be provided for the 10th to 12th years. The Ministry of Labour also runs a long-established vocational guidance service. It does not seem, however, that the guidance service about working life is as yet at all well developed within the education system itself. We can only recommend that improvements should be implemented rapidly. We are not entirely convinced of the feasibility of the plan to train under one programme career advisers for all sectors of the school system: neither are the practical workings of the plan to extend and reinforce the links between educational institutions and the world of work, above all at the school level, entirely clear. We would recommend that particular efforts should be made to ensure the participation of parents and the social partners.

The arrangements for the extended guidance and counselling service introduced by the Ministry of Education since 1977 represent a useful degree of continuity in the system.

The Organisational and Institutional Issues

We should like to conclude this chapter with some general remarks about the conditions under which manpower policy in relation to youth is operated. We have already indicated in Chapter III the organisational structure of youth employment initiatives in Denmark. It is a complicated structure which involves responsibility for revenue raising at both the national and local level; responsibility for programme operation and supervision at both national and local level; varying degrees of involvement and control by the social partners - ranging from almost absolute in the case of apprenticeship to not much more than token in other cases; it involves operating responsibility for some independent groups (youth groups, church groups, etc.) as contractors to either local or national authorities; it involves a structure of specialist advisory committees at national and local level; it involves the local labour market boards and the national labour market board; it involves the national associations of the municipal and county associations. This extensive plurality of involvement has produced extensive inter-jurisdictional consultation and sometimes co-operation between the levels of government and the major interest groups in Danish society. Without doubt, it has contributed to most sectors of the economy and the society being aware of the problem and some in being involved in doing something about it.

We would, however, wish to comment that it has perhaps contributed to a lack of clear direction in Danish youth policies and resulted in considerable problems in co-ordinating programmes and in policy development and rationalisation. We have commented earlier in this report on the trends in Danish society towards the decentralisation of government to the local level, and in particular the responsibilities of locally elected authorities to have revenue-raising responsibilities for youth programmes. We have further indicated the almost exclusive role played by the social partners in controlling terms and conditions of employment, entry patterns, and the extent to which government can intervene in the labour market. Finally, we have commented on the need for a positive relationship between industrial and education policy.

We would wish to propose that the responsible ministries - Finance, Commerce, Labour, Education and Interior - be <u>centrally responsible</u> for the setting up of overall policy objectives, policy evaluation, development and co-ordination, with the local and county authorities being responsible for detailed programme design and implementation. The social partners should provide an advisory role at both the national and local level. For the apprenticeship system we would wish to propose that the social partners continue to have operating responsibility for programmes but should abide by broad policy objectives and precise targets established at the national level. We believe it is essential that clearly delineated responsibilities with regard to each of these areas be established so that communication and co-operation can be effective and not confusing.

Within the area of central policy responsibility we would suggest the following important policy considerations:

i) Apprenticeship targets should be determined in light of the expected demand for skilled manpower in the medium term. The structure of incentives and financial support should be designed in a sufficiently flexible way to ensure that training occurs in those local labour markets where the expected demand is likely to occur.

ii) The need for an adequate supply of skilled manpower for export-related industries and for energy conservation and substitution measures.

iii) The allocation of resources between academic secondary and higher education and vocational education and training schemes.

We have stressed the need to clarify the role of different parties in youth programmes and to make sure that each knows what his or her responsibility is. We saw evidence of fragmentation and the development of dual or parallel systems, for example, in the field of labour market information. Representatives of the labour exchanges reported that in some communities the local and county authorities were providing parallel services.

We have noted in Chapter II that whilst the regional distribution of unemployment has narrowed, regional variations still remain substantial. Rates of unemployment also vary considerably within regions. We have noted that the local authorities are responsible for raising fixed sums of money (Kr. 20 per inhabitant by county authorities and Kr. 40 per inhabitant by municipal authorities) to provide some 60 per cent of the total cost of special youth programmes under the Employment Plan. The money raised by each local authority is dispersed within its own jurisdiction. The financial allocations from the central authorities are principally based not on the proportion of young people unemployed but on the number of participants in special programmes there are in each local authority. However, the initiative for seeking a financial application rests with the local authority; money is not automatically allocated to local authorities. The result of this structure of jointly-shared financial responsibility is that there is relatively more money available to tackle youth unemployment in those areas where the problem is less acute. The financial structure of these programmes is therefore likely to reinforce inequality of provision, we believe, rather, that it should modify it.

We suspect that the trend towards local revenue raising is irreversible not only for reasons of ideology but also because of high levels of national taxation. Nonetheless, the problem remains of getting the money to those areas and those parts of local and county authorities where the problem is most severe. This may, however, mean getting money to certain parts of local and county authorities rather than to them as whole areas. We would strongly recommend that the central authorities organise their system of financial support in such a way that their 40 per cent of the total youth employment budget redresses the balance. This might be organised in the following way: 50 per cent of central expenditure would be distributed on a basis of reported levels of youth unemployment on a pro-rata basis; the remaining 50 per cent might be dispersed on a basis of a formula to include the following factors:

i) relative level of unemployment above the national average;
ii) the percentage of young people out of work for more than three months;
iii) sex-distribution of the unemployed and how this differs from their proportion of the age group.

We only suggest this as one possible approach in the light of our concern that the existing funding arrangements are not getting the money to those areas where it is most needed.

Policy Evaluation and Research

We have noted elsewhere in this report the large amount of policy experimentation which exists within Danish youth employment policies. We have also noted that sometimes there appears to exist a lack of clearly stated policy aims and objectives. Whilst we regard it as very important that youth employment programmes maintain an experimental element, each programme should be the subject of rigorous assessment and evaluation in order to build on the most promising and proven programmes and to eliminate unsuccessful approaches. In this regard, we were concerned that the programme of research which was explained to us did not seem to be sufficiently directed to serving the needs of policy or evaluation and development. We would strongly recommend that the Danish authorities (at the central level) invest in an evaluation of the costs and benefits of each of their programmes. Such an evaluation would illuminate the effect of different programmes on their participants, in comparison with the histories of those who do not participate.

In conclusion

We see the Danish policy for tackling youth unemployment essentially as a strategy aimed at helping young people to enter the labour market by additional programmes of training in its widest sense. Special emphasis is placed on the most disadvantaged group of young people (the "restgruppen"). Within this strategy, the programmes put into action appear concrete, imaginative and generally non-bureaucratic. However, we must ask ourselves if the strategy employed is capable of meeting the gravity of the present crisis.

V

THE WIDER CONTEXT: THE ECONOMY,
THE LABOUR MARKET
AND THE EDUCATION SYSTEM

In Chapter II we commented on the fact that those we talked with during our visit to Denmark scarcely mentioned the overall context in which the youth unemployment problem arises and that, in general, they did not interpret youth unemployment in relation to general unemployment, to the wider labour market or the macro-economic position of the Danish economy. This attitude runs the risk of obscuring more ambitious possibilities for tackling the problem. It has not been our role to consider the current Danish economic situation and the policies adopted towards it. However, given what we have said about the importance of demand deficiency in accounting for the current high levels of youth unemployment, we should like to make certain remarks.

Danish youth employment policies seem to us to represent something of a contradiction. In making our diagnosis we are hampered by a lack of information and a less than adequate statistical base. With between 7-8 per cent unemployment in 1978, Denmark had one of the highest levels of unemployment in the OECD. This rate represents a dramatic rise from 1 per cent before the crisis of 1973. Nor does the recent drop in unemployment in 1979 reflect a sustained improvement in Danish economic performance. It stems principally from early retirement, an increase in public sector employment and the special measures.

Real growth prospects in the Danish economy are poor in the next few years, and the economy faces particularly severe constraints with an external balance in constant current deficit financed only through foreign capital imports.

If our diagnosis of the general macro-economic situation is broadly correct, the strategy adopted to tackle youth unemployment appears inadequate in relation to the size of the problem.

It seemed to us that youth employment policy (excluding apprenticeship) has a stronger social orientation than an economic one. We feel that the Danish authorities should consider bringing youth employment policy closer to their broader economic policy aims. In this regard, we noted that whilst there were widely reported skill shortages, the available statistics on job vacancies were too poorly reported to provide a reasonable picture of the sorts of jobs available and the locations in which they arose. Until such time as effective arrangements exist for reporting vacancies, the/problem of mismatch will be more serious than it needs to be. On the basis of reliable data about skill shortages it should be possible to mount training programmes to redress the mismatch. Dealing with the mismatch problem will not only involve a clearer economic direction of manpower policy by the central government but also a broader interpretation of economic interest by the social partners.

We have commented in Chapter IV that the apprenticeship system needs to be geared to training targets established in the light of expected future demand for skilled manpower. We have stressed the critical importance of this in regard to export-related industries. Central forecasting, based on expected developments in demand disaggregated by sector, and on the projected retirement of skilled workers in the upper age ranges, is essential.

We have noted elsewhere that some of the Employment Projects appeared to offer prospects of commercial viability - for example the Vejle and Copenhagen Employment Projects. Projects such as these could do a great deal to encourage entrepreneurship among the young. Such schemes could be used to pioneer new approaches, especially where existing small companies are unable to finance the risks of pioneering technological innovations. The embryo for such an approach in Denmark exists; we would strongly recommend that these experiments be allowed to breathe; they could be suffocated by bureaucratic concerns and inhibitions.

Many of those involved in the Danish guidance and information services are recruited from social work and educational backgrounds. We commented in Chapter IV on the attitudes of the teaching profession to the world of work. We strongly recommend that the Danish authorities seek to recruit into these two areas people with experience of the industrial and commercial world. Further, we would want to encourage reciprocal exchanges between those in the productive sector and those in education so that the evident hostility between the two groups could be reduced and so that young people are able to enjoy an education more related to the world of work.

In Chapter II we indicated that the Danish productive sector is characterised by little direct government intervention and that the Danish labour market was almost exclusively regulated by the social partners. We believe that there is a strong case for a reappraisal of these attitudes. We have indicated the need to correct the role (or lack of it) of government in the apprenticeship system; we are, however, concerned that small firms in particular (the backbone of the Danish economy) need help in training skilled workers, in obtaining the services of professionally qualified engineers and specialists,

and often in making the jump to new technologies. Meeting these
particular needs will require government support though not necessarily government intervention. Manpower policy - in terms of sharing
the costs of training expensive highly qualified manpower - could make
a useful contribution. Total employment in the productive sector is
still declining in Denmark and, even though productivity performance
is relatively good, a country so dependent on the export of manufac-
tures must pay special regard to sustaining employment in the productive sector. The recent initiative of the Danish government to encourage pension funds and insurance companies to channel some D.Kr.
5 billion ($820 million) into risk investment is encouraging. The idea
is to make insurance and pension fund money available at favourable
interest rates in return for a higher rate of return to the investor
if the scheme is successful. Whilst such a scheme has many risks, and
there is no guarantee that the availability of cash will encourage
business to invest, it may help to reverse the decline in industrial
employment.(1)

Wages and the Youth Labour Market

We have noted that the labour market is highly regulated by collective agreements between employers and unions but that this is not
the case for workers under 18 years of age. Whilst workers of 18
years and over receive a guaranteed minimum wage of D.Kr.35.75 per hour,
in 1979 rates of pay for younger workers average some 50-70 per cent
of this figure. A few are, however, regulated by collective agreement.
Two major problems have developed from this set of arrangements:

  i) A secondary labour market for young workers between
     15-18 has been created;
 ii) There is a sharp change in employers' attitudes towards
     the employment of young people over 18 whose costs of
     employment rise substantially and immediately on their
     eighteenth birthday.

Whilst unemployment rates are much lower for the 15-18-year age
group, the labour market these young workers find themselves in is an
unhealthy environment in which to start working life. We have received many reports that jobs for them are casual, dead-end and provide little opportunity for advancement. Further, we note that the
majority of young workers in these jobs are drawn from the so-called
"restgruppen", i.e. those most vulnerable in the labour market in
later years, who often find themselves unemployed when they become
18 years of age. Poor or dirty jobs exist and need to be filled, but

---

1) We note that subsequent to our visit to Denmark these proposals
   have been withdrawn.

we are concerned about the lack of regulation of terms and conditions of unemployment for the 15-18-year-olds, in marked contrast to a highly regulated labour market for other workers, and the way it has contributed to the growth of a juvenile secondary labour market. It is those most at risk of unemployment later on who start their working lives in this environment, often becoming participants in special measures programmes which seek to reverse some of the damage done during this period.

We have received many reports of young people being dismissed from employment on or soon after their eighteenth birthday. The attitude of employers to the over-18-year-old group changes because of greatly increased wage costs which may not be reflected in correspondingly increased productivity. It seems to us that this sudden jump in wages must, to some considerable degree, account for the substantial increase in unemployment experienced by the over-18-year-old group. The Danish authorities might consider introducing measures to extend labour market regulation for the 15-18-year-old age group whilst arranging for a more gradual progression to full adult minimum rates of pay. Whatever regulation of terms and conditions is introduced will need to be supplemented by integrated education and training measures for these young workers, in order to help ensure them a firm position as well as a first position in the labour market.

Segmentation in the Labour Market

We have already made specific proposals for tackling labour market discrimination on grounds of sex through reform in the education system, the apprenticeship system, and special measures programmes. We have also indicated the need for financial incentives to help overcome discrimination. Measures to tackle segmentation will take time to produce results, perhaps most importantly because they require major changes in attitudes not only on the part of men, but also of women. The role of the education system in this regard will be crucial. Change can be encouraged through example, and in this regard employment policy in public bodies - government departments, local government and the like - should set the right example by establishing equal opportunity career policies for men and women.

Academic Secondary Education and Vocational Education

We have commented that there are two different financial systems for providing academic upper secondary education (the gymnasium) and vocational education. Local education authorities are obliged by law to provide sufficient places in gymnasia to meet the demand in their locality. Conversely, central government provides the finance for vocational schools but faces no legal requirement to meet demand. The range of vocational education opportunities is much more limited

than the range of academic schools. We believe that there is a need
to introduce some better balance of provision between the two systems.
This might be assisted by introducing vocational education elements
into the gymnasium. We recognise this is a complex issue and one
which goes to the heart of the question of parental choice. Nonetheless, many young people find a vocationally based upper secondary education interesting and rewarding. Gymnasium intakes are increasingly
heterogeneous. The introduction of numerus clausus upon entrants into
higher education and the restrictions on intake into the teaching
profession will limit opportunities for the traditional gymnasium
alumnus.

A Youth Guarantee

Finally, before concluding this chapter, we should like to comment on the Danish proposals for a Youth Guarantee. We are uncertain
as to the exact nature of this guarantee but the purpose seemed to be
to ensure that all young people can be provided with a suitable and
constructive alternative to unemployment.

As with a commercial guarantee, a youth guarantee would vary in
both content and value. It would not necessarily imply some automatic set of rights but would be rather a safety-net providing a
minimum level of support and protection available to all young people.
The eligibility terms for, and the contents of, a youth guarantee
have major implications - not least for the cost of realising such a
policy declaration. A guaranteed place on a programme for all young
people is likely to be very expensive; but a guaranteed place for
all young people unemployed for say a year or more is unlikely to
involve much more provision than is currently available. A compromise
might be found by guaranteeing such a place to those still unemployed
six months after completing their schooling. In our view a guarantee
would be more valuable if the reforms set out in this report could be
introduced, for then the opportunity of moving into permanent and
worthwhile jobs from a place on a special youth programme would have
been considerably enhanced.

VI

In light of the many short-term measures introduced to tackle youth employment, education and training needs, there is now a need for a long-term strategy based on co-ordinated labour and educational policies at the national and local level.

The problem of youth unemployment should be clearly considered within the context of general economic considerations. Whilst measures directed at the transition from school to work, or at structural unemployment, certainly have their place, they are no substitute for general economic policies intended to restore full employment.

A clear long-term objective for tackling youth unemployment might be to bring demand-management, industrial and labour market measures together by training many more young people for export-related industries, trades and professions, or for those that save imports, such as energy conservation measures.

Tackling the problem of the secondary labour market for workers under 18 years of age requires changes in the structure and extent of training provision, an extension of labour market regulation for young workers under 18 years of age and a more gradual move to the full adult wage.

The operating conditions for employment subsidies for the additional recruitment of young people require review in order to encourage employers to hire and train less qualified young people.

Provision of labour market information and counselling should be strengthened and a greater emphasis on the labour market be introduced into these services.

Measures to tackle the labour market problems of the "restgruppen" need to go further than extension of labour market regulation. Two particular approaches might be considered; first, an effective structure of recurrent education and training aimed at this group from, say, 20 years of age onwards. Second, emphasis with programmes should be placed on the development of independence and initiative, through learning by doing.

Manpower policy should be closely related to industrial policy.

The issue of financial support during the first year of EFG training may well be crucial. The most satisfactory answer is to make

83

student grants available to boys and girls in full-time education and training from the age at which education ceases to be compulsory. Such a scheme would cover both the first basic year of EFG training and the optional school years after the ninth grade.

Financial inducements to employers to provide more apprenticeship places for those who have completed the first year of EFG training are required. A further extension of the extraordinary apprenticeship measures could be implemented quickly.

If there is to be a gradual move towards providing allowances for the first year's participation in the EFG scheme, priority could be given to boys and girls who undertake courses for areas of employment not traditionally associated with their own sex. Further, the State might offer incentives to employers to provide apprenticeship openings after the completion of the basic year to young women seeking work in such areas.

As part of the proposed structure of recurrent education, the Danish authorities should consider establishing a second route of entry into apprenticeship for the 20-24 age group.

The Ministries of Education and Labour should consider establishing minimum quotas for apprenticeship intake for each sector of the Danish economy with provision for instituting training levies on those firms not reaching the required target.

Any structure of incentives to encourage employers to train should take account of the particular constraints in them which small firms operate. In particular, we would suggest that Group-Training Associations might be encouraged.

It is important that an integrated approach to work and education is developed in Employment Projects. Greater control needs to be exercised over the approval and reapproval of projects, and consideration should be given to establishing a team of specialist advisers to help integrate training into projects.

Consideration should be given to the career development needs of trainers working on special programmes.

When considering the intake of young people into projects, a finer distinction should be drawn between those unemployed for reasons of general demand deficiency and those unemployed by virtue of long-standing social and educational disadvantages.

We would strongly recommend that, wherever possible, employment projects be encouraged to sell their output and move towards commercial viability.

Consideration should be given to a stronger emphasis on practical experience in EIFU courses, improving progression after clearer definition of the target group for these programmes.

Within employment subsidy programmes, larger subsidies could be provided to those employers recruiting young women in areas of employment with which they are not traditionally associated.

Comparative longitudinal studies of continuation school graduates in comparison with those who do not attend these schools should be undertaken.

Specific efforts are required to heighten teachers' awareness of the practical, pedagogic and organisational implications of a closer relationship between education and employment, by such routes as secondments between professional educators and industry and commerce.

The role of the careers guidance system within schools needs strengthening and efforts should be made to involve parents and the social partners in providing and accepting advice about the world of work.

Central policy objectives about youth employment should be decided by the Ministries of Finance, Commerce, Labour, Education and Interior. Operational responsibility should rest with local and county authorities. For the apprenticeship system the social partnesr should maintain operating responsibility but abide by broad policy objectives and precise targets established at the national level.

Apprenticeship training targets need to be established in light of the expected demand for skilled manpower in the medium term.

The system of financing youth employment measures needs to ensure that funds are directed to those areas where the problem is most acute.

We would strongly recommend that the Danish authorities (at the central level) invest in an evaluation of the costs and benefits of each of their programmes.

Dealing with the "mismatch problem" will require a better system for reporting vacancies and a more economic direction within manpower policy.

Employment projects could do a great deal to encourage entrepreneurship among the young. Such schemes should be used to encourage new approaches, especially where small companies are unable to finance the risks of pioneering technological innovations. We would strongly recommend that those experimental projects tackling these problems should be allowed to breathe and not be suffocated by bureaucratic concerns and inhibitions.

The labour market for 15-18-year-olds needs to be effectively regulated and in particular there needs to be a more gradual progression to full adult minimum rates of pay.

Equal opportunity career policies for men and women should be established in all public bodies.

A better balance between the academic and vocational education systems is required which may involve changes in the financing of these two systems. Vocational education elements should be introduced into the gymnasium.

A youth guarantee might be provided for all young people unemployed for six months or more; however, its success in enabling
young people to progress into permanent and worthwhile jobs is
dependent on wider educational and labour market reforms.

Part Three

A REVIEW OF YOUTH EMPLOYMENT POLICIES IN GERMANY

THE OECD EXAMINERS

The Rt. Hon. Mrs. Shirley Williams, P.C.
Chairman

- Senior Research Fellow at the Policy Studies Institute
  (formerly Secretary of State for Education and Science),
  the United Kingdom

Mr. Jacques Legendre

- Then Secrétaire d'Etat auprès du Premier ministre chargé de
  la formation professionnelle, France

Professor Sar Levitan

- Professor and Director of the Centre for Social Policy
  Studies, the George Washington University, United States

INTRODUCTION

In several OECD countries there has been a shift from an era of rapid economic growth to slower growth in the 1970s which brought about fundamental changes in their labour markets. Unemployment has risen to high levels, and its burden has fallen especially heavily on those least able to compete for jobs, notably young people.

In several respects the problem of youth unemployment differs in Germany from that in other OECD countries. Its post-war baby-boom came later, peaked in 1964, and was followed by a sharp decline in fertility. Consequently, the labour market in the later 1970s has had to absorb sudden increases in the numbers of adolescents, a trend that will continue into the 1980s and then be followed by a fall in a few years.

The ways of dealing with the problem of youth unemployment are different too. Unlike many other countries, Germany makes relatively little use of job creation measures. Instead, strenuous efforts have been made to reduce the number entering the labour force direct from school, and its well-established system of vocational education and training has been expanded to absorb more adolescents.

Our report is based on a background report prepared by the Federal Ministry of Labour, statements from the Federal Ministry of Education, and a brief 8-day visit to Germany in January 1980. During our visit we had discussions with representatives of the Federal Ministries of Labour, Education and Economics of the governments of the Rhineland-Palatinate and of North-Rhine Westphalia; the President of the Federal Institute for Employment in Nuremberg; the General Secretary of the Federal Training Institute; the Federation of German Employers' Associations; the German Trade Union Confederation; the German Confederation of Chambers of Industry and Commerce; and the Chamber of Handicrafts at Düsseldorf whose training workshops we also visited. We visited the local Labour Office in Nuremberg; the training workshops of the BASF, a large private enterprise in Ludwigshafen; vocational schools in Mainz and Cologne, and the counselling centre in Dortmund. We also had a discussion with Burkhart Lutz, Director of the Institute for Social Science Research in Munich.

We are grateful to those we met for their co-operation, their willingness to share their expertise with us and to respond to our many questions. Their thoughtful presentations and comments reflected the widespread concern throughout Germany to find ways not only to keep youth unemployment low but to give young people opportunities to find their places in the labour market and in the community. In the course of our review we have concentrated our thoughts on the most central questions. We have reviewed what has so far been done to keep youth unemployment down. We have also tried to look ahead. The very success of German policies so far has created problems that need to be recognised if Germany is to bring to bear on them the same political will that has inspired its efforts so far.

I

YOUTH UNEMPLOYMENT

The German Economy since 1950

During the past three decades Germany has enjoyed continued
economic growth, interrupted briefly in 1967 and more severely during
the economic recession in the mid-1970s. Real GNP during the period
multiplied six-fold. This remarkable growth was achieved with an increase of only 20 per cent in the labour force. Sustained growth was
made possible by an uninterrupted growth in productivity. Output per
working hour more than quintupled during the same period. Real annual
wages did not keep pace with rising productivity, but still trebled
during the post-World War II period. The reason why real wages rose
more slowly than productivity was that Germany invested part of its
rising productivity in increased leisure. After World War II average
hours of work per week in Germany declined from 48.1 hours in 1950 to
41.9 hours in 1979.

The unprecedented growth of the economy during the first generation following World War II slowed down in 1973, but progress did
not stop even after the shock of the increased oil prices exacted by
the OPEC nations. After a drop of almost 2 per cent in real GNP in
1975, the German economy rebounded the next year, showing a hefty
growth of more than 5 per cent in 1976 (Table 1). During the final
three years of the past decade the rise in real GNP averaged 3.6 per
cent, and productivity per hour during the four years following the
recession rose by an annual average of more than 4 per cent.

Table 1

GROWTH OF GROSS NATIONAL PRODUCT AT CONSTANT (1970) PRICES
(percentage rate of growth)

1966-1977	3.6
1975	-1.8
1976	5.3
1977	2.8
1978	3.6
1979	4.5
1980	1.3/4*

* Estimate.
Source: OECD, National Accounts of OECD Countries, 1961-1978, Paris,
1980, and OECD, Economic Outlook, No. 28, Paris, July 1980.

By 1960 Germany had recovered from the devastation caused by World War II. During the next 14 years it experienced full employment until the 1974 economic crisis hit the industrial world (Table 2).

Table 2

UNEMPLOYMENT

(percentages)

1964–1973	0.9
1974	2.2
1975	4.1
1976	4.1
1977	4.0
1978	3.8
1979	3.3

Source: OECD, Labour Force Statistics as updated by the Quarterly Supplement, Paris, 1980.

Current labour market statistics have, however, lost much of their validity in modern industrial countries. As long as the only option for most people was to work or to starve, unemployment was properly identified with economic hardship. The level of unemployment was therefore a sound measure of the state of the economy. In today's Welfare State the unemployed worker forced into idleness has various sources of support. So do retired people and those who, because of ill-health or other reasons, are unable to work. In 1979, total disposable income available to the 61 million people in Germany amounted to DM.876 billion, of which transfer payments accounted to 26.8 per cent. The share of total income distributed through transfer payments is higher in Germany than in most other advanced industrial countries.

During the 1970s inflation became the dominant spectre haunting major industrial economies. But rising energy and raw material prices were not the only cause of inflation. Excess demand during the early 1970s was also a source, and inflationary expectations combined with cost-push inflation on the supply side have made the situation more difficult.

Conventional wisdom held that inflation and unemployment could not exist side by side. Rising unemployment reflected declining economic activity which in turn depressed prices. Conversely, a rise of wages could not happen as long as idle labour was competing for scarce jobs. The same was believed about the prices of commodities: their prices would not rise if firms faced massive inventories of unsold goods.

The challenge to post-World War II economic policy makers has been to create an economic climate that would strike the most acceptable balance between the ills of inflation and unemployment. But this

goal has remained elusive. To capture the combined impact of the two
ills, the late American economist Arthur Okun suggested the use of a
"discomfort index", the simple addition of the unemployment and inflation rates. For example, given an unemployment rate of 5 per cent
and inflation of 4 per cent, the discomfort index would be 9 per cent.

Based on this discomfort index, the German economic miracle continued in the 1970s, albeit not at the phenomenal level of the previous
decade (Table 3). Compared, however, with the record of other major
OECD partners, the German economy has continued to operate at a remarkably high level of activity with a minimum of inflation. The discomfort index for Germany was, at its peak, less than half as high as
in other major OECD countries.

Table 3

DISCOMFORT INDEXES, 1st QUARTER, 1980

Country	Inflation (at annual rate)	Unemployment (latest month)	Discomfort index
Germany	5.8	3.4	9.2
France	13.9	6.0	19.9
Italy	20.9	7.7	28.6
United Kingdom	21.8	5.8	27.6
United States	14.7	5.8	20.5

Source: Derived from data in OECD, Labour Force Statistics, Paris,
        1980 and OECD, Main Economic Indicators, Paris, 1980.

A major factor contributing to the relatively low German discomfort index is the fact that the growth in the productivity of its
labour force during the 1970s has exceeded that of other OECD
countries (Table 4). Increases in productivity have permitted gains
in the real standard of living in industrial countries. Any increases

Table 4

RATIO OF GNP TO EMPLOYMENT,
AVERAGE ANNUAL CHANGE, 1973-1980
(percentages)

Germany	3.1
France	2.7
Italy	1.9
United Kingdom	0.4
United States	0.0

Source: OECD, Main Economic Indicators, Paris, 1980.

in wages and salaries above the rise in productivity are likely to result in higher inflation. In most OECD countries the rate of productivity growth declined during the 1970s compared with the 1960s. In some countries productivity has actually stagnated during recent years, and there have been no increases in the real standard of living. The growth of German productivity has, however, continued significantly to exceed that of its neighbours.

The productivity data that are most appropriate for purposes of comparisons are for manufacturing. The growth of German productivity in manufacturing during the 1970s was more than double that of the United States or of the United Kingdom. It even exceeded the productivity growth of Japan, which also experienced sustained and phenomenally high growth during the post-World War II era. The growth of German productivity per work hour continued at the remarkable level of close to 5 per cent during the 1970s.

Youth Employment and Unemployment

Turning to the official comparisons of youth unemployment the German record is equally remarkable. During the first half of the 1970s the number of unemployed adolescents rose more quickly than total unemployment. The increase was especially sharp in 1974 and 1975. In September 1975 there were 116,000 adolescents unemployed. However the number unemployed fell in 1978 and 1979, and by September 1979 it had fallen to 68,600. But youth unemployment rates in several OECD countries were at least three times as high as in Germany (Figure 1).

In most OECD countries unemployment has borne more heavily on young people than on adults. The youth unemployment rate has exceeded that of adults by a factor of about two in Canada, Finland and Japan; by a factor of about three in Australia, France, Sweden, the United Kingdom and the United States; by more than four in Portugal and Spain; and by more than six in Italy. Yet Germany has succeeded in keeping youth unemployment at a rate close to that of adults (Table 5).

It is not surprising that the rate of unemployment of young people should nevertheless still be higher than that of adults. In most OECD countries the ability of young people to compete for jobs is weakened by legislation intended to protect them. In Germany, under the Youth Labour Protection Law of 1976, which greatly extended the provisions of an earlier law of 1960, the employment of young people under 18 is regulated. The minimum age at which they can be employed has been raised from 14 to 15. Under 18, young people must have a minimum of 8 hours a week off work to go to vocational school. The maximum work-week has been reduced from 44 hours to 40, and the maximum length of shift is 10 hours a day except in restaurants, where

94

Figure 1
YOUTH UNEMPLOYMENT RATES, 1970-1979

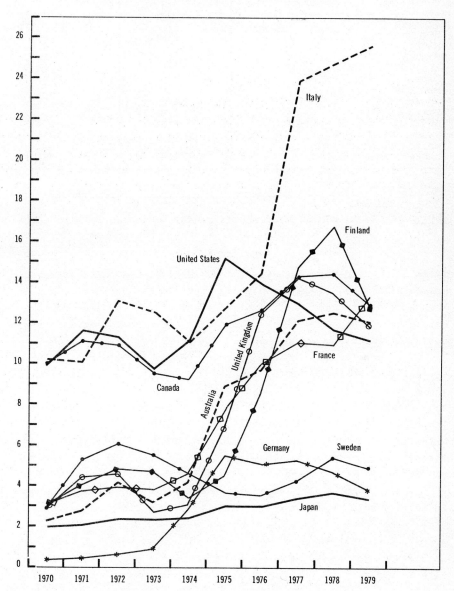

Source : OECD, *Youth Unemployment : The Causes and Consequences,* Paris, 1980.

Table 5

RATIO OF YOUTH(a) TO ADULT(e) UNEMPLOYMENT RATES

	1978	1979
Australia	3.2	3.4
Canada	2.3	2.4
Denmark	2.0	..
Germany	1.7	1.4
Finland	2.7	2.4
France	3.1	3.3
Italy(d)	7.0	6.6
Japan	1.9	1.9
New Zealand(c)(f)	5.5	4.5
Norway(b)	5.4	6.0
Portugal	4.8	4.5
Spain(d)	4.3	4.1
Sweden(b)	3.5	3.3
United Kingdom(b)	3.5	3.3
United States(b)	2.9	2.9

Source: OECD, Youth Unemployment: The Causes and Consequences, op.cit.

Notes: a) Young people aged 15 to 24. b) Young people aged 16 to 24.
c) Young people aged 15 to 29. d) Young people aged 14 to 24.
e) Adults aged 25 to 64. f) Adults aged 29 to 64.

it is 11. Piece-work is not allowed. Medical examinations are required each year. Young people are given longer vacations, and if
they work at weekends must be given a day off in the week to compensate. This protection raises the cost, including the administrative
costs, of employing young people.

The competitive position of young people in Germany, as in
several other OECD countries is also weakened by the protection of
older workers. The Works Constitution Law of 1972 introduced protection for regulating the lay-off and compensation of redundant workers.
Their position is also achieved through collective bargaining which
establishes strict seniority rules. In addition, enterprises over a
certain size are required to employ a quota of handicapped workers
and disabled war veterans or to pay a penalty.

The share of young people in the labour force is much the same
in Germany as in the other six major OECD countries: 7 per cent are
adolescents aged 15 to 19, and 13 per cent are young adults aged 20
to 24. But their share of the burden of unemployment is much less
in Germany: adolescents are 9 per cent of the unemployed compared
with 22 per cent in the other six countries; and young adults are
17 per cent compared with 24 per cent (Table 6).

Statistical problems

This is not, however, the whole story. There is considerable
controversy about the true rate of German youth unemployment. The

Table 6

SHARES OF THE LABOUR FORCE AND OF UNEMPLOYMENT
IN THE SEVEN LARGER OECD COUNTRIES, 1979
(percentage)

	Germany	Canada, France, Italy, Japan, United Kingdom, United States (a)
Adolescents (15-19)		
Share of unemployment	9.3	22.4
Share of labour force	7.1	7.1
Young adults (20-24)		
Share of unemployment	16.8	23.7
Share of labour force	12.6	13.0

Notes: a) Weighted averages.

Source: OECD, Labour Force Statistics as updated by the Quarterly Supplement, consistent with national statistics, Paris, 1980.

confusion stems partly from the availability of two sets of estimates based on two different sources: the unemployment registration by the employment offices, and the annual sample population survey (the microcensus).

The data-gathering functions of the employment offices are a by-product of their operational responsibilities for helping place unemployed persons and paying them benefits. Their unemployment count excludes all persons enrolled in school, and also those school-leavers who are only looking for a training place in the dual system.

The microcensus data are, however, more comprehensive and are based upon ILO labour force definitions and concepts, although they are not identical. Accordingly, the 1 per cent population survey, which is taken in April each year, includes persons looking for work who do not register with the employment office. They are counted even if they are seeking short-term employment of less than three months or part-time employment of less than 20 hours per week, and regardless of whether or not they are enrolled in school. The sample survey also counts school-leavers who are looking for a training place rather than for paid employment.

The difference between the microcensus and employment office data can be significant. As might be expected, the estimates of unemployment, or more precisely of those seeking work or training places, based on the sample survey, are higher than the unemployment registered by the employment office. For example, in May 1977 unemployment among adolescents aged 15 to 20 estimated from the sample survey was one-third higher than that measured by the employment office: 116,000 compared to 87,000.

If unsuccessful applicants for training places had been counted as unemployed in September 1977, the unemployment rate of the 15-to-20-year-olds would have been 5.8 per cent instead of the official 5.0 per cent. It was estimated in 1977 that only 60 per cent of young people without training places but taking the required part-time vocational training bothered to register, and that some 29,000 young unemployed people were not counted in the statistics. According to the Federal Institute for Employment in September 1979, of the 20,200 applicants for training places who had not succeeded in obtaining one, only 5,500 were ready to take up an ordinary job. Thus only about a quarter of the unsuccessful applicants were counted as unemployed. In addition, workers on short-time, or even those laid off but not formally redundant, are not included either. Girls living at home and doing domestic work are often excluded. The German trade unions (DGB) estimated to us in January 1980 that actual youth unemployment was probably twice as high as the published figures indicate. A recent study by the Carnegie Council on Policy Studies and Higher Education (1) cited several surveys which suggest that both sets of official statistics significantly undercount unemployed young people. One of these studies concluded that the true unemployment of 15-to-18-year-olds might be as much as 60 per cent higher than the official figures indicate. A local study in the Dortmund area found 6,200 adolescents looking for work or training places in the area compared with the 1,847 officially reported. The Carnegie study concludes, "If the results of this survey were extended to the entire Federal Republic of Germany, actual youth unemployment would be more than three times as high as the official figures indicate".(2)

There is general agreement that the unemployment rates of foreign-born young people and children of foreign workers are grossly underestimated. Although the laws prohibiting foreign young people from obtaining work permits were amended in 1979, the children of foreign workers who enter Germany to join their families still have to wait two years before they get a work permit. This period can be shortened if the young immigrant participates in a full-time voca- tional course for at least ten months. The OECD estimated the number of non-registered foreign unemployed youth in 1978 at about 40,000 or 50,000.

It is beyond the scope of this report to attempt any detailed analysis of the two official rates of adolescent unemployment in Germany, and whatever new estimates might be used would require the adoption of revised concepts and definitions of labour force partic- ipation and measures of unemployment. Yet even given some statistical

1) Klaus von Dohnanyi, Education and Youth Employment in the Federal Republic of Germany, The Carnegie Foundation, New York, 1978, pp. 35-38.
2) Ibid., p. 38.

discrepancies it is quite clear that Germany has succeeded in achieving a lower rate of unemployment among young people than the other major OECD countries, many of which also underestimate their unemployment rates.

Reductions in the Supply of Labour

The success of the German economy in attaining a high rate of growth of productivity in the 1950s and 1960s permitted only a slow expansion of employment, and during the recession of the mid-1970s total employment fell. The net number of jobs lost in Germany in the four years 1973-1977 totalled 1.7 million. In manufacturing and mining, 1,246,000 jobs disappeared between 1970 and 1977, despite shorter hours and longer holidays. The numbers employed fell by 14.5 per cent, and the volume of employment (people multiplied by hours worked) by 21.3 per cent. Yet manufacturing production, because of the growth of productivity, increased no less than 13.5 per cent.

During the mild recession of 1973 to 1977 unemployment rose four-fold, but Germany was able to avoid, or at least postpone, a much more serious rise in unemployment during these years partly because of favourable social factors and partly because of policy decisions which reduced the supply of labour. The social factors were a decline in labour force participation; the continued decline in hours worked; a trend towards earlier retirement; the relatively late arrival of young people on the labour market compared with most other OECD countries; and increasing enrolments in higher education. The policy decisions were the repatriation of foreign workers (Gastarbeiter) when their contracts came to an end and a virtual stop to their re-cruitment; the encouragement of short-time working by income mainten-ance arrangements; extended education or expansion of training places, both mainly for young people.

The civilian labour force fell from 26.5 million in 1973 to 25.5 million in 1977, resuming in the next two years its previous slow growth (Table 7).

Table 7

CIVILIAN LABOUR FORCE, EMPLOYMENT AND UNEMPLOYMENT
(thousands)

	Labour Force	Employed	Unemployed
1970	26,318	26,169	149
1973	26,474	26,201	273
1974	26,270	25,688	582
1975	25,872	24,798	1,074
1976	25,616	24,556	1,060
1977	25,541	24,511	1,030
1978	25,693	24,700	993
1979	25,893	25,017	876

Source: OECD, Labour Force Statistics, Paris, 1980.

One important factor in the reduction of the labour force has
been a decline in labour force participation, which is in common with
the experience of most other advanced industrial countries. The fall
in total labour force participation during the 1970s was entirely due
to a decline in male participation (Table 8). The decline in labour
force participation was particularly marked among young people during
the 1960s and 1970s as a result of the expansion of education (Figure
(Figure 2). Female labour force participation remained stable during
the 1970s within about half a percentage point (Table 8): a slow
rise in the participation of married women was balanced by the declining participation of young women and girls.

Table 8

LABOUR FORCE PARTICIPATION RATES(a)

	Males	Females	Total
1970	92.5	48.1	69.5
1973	88.9	48.7	68.3
1977	83.5	48.4	65.6
1978	83.2	48.7	65.6

Note: a) $\dfrac{\text{Labour force}}{\text{Population aged 15 to 64}} \times 100$

Source: OECD, Labour Force Statistics, Paris, 1980.

German experience diverges markedly from that of the other major
OECD countries in the activity rates of girls and women, i.e. the
proportions of working age who are in paid employment. Female participation in the labour market not only affects the number of girls
looking for jobs, but also the extent to which existing jobs are
filled by married women. In Sweden, the United Kingdom and the
United States, activity rates among women and girls have risen mas-
sively in the last 30 years. For many jobs, married women and new
entrants to the labour market compete. This is not so in Germany.
The activity rate among women has increased only 4 per cent in the
past 30 years, and is still well below that of the English-speaking
and Scandinavian countries. During the 1975-1977 recession there was
no increase in female participation. One suspects that the revolu-
tion of sexual equality has not yet really affected Germany as profoundly as it has affected the Scandinavian countries, the United
States of America or the United Kingdom. Further evidence of this is
the remarkably traditional pattern of female occupations and of female
apprenticeship.

Early retirement has been a significant element in the reduction
of the labour force. The early retirement of workers aged 60 to 65

100

Figure 2

LABOUR FORCE PARTICIPATION RATES AS A PROPORTION
OF THE AGE GROUP (MEN AND WOMEN) 1962 TO 1979

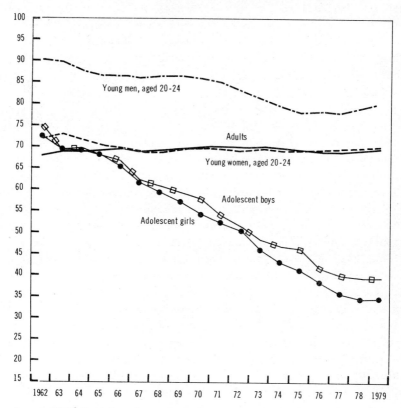

Source : OECD, *Youth Unemployment : The Causes and Consequences, op.cit.*

removed some 300,000 people from the labour market between 1973 and 1977.

The total labour supply was also reduced by a decline in hours worked. The long-term trend is for total hours worked in Germany to decline at the rate of about 1 per cent a year.

To rectify the serious labour shortages which emerged during the 1960s, Germany depended to an increasing extent on foreign workers to operate its expanding economy. By 1973 Germany had taken in some 2.6 million foreign workers, mostly from Turkey, Yugoslavia, Italy, Greece and Spain. They formed about 10 per cent of the working population. During the next four years some 650,000 foreign workers, most of whom left Germany when their contracts ended, returned to their countries of origin. This brought the total active foreign population down to 1.95 million. When the unemployment rate began

to rise one of the Laender decided to pay up to DM.10,000 as a lump
sum and to provide transportation for any foreign worker who went home,
but the offer was open for only a short time and not many took advantage of it. In addition, some enterprises which had made extensive
lay-offs of foreign workers gave them some financial help to return
home. Since November 1973 the recruitment of new foreign workers from
countries outside the free labour market of the European Economic
Community has been banned. From a peak of 519,625 in 1970 the number
of new foreign workers fell to 19,521 in 1978. The return home of
foreign workers, combined with the sharp reduction in the number of
new foreign workers recruited, has been the largest single element in
the reduction of total labour supply in Germany.

It has been possible for foreign workers other than those from
EEC countries to be used as an employment buffer in Germany because
they have to have both residence permits and work permits. From 1974
to 1978 5.9 million work permits were issued for renewed employment or
for the continuation of existing employment. Of a total of 6.37 million applications for work permits (including those for first employment) only 152,000, i.e. 2.4 per cent, were rejected. There is only
one substantial group of workers from outside Germany which is not
subject to such stringent control: refugees from the Eastern European
countries. Unlike France or Britain, Germany does not have large communities of immigrants from the old Empires, nor does it have the
problem of vast illegal population movements across the border, as is
the case in the United States.(1) There has been no major return flow
from Britain or France back to countries of origin. Nor is there
likely to be one.

Germany has also used short-time working (Kurzarbeit) successfully as a means to combat unemployment. Under this programme, a
firm or a section of a firm facing a drop in demand for its products
or services, instead of laying off surplus labour, divides the available work among some or all the employed workers by cutting the number
of hours worked. This is done without reducing too sharply the income of individual workers or the workforce as a whole by paying
partial unemployment insurance amounting to 68 per cent of the wages
lost due to reduced hours. During the depth of the recession in the
mid-1970s Germany placed a monthly average of 773,000 workers on short-
time work and claimed that the programme saved 175,000 jobs in 1975.(2)

1) There is however a steady flow of foreigners, mainly from Turkey,
   India and Pakistan, entering West Germany from Austria, or West
   Berlin from East Berlin, claiming political asylum. Many of them
   pretend to claim political asylum in order to circumvent the recruitment ban. Because legal procedures to determine whether an
   individual is entitled to political asylum are slow, there is a
   resident population awaiting legal decisions, and meanwhile looking
   for jobs or living on welfare. It is, one might say, an immigrant
   population in suspense.
2) Mitteilungen des Instituts für Arbeitsmarkt und Berufsforschung
   Mitt AB 1/78, p. 61.

Short-time working continued during the recovery and by 1979 an average of 88,000 workers still remained on short time. No doubt, if the employment situation worsens, more workers will be placed on short time.

The population pattern in Germany, as in most other OECD countries, is one in which the large numbers of children born in the late 1950s and early 1960s are now reaching working age. Germany has made strenuous efforts to match this rising supply of young people with training places, extended education and jobs, despite the less favourable economic context. There has been an impressive expansion of post-compulsory full-time school education (1) of all kinds. In the traditional forms of the intermediate school (Realschule) enrolments rose from 0.57 m. pupils in 1965 to 1.22 m. in 1976, an increase of 113 per cent. Numbers attending the grammar school or academic school (Gymnasium), where pupils usually expect to take examinations preparatory to higher education, were up from 0.96 m. pupils in 1965 to 1.91 m. in 1976, an increase of nearly 100 per cent. There have also been significant increases in new forms of further education, such as the two-year full-time schools (Fachoberschule) and the polytechnics (Fachhochschule) established in 1970. The universities have more than doubled their entry, and a major effort has been made to loosen the constraints of numerus clausus in particular faculties.

Nor has Germany relied only on the education system to absorb young people. From 1972 to 1975 the number of training places offered by enterprises fell from 637,990 to 480,198 while the number of places demanded by young people rose from 466,000 to 485,559. The 1976 Training Places Promotion Act, passed after major political controversy, called on employers to produce 12.5 per cent more training places than the estimated number of applicants, with the threat of moving to a compulsory levy system if sufficient places were not forthcoming. Being deeply hostile to the idea of stricter government control and a levy-financed system of training, employers responded impressively. Starting in 1976, the number of training places on offer rose to 625,000 in 1979, and in that year places did indeed substantially exceed registered applicants. The federal government and the Laender have also developed new types of courses for those pupils who wanted to, or had to, undertake a first basic vocational education year (Berufsgrundbildungsjahr or BGJ) before entering an apprenticeship. There are variants of this basic year for school-leavers whose handicaps or inadequate educational attainment render them unable to start an apprenticeship either immediately or at all. They include, for example, the pre-vocational year (Berufsvorbereitungsjahr or BVJ) and

---

1) Compulsory full-time education in school ends at 15 (9th grade) except for West Berlin and three other Laender, where it is 16 (10th grade).

the year of full-time schooling (Berufsgrundschuljahr or BGS). In
addition, the Federal Institute for Employment has made an important
contribution to reducing youth unemployment by financing training
courses outside schools for adolescents without qualifications. They
were provided by the Federal Institute for Employment or in private
institutions, including voluntary bodies.

Thus in Germany the emphasis in the armoury of youth employment
policies is on finding places in educational establishments or in
training firms and workshops. Any description of that armoury is
necessarily dominated by an analysis of the dual system of training,
its variants and developments, as it would be in no other country
save two neighbours: in German-speaking Austria and in Switzerland,
where German is also a major language. In addition to the normal
route of the dual system for the majority of young people, training
is the main instrument used to help disadvantaged groups such as
young women and girls, the handicapped, young foreigners, and young
workers who are unemployed or who do not qualify for apprenticeships.
The use of subsidies to create jobs is kept to a minimum, although
Germany has not wholly eschewed such measures. Under the Employment
Promotion Law the Federal Institute for Employment can pay an employer
a subsidy of up to 60 per cent of normal or negotiated wages for up
to a year to employ someone who is hard to place under normal labour
market conditions. A higher subsidy of up to 80 per cent of wages
for up to two years can be paid to an employer who takes on a young
person who has been unemployed for more than six months; but in 1979
a monthly average of only 4,800 young people under the age of 20 was
employed in this way. Young people can also obtain financial help in
searching for a job to meet costs of applying for work, travel or
special work clothing.

The number of young people looking for work is also reduced by
conscription. In 1979 military service removed 236,000 from the
labour market for fifteen months, equivalent to 295,000 man years.
Many other European countries have conscription, so that this factor
only seriously affects comparisons with the English-speaking countries,
which do not.

Obviously these substantial withdrawals from the labour force
did not benefit young people exclusively; but, by improving the
overall balance between supply and demand for labour, they helped
young people among others get jobs, and kept down the unemployment
rate. The net result of the favourable economic and social trends
and public policies has been to reduce the numbers of unemployed
during the last few years. From May 1975 to May 1979 the total number
unemployed in all age groups fell from 1,017,903 to 775,548. It fell
5.5 per cent among workers aged 45 or more; 34.8 per cent among those
aged 35 to 44; 29.1 per cent among those aged 25 to 34; 24.2 per

cent among young adults, aged 20 to 24; and 33.1 per cent among
adolescents of 15 to 19 (Table 9). It is a remarkable achievement.

Table 9

UNEMPLOYMENT BY AGE GROUPS IN MAY OF EACH YEAR
(percentage rates)

Age	Less than 20	20 to 24	25 to 34	35 to 44	45 and over	All age groups
1974	2.0	2.5	2.1	1.7	2.1	2.0
1975	4.6	6.4	5.0	3.9	3.8	4.4
1976	3.8	6.2	4.6	3.4	4.0	4.2
1977	4.1	6.3	4.7	3.2	3.9	4.2
1978	3.7	5.9	4.5	3.0	3.9	4.0
1979	2.7	4.6	3.8	2.4	3.7	3.4

Source: Institute of Labour and Occupational Research, Nuremberg.

By placing emphasis on the employment needs of young people immediately after leaving school, the needs of older adolescents and
young adults may have been sacrificed. A breakdown of adolescent unemployment shows that unemployment among 19-year-olds is double that
for 17-year-olds. This includes young people who have dropped out of
apprenticeship, full-time school or university and have not completed
their education or training. In addition there may be insufficient
opportunities for absorbing them into employment. The unemployment
rate of young adults aged 20-24 has been consistently higher than for
adolescents by as much as 50 per cent or more. Even for the month of
September, when many school leavers have not yet been absorbed in the
labour market, the unemployment rate of young adults aged 20 to 24
years typically has exceeded that of teenagers. By May of each year,
the unemployment differential is even greater. For example, in May
1979 the unemployment rate among young adults (4.6 per cent) was 70
per cent higher than that for adolescents (2.7 per cent). But
periods of unemployment are relatively short.

The German record is impressive, and that should be stated un-
ambiguously in a report which will also necessarily make certain
criticisms. The well-established dual training system, which has a
long tradition going back to the mediaeval guilds of craftsmen and
meisters, has served Germany well in training large numbers of young
people. The size and flexible capacity of the dual system has made
it possible to save large numbers of young people from unemployment.

The Outlook

The favourable social trends will not continue during the next
few years. The peak in the numbers of births was in 1964 (Figure 3).

105

Figure 3
NUMBER OF BIRTHS, SCHOOL LEAVERS FROM COMPULSORY EDUCATION, TRAINING PLACES DEMANDED AND YOUNG PEOPLE UNEMPLOYED

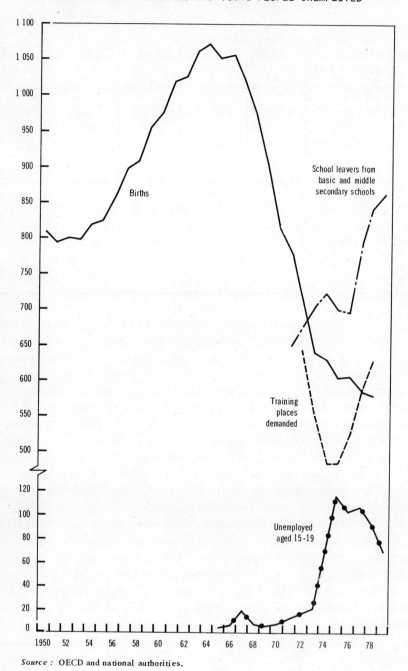

Source : OECD and national authorities.

Pressure on training places is now at its height. Pressure on places in higher education, including the universities, will reach a maximum in two to four years' time.

The peak number of young people entering the labour market in 1980 coincides with a slowdown in the German economic growth, and a severe recession in other OECD countries. This will inevitably limit the number of new jobs that can be created in the private sector. The public sector has been an important source of jobs in Germany as elsewhere, especially for more highly educated young people, but this cannot be assumed for the future either.

Furthermore, Germany is beginning to feel the impact of new technologies (notably of microelectronics) on jobs in administration, offices and some sectors of manufacturing. It is in the technologically advanced sectors, like plastics and data-processing machinery, that productivity has increased most. In the latter case, productivity per hour more than doubled between 1970 and 1977, and the number employed fell by more than a quarter. Major strides towards standardising and automating jobs are on the way. In 1979, a number of major companies, including several in car manufacture, set up assembly lines and other processes using robots. Office equipment manufacturers estimate a major breakthrough in respect of clerical and office work in the current decade. For example, an unpublished paper by Siemens SG estimated that 43 per cent of office jobs could be standardised, and between 25 per cent and 30 per cent could be automated, figures that rise to 75 per cent and 38 per cent respectively in the case of public administration. Of course many new jobs will be created too, especially skilled jobs. As in other OECD countries it is impossible to anticipate the net effect of technology on employment. What is important is that the widening application of new technologies is transforming patterns of employment, and therefore the skills needed, in both the sectors where they are pronounced and in those that use them.

The scope for a further reduction of foreign workers is slight, and indeed Germany's remaining foreign workers are transforming themselves from foreigners into permanent immigrants by their unwillingness to return home. Indeed, for many of the million children under 16, Germany is home: 47.7 per cent were born in Germany. Because most of their parents have been German residents for eight years or more, they and their children have the right to remain. In addition, children still living in other countries have a right to join their parents and in recent years have been doing so at the rate of about 100,000 a year. Moreover, foreign workers have significantly higher birth-rates than native-born Germans. For these reasons the population of immigrants seems sure to increase. By 1995 one in five of the 15-18-year-olds in Germany will be the children of foreign workers,

half of them Turkish. At present they constitute one in fourteen of
that age group. Until recently the German authorities have been ambivalent about these foreign youngsters. The illusion that many would
return sooner or later to Turkey or Spain or Italy has until recently
inhibited serious proposals to integrate them into German society.
But there is evidence now of a more constructive approach by the
federal government in particular.

The number of people seeking early retirement is unlikely to
rise, since Western Europe is in the years of low age cohorts born
during and after the First World War. As for participation among
women, it is remarkable that this has changed so little since 1950.
Surely even Germany will sooner or later be caught up in the demands
for full-time jobs and careers for women. If and when this happens,
Germany will have a more difficult time solving its employment problems.

There are no longer any obvious ways to reduce labour supply on
a large scale. The policy decisions have a once-for-all element
which cannot be repeated, and social factors are unlikely to continue
to moderate unemployment. Much depends on the future trend of productivity which is strongly influenced by fixed investment, technology,
wage rates and interest rates and cannot be forecast. The risk is
that if it continues to rise the rate of growth may not suffice to
absorb new workers, whether young people including second-generation
immigrants or married women, and unemployment could reach more serious
levels in the next five years. However, Germany, like several other
OECD countries, appears to have scarcities of manpower in some sectors.
According to the Federal Ministry of Labour employers have "for years
been complaining about a lack of skilled labour". The Ministry reports
that there are, in 1980, some 200,000 vacancies for skilled and unskilled workers in the craft trades, for qualified workers in retail
trade, and for skilled workers in construction.

In a highly organised labour market the trade unions are bound
to protect the interests of their members against the interests of
would-be entrants to the labour market. The position of the less
highly qualified, the educationally disadvantaged, girls and foreign
workers' children could become more serious in circumstances of substantial unemployment. The OECD expects that youth unemployment will
rise during 1980 and 1981, but that Germany will still succeed in
keeping youth unemployment at a low rate compared with other countries
(Table 10).

Whatever youth unemployment problems Germany may be facing in
the next few years, demographic factors indicate that before the end
of this decade the situation will change. In 1980 Germany had 4.8
million young people aged 15-19. By the end of the decade the number
of young people in this age category will decline to 3 million, reflecting the low birth rates of the late 1960s. Therefore, barring

Table 10

ACTUAL AND PROJECTED RATES OF YOUTH(a) UNEMPLOYMENT
(percentage)

	Actual		Projected	
	1978	1979	1980	1981
Canada	14.3	13.0	$13\frac{1}{2}$	$14\frac{1}{4}$
Germany	4.8	3.7	4	$5\frac{3}{4}$
France	11.0	13.3	$14\frac{3}{4}$	$17\frac{1}{2}$
Italy	24.8	25.6	$27\frac{1}{4}$	$30\frac{1}{4}$
Japan	3.8	3.5	$3\frac{1}{2}$	4
United Kingdom(b)(c)	8.9	8.0	10.6	$16\frac{1}{4}$
United States(b)	11.7	11.2	14	$15\frac{3}{4}$
Average(d)	10.8	10.5	12.4	14.5

Notes: a) Young people aged 15 to 24. b) Young people aged 16 to 24.
c) Data are for Great Britain only, exclude school-leavers
and adult students, and are for July of each year. The 1980
figure is the actual rate, not a projection. d) Weighted by
the youth labour force.

Source: The calculation on which the projections are based is described in OECD, Youth Unemployment: The Causes and Consequences,
op.cit.

an influx of unprecedented proportions of new adolescent immigrants,
Germany will have far fewer adolescents by 1990 and, unless dramatic
technological changes eliminate the need for young workers, they will
once more be at a premium and the labour market will have to readjust
to shortage conditions. One possibility is that the proportion of
girls and women entering the labour force might increase to fill the
shortage of potential new entrants. Another is that unskilled older
workers may be drawn back into the labour force.

II

TRAINING FOR THE LABOUR MARKET AND NEW TECHNOLOGIES

In Chapter I we have shown what a massive effort Germany has made to keep the increasing numbers of adolescents out of the adult labour market by placing them in what has come to be known in Germany as the market for training places. It was pointed out to us that this reduces the normal working life of each worker by one year in forty for each year in training, i.e. by 7.5 per cent for three years' training. Thus the education and training system absorbs a very large part of the potential labour supply: much more than in most OECD countries, where fewer young people are taken into training and where the training period is also shorter. Eventually, however, these young people will enter the adult labour market. Does the training they receive adequately prepare them to compete for the jobs that are available and for the changes that must be anticipated in the kinds of work to be done?

The time adolescents spend in the dual system has three main functions for them: it helps them make the transition from school to work; it provides an occupational qualification through theoretical and practical training and work experience; and the training allowance provides them with a source of income. Correspondingly for employers it provides them with an opportunity to introduce young people to the labour market, the means of training personnel for the years ahead, and to a limited extent with a source of manpower.

Are Apprentices Cheap Labour?

It is sometimes alleged that apprenticeship systems are sources of cheap labour. In Germany an apprentice receives an allowance from the employer. There are no statutory minimum wages. Instead, under the 1969 Vocational Training Act, allowances are set by collective agreements, and increase each year. In 1978 the average monthly allowance of apprentices was DM.453 in the first year, DM.523 in the second, DM.606 in the third, and DM.645 in the fourth. This places the average allowance for apprentices in the first year at about one-fifth the average wage of all male workers in the private sector. Even in the third year the average allowance is still less than one-third the average wage.

Allowances vary greatly among occupations. A more appropriate comparison might be made of training allowances with the initial gross earnings of newly qualified craftsmen in the same occupations (Table 11). In 1978, the 20 occupations with the highest number of trainees accounted for 842,000 of the 1.5 million enrolled in the dual system. Their first-year allowances ranged from 15 per cent of earnings of newly qualified craftsmen to 37 per cent. In the third or fourth year trainees in only two occupations received allowances equal to 50 per cent or more of initial wages received by craftsmen.

Table 11

TRAINEES' ALLOWANCES AS PERCENTAGE OF GROSS
WAGES PAID TO NEWLY QUALIFIED CRAFTSMEN, 1978

Occupation	Number of trainees	1st year	2nd year	3rd year	4th year
Motor mechanic	88,633	21	22	25	..
Salesperson (first stage)	84,890	37	42	..	..
Hairdresser	68,584	26	30	36	..
Industrial clerk	54,744	34	36	40	45
Electrician/fitter	48,614	17	21	24	28
Clerk in wholesale and foreign trade	45,691	37	43	49	..
Office clerk	45,647	29	31	35	40
Machine fitter	41,571	28	31	34	39
Retail clerk (second stage)	38,442	..	..	50	..
Bank clerk	37,819	36	40	45	..
Salesperson in food sector	37,188	34	43	54	..
Joiner	35,139	15	18	21	..
Painter and varnisher	34,370	17	20	26	..
Doctor's assistant	31,438	31	35	..	..
Bricklayer	29,936	24	37	47	..
Gas and water fitter	27,938	26	28	32	36
Baker	23,884	23	29	38	..
Dentist's assistant	23,827	31	32	40	..
Butcher	22,200	27	29	35	..
Toolmaker	21,269	28	31	34	39

Source: Data provided by the German Ministry of Labour.

Allowances also vary greatly among local labour markets. For example, in the first year allowances for heating installation plumbers (Heizungsbauer) for 1980 ranged from DM.250 in Schleswig-Holstein to

DM.489 in Suedwuerttemberg-Hohenzollern; and in the fourth year from
DM.412 in Bremerhaven to DM.698 in Berlin.

The relatively low allowances raise questions about the equity
of the system and whether it enables some employers to obtain labour
at low wages sanctioned by unions and others who do the bargaining to
determine training allowances.

Such comparisons take no account of the trainees' lack of experience and the fact that they spend 8 to 12 hours a week in vocational school and not at work. So the averages may hide more than
they reveal. The question whether the dual system is a source of
cheap labour can be seen from two different points of view. From the
point of view of enterprises some of them may get more than they invest on training by securing low cost labour, while others receive
little output during training. According to the Edding Commission
the value of the work done by apprentices amounted on the average to
44 per cent of the costs of the enterprises providing training (1)
showing a broad correspondence between apprentices' allowances and
the value of their work, but since that time training regulations
have been overhauled and training requirements raised. The proportion of training costs covered by the value of apprentices' work is
almost certainly lower now.

In addition to the allowances paid by employers, young people
in need can receive assistance under the Employment Promotion Act.
The rates set depend on the age of the trainee, whether he or she is
living at home or elsewhere, and on the training institution. The
aim is to encourage young people to prefer training to unskilled work.

As in several other OECD countries traditional views persist
among parents and employers and girls about the role of women in
employment. Girls in the dual system are still concentrated in
training leading to sales, clerical, and health occupations, and to
hairdressing. Girls accounted for a majority of trainees in 9 of the
20 top training occupations. More than half of them were enrolled in
these occupations. The average allowances to women were well below
those for men. In 1978, the unweighted average monthly wage of newly
hired workers in these occupations was DM.1,230 compared with an
average monthly wage of DM.1,640 in the remaining top 11 occupations
in which men predominated. Excluding clerks in wholesale and foreign
trade, the top 10 occupations in which men constituted the majority
of trainees accounted for 373,000 training places. Only some 3,000
women were enrolled in these 10 occupations. In addition, girls in
the "social year" receive very low allowances (see Chapter V).
However, we were told that more girls are applying for and being

---

1) Abschlussbericht der Sachverstaendigenkommission, Kosten und
   Finanzierung der beruflichen Bildung, Bonn, 1974. Cf. Summary in
   Annex III, pp. 169-170 of this volume.

accepted into occupations which used to be exclusively the domain of
men; and in several workshops we saw a few girls learning traditional
male jobs such as metal-working or printing. Nevertheless, the
majority of girls were still heavily concentrated in traditional
women's occupations.

The Transition from School to Working Life

In several other OECD countries help in making the transition
from school to the world of work is given to those school-leavers who
are socially and educationally disadvantaged. This is done through
programmes to provide work experience, which give participants opportunities to discover about the labour market. Opportunities under
such programmes mostly last from four to six months. Young Germans
entering the dual system have the opportunity to learn about the world
of work throughout their periods of work in the enterprise to which
they are apprenticed.

The retention rate of the system is phenomenally high. In 1978
a dropout rate of only 4.6 per cent was recorded: of the 1.5 million
enrolled in the system during 1978, only 69,000 participants terminated
their training before completion.(1) Considering that the bulk of the
trainees are between the ages of 15 and 18, when young people are
prone to undergo rapid changes in their lives and ambitions, this ter-
mination rate is low. More than half of the dropouts occur during the
first year of training. Apparently, once a young person gets into the
system, he or she normally stays until completion.

Training is not limited to learning about the technical tasks of
an occupation. In the modern world of industrial participation, it
should also prepare young people to take part in collective bargaining
and in the functioning of Works Councils. Training should give employees more confidence, greater capacity for managing themselves and
greater flexibility. In Germany, there is considerable evidence to
show that the training system contributes substantially to these objectives. Young people have the right to elect their own representatives to the Work Council of the enterprise.

Training for the Future

The crucial question is whether the dual system is an effective
means of training. At first glance, it appears that it is a definite
success. Adolescent unemployment in Germany, as pointed out in
Chapter I, is significantly lower than in all other major OECD
countries. There is also little question that the German labour force
is highly productive and training undoubtedly contributes to the

---

1) Statistisches Bundesamt, Wiesbaden, Bildung und Kultur, Berufliche
   Bildung, Fachserie 11, 1978.

continuing high German competitiveness in the world market. The
latter is particularly important to the country because nearly a
fifth of its gross domestic product arises from exports. Still, the
debate about direct governmental intervention, requiring the expansion of training places, has raised questions about the system.
Since it is difficult to measure precisely the costs and benefits of
the programme, any review of the dual system involves value judgements,
including one's assumptions and views about the future of Germany's
society and economy.

The majority of apprentices are trained in about 20 occupations.
These occupations absorbed 56 per cent of trainees in 1967 and 56 per
cent in 1977. A considerable proportion is relatively low-skilled
service occupations for which the training lasts three years. Many
apprentices will not be able to find jobs in the occupations for
which they have trained.

Since half the trainees leave the enterprise where they receive
their training within two years of completing it, it is not known to
what extent training is being utilised in future employment. Nor is
the training an employee receives during the three- to four-year training course always relevant to his future work, even if the trainee
stays with the employer who provided the training. Critics might
argue that a much briefer period of on-the-job training would suffice
for many of the occupations included in Germany's dual training system,
at a much lower resource cost. Furthermore, young people would not
be spending long periods of time learning an occupation they may never
be able to practise. The expansion of training places since 1976 has
been most marked in handicrafts and in certain traditional trades like
retail selling, bakers and butchers. It seems highly unlikely that
all the apprentices in these trades will find permanent employment
within them. One is bound to ask whether the government's laudable
desire to keep down youth unemployment, and the employers' anxiety to
avoid greater government intervention and a compulsory levy, encouraged
both to welcome an expansion of the quantity of training places without
asking too many questions about their relevance to Germany's future
economy. Certainly the expansion of 104 per cent in training places
for sales-people, 73 per cent for bakers and 32 per cent for butchers
in the period 1966 to 1978, when the German population rose only 3.5
per cent, seems rather out of balance.

Proponents of Germany's dual training system argue that it pre-
pares trainees for changing conditions in the labour market, makes them
more readily employable, and produces a responsible, flexible and well-
based labour force. It is often pointed out that young people who
have not completed a training course are disproportionately represented
among the unemployed. It may of course be argued that those very
characteristics that contributed to a trainee's ability to complete
his or her course would make him or her readily employable even without

having gone through training. High school drop-outs, for instance, are much more likely to be unemployed in the United States than those who complete their schooling. But it is undeniable that training does help young people to get jobs. For example, in Nuremberg we were told that the number of the unemployed had declined from 1,190 in 1977 to 950 in 1979, and of those totals the proportion without training had risen from 75 per cent to 86 per cent.

German employers have often advocated the need for more skilled workers. This shortage could become more acute during the late 1980s when the number of new young entrants to the labour force will decline sharply. Undoubtedly some of the training being done now will provide a future "back-up" of trained people to be drawn on as the number of new entrants falls. But since many will be inappropriately trained for their future occupations, retraining will be needed. For the reasons set out in the subsequent paragraphs, it may well be true that "any training is better than none", a view urged upon us by sources as diverse as officials of the German Federation of Trade Unions, the German Employers' Association, the Federal Secretary of State for Labour, and the principals and staff of the training schools we visited. It may be better but it will not be sufficient.

The Adaptation of Training to New Technologies

Economists since Adam Smith have recognised that education and training enhance the value of labour as a factor of production. More recently economists, attempting to qualify the impact various factors have had on productivity growth, have found that they could not explain the entire growth in output per worker by measuring only increases in capital goods or natural resources. Accordingly, they reasoned that the unexplained residual was a product not only of education but of technological change. Not only were there more capital goods, but the new ones were better than the older vintages. However, beyond machines there has also been an investment in the health, education, and skill level of workers. In Germany it is argued that since the country has few natural resources, its continued economic progress is largely dependent on the skills of the labour force in applying sophisticated technology.

This important concept of investment in human capital provides one rationale for the emphasis on longer education and training. Of course, other reasons have also contributed to the extension of training. In a modern industrial society the jobs that were traditionally performed by young people are continually declining in number, and some are disappearing altogether. The solution arrived at by affluent societies has been to delay entry into the labour force, using education and training to enrich young people's knowledge and to allow them to mature before they enter active labour markets. Aside from these

115

practical considerations, traditions die slowly: in European
countries apprenticeship has had a long and pervasive tradition,
especially so in Germany.

The close links between training, the organisation of work,
productivity, management and industrial relations are well illustrated
by a comparative study of France and Germany.(1) It compared enterprises in the two countries that were almost identical in industry
branch, product mix, technical production function and factor proportions. It found marked differences in levels of training of the employees, the organisation of work and responsibility and the distribution of pay. In Germany, compared with France, production depended
more on the flexible use of skilled workers on several tasks, including management, control and implementation. The lower strata of
the labour force were comparatively better paid. There were more
trained workers in the German enterprises, they had more training in
the enterprise, and more opportunities to move ahead. They were less
closely supervised, and had more responsibility than their French
counterparts. This is a testimony to the quality of their training
and the imaginative use made of skilled workers in German firms.

We share the value that Germany places on the training of young
people, and in particular on a systematic transition from school to
work. We also believe, as the comparative study of France and Germany
indicates, that a well-trained labour force can be used more flexibly.
Moreover, it can contribute to joint consultation more effectively
and is the essential starting point for a more advanced system of industrial democracy. But there are questions to be asked about the
philosophy of "any training being better than none". In particular,
it is important to avoid training people for jobs that are not available, not only because of money being wasted, but because of the dis-
illusion caused to the young people involved in pointless training.

Clearly it is important to do everything possible to avoid training people for jobs that will not be available. When we asked about
how this was avoided in Germany we received various replies: that
the counselling process reconciles individuals and the available
training places; that the pattern of courses given in vocational
schools reflects the pattern of employment in the local labour market;
and that training could be more broadly based.

Young people trained for skills which they cannot use either have
to seek unskilled jobs in the secondary labour market or train for
other occupations. Completion of the programme does not mean that a
young person remains with the employer or even in the occupation for
which he or she was trained. Indeed by law an employer may not offer

---

1) Burkhart Lutz, "Zur Analyse der Entwicklungstendenzen der Qualifi-
   kationsstruktur und der Beziehung Bildung-Beschaeftigung", 1978,
   unpublished manuscript.

an apprentice a contract of employment until he has completed his
training. A study of 30,000 gainfully employed persons conducted by
the Federal Ministry of Education and Science and published in 1980
found that one of every five trainees leaves his or her employer immediately upon the completion of the programme, and less than half of
the trainees are still with the same employer two years after the
completion of the apprenticeship. But some remained with the same
employer for decades and even during their whole working career.
Fifteen per cent of the employees surveyed who completed their training prior to 1960 were still employed by the same establishment 20
years later. The reasons for leaving employers included entry into
military service, dissatisfaction with working conditions, the pursuit
of better pay, and the search for additional training. Many also
leave the industry in which they have been trained. About one of every
three completers who left their employers upon finishing their training moved to different industry groups and presumably different occupations.(1) In either case the cost to society is high.

An adequate supply of skilled workers can be an engine of economic growth. In some respects Germany seems to be moving in this
direction. The composition of the labour force is changing (Table 12).

Table 12

COMPOSITION OF THE LABOUR FORCE BY
LEVEL OF EDUCATION AND TRAINING

	1961	1970	1980	1990
Higher education	3	4	8	12
Occupational qualification	..	57	..	69
No occupational qualification	..	37	..	20

Source: Data provided by the German Ministry of Labour.

In our meeting with the Minister of Labour in North Rhine-
Westphalia, Mr. Farthmann, he observed that there is no escape from
technical progress. The main question is whether the dual system is
capable of adapting to provide training for the new occupations that
will be created by the widespread application of new technologies and
for the changes that will be needed in the training content of others.
In Germany training can only legally be given to a young person for a
recognised occupation, so the process of recognition is crucial. One
of the most powerful arguments for training in enterprises is that
young people are trained where innovations in markets, in the organisation of production and in technology, are being made.

1) Berufsbildungsbericht der Bundesregierung, 1980, pp. 46-51.

Small enterprises with few or no training facilities need help in adapting to new technologies. The federal government of Germany is supporting the expansion of inter-enterprise training facilities with funds amounting to nearly DM.1,000 million.

The Federal Training Institute has completed the task of bringing up to date the curricula of about a quarter of the 451 trades recognised in Germany. The regulations for some trades are now very modern and include new techniques such as micro-electronics, although others belong to the distant past. Some kinds of work no longer exist, such as making lead joints in plumbing, while others are emerging, such as control mechanics. One of the larger industry groups, metal-working, covers 65 distinct trades that have all recently been brought up to date. The metal-working industry has recently introduced a co-operative year comprising 12 to 24 hours a week of technical instruction, the remainder of the time being given to practical work in training workshops (Lehrwerkstaetten) of a high standard of competence.

The continuing review and updating of training curricula and regulations is an impressive feature of the German dual system, since necessarily curricula in some occupations are rendered obsolete by the speed of technical change. The rate of technical change is likely to become even more rapid, and its impact even more far-reaching, as micro-electronics and other revolutionary new technologies move in to more and more industries and services. The question therefore is whether Germany's elaborate dual training system can adapt fast enough, and whether training in certain rather narrow occupations in a single enterprise provides a broad enough base for a whole lifetime of employment. The federal and Laender authorities are clearly aware of the challenge: hence the new emphasis on group training schemes, training workshops, and new patterns of vocational education and training like the co-operative year.

A broad foundation year, like the Berufsgrundbildungsjahr (BJG) followed by two years of dual education and training gets over some of the limitations implicit in the three-year dual system. We also believe the proposal made several years ago by the Young German Employers for apprentices to get experience of more than one enterprise, especially where the enterprise is small or monolithic in skills, has much to commend it. The modern skilled worker will need to be flexible and multi-skilled ("polyvalent" in technical language) rather than narrowly trained to a single occupation which may become obsolescent. Any reform on these lines, a requirement of a foundation year followed by experience in more than one enterprise, would require changes in the present dual system. We recognise the undoubted achievements of that system, but we commend to the German authorities these considerations for the future.

III

<u>VOCATIONAL EDUCATION, TRAINING AND SOCIAL OPPORTUNITY</u>

The Place of Dual System in Education

The German education system, administered by the Laender, or
state governments, retains some at least of the elitist and merito-
cratic divisions of the past, though they have been modified by a big
expansion of higher and post-compulsory education and to some extent
by easier movement between different educational channels. Basically,
the Laender require nine years of full-time schooling, from 6 to 15.
Children normally stay at the primary school (<u>Grundschule</u>) until the
fifth grade when they are 10 or 11. They then move on to one of
three types of secondary school. The basic secondary school (<u>Haupt-
schule</u>) takes them up to the ninth or tenth grade and a certificate
of completion known as the <u>Hauptschulabschluss</u>. There is an intermediate secondary school (<u>Realschule</u>) whose alumni often move on to
professional or technical training after completing their Realschule
certificate (<u>Mittlerereife</u>) in the tenth grade. The prestigious
traditional academy (the <u>Gymnasium</u>) leads to a final examination (the
<u>Abitur</u>), taken in the thirteenth grade, which is the gateway to uni-
versity. For those who go into the labour force after the end of
compulsory school, three years of part-time vocational education are
required, comprising a minimum of eight hours day-release a week, or
its equivalent in block release.

After compulsory full-time schooling over 90 per cent of all
school-leavers enter further vocational or general education. The
great majority, approximately two-thirds of each year's cohort, is
trained under the dual system (Table 13). Each apprentice has an
individual contract with his employer. The employer is obliged to
offer him or her an individual training course, combining practical
on-the-job training with vocational and theoretical education in a
vocational school (<u>Berufsschule</u>). This is normally between 8 and 12
hours each week. The apprentice must pass written and practical
examinations in order to become a qualified journeyman.

There are variations on this theme. Some apprentices attend the
vocational school for block release, i.e. full-time attendance for
several weeks (<u>Blockunterricht</u>) rather than day release. This is
more often the case if the apprentice is in a rural area, or works
for a small enterprise which is part of a group training scheme.

Table 13

YOUNG PEOPLE LEAVING COMPULSORY EDUCATION IN OECD COUNTRIES IN MOST RECENT YEARS

DISTRIBUTION AMONG FULL-TIME EDUCATION, LABOUR FORCE AND OTHER ACTIVITIES

(percentages)

Country	Year	Full-time education			Labour force		Outside labour force	Not known	Total (4+5+6+7+8)
		Secondary General (a)	Secondary Vocational (b)	Total (2+3)	Apprentice- ship (c)	Other			
	1	2	3	4	5	6	7	8	9
Australia (e)	1975	..	..	60	..(p)	29	..(d)	..(d)	100
Austria (e)	1976	15	24	39	54	7	..(d)	..(d)	100
Denmark (f)	1976	69	1	70	..	..	..	..	100
Finland (e)	1977	43	20	63	1	25	..	11	100
France (e)	1975	34	36	70	8	22	..(d)	..(d)	100
Germany (g)	1977	..	..	31	64	4	1	..(d)	100
Greece	1974	70	10	80	3	17	..(d)	..(h)	100
Ireland (f)	1976	50	14	64	4	26	1	..(d)	100
Japan (m)	1977	61	32	93	-	3(n)	5	..(h)	100
Netherlands (e)	1968-9	..	..	82	5	6	4(o)	-	100
Norway	1975	45	31	76	5	19	7	..(h)	100
Portugal	1975	..	..	69	3	20	..(d)	..	100
Sweden (e)	1974	37(j)	30(k)	68(l)	..(d)	28	4	8	100
Switzerland (e)	1975	..	..	17	55	28	..(d)	..(d)	100
United Kingdom	1974	..	..	21	18	51	..(d)	..(h)	100
England and Wales	1976	..	..	22	..	..	10	..(h)	100

Notes:
a) Some students in this category may later proceed to vocational training.
b) Excluding apprentices who are enrolled in part-time education.
c) Numbers entering apprenticeship. In the official statistics apprentices are included in the employed labour force.
d) Included in column 6.
e) Young people becoming 16 during the year and having completed compulsory education.
f) Age 16, completion of school beyond compulsory.
g) Plans of school-leavers mostly aged 15-16, (Berufsbildungsbericht, 1978, Table 27).
h) Included in column 7.
j) Theoretical lines in the comprehensive school.
k) Vocational lines in the comprehensive school.
l) Includes 0.5 per cent in other forms of education.
m) Includes 0.5 per cent in other secondary education.
n) Graduates from lower secondary education.
o) Excludes students in upper secondary education with jobs.
p) Includes entrants into special training schools.
r) Not available. However it is known that 15 per cent of young people aged 16 enter apprenticeship.

Sources: Estimates by national authorities.

120

We discuss in Chapter IV how the apprenticeship system is managed, regulated and monitored. In this chapter, we need only point out that the traditional vocational schools (Berufsschulen) are not highly regarded. They are short of teachers of general education, including German and mathematics, since the job is far less prestigious than teaching in a Gymnasium, a Realschule or a Fachschule. The trainers in the Berufsschule have a lower status than the teachers, and are paid less. Furthermore, student absenteeism is high, especially among pupils not in apprenticeship. One of the motives for developing a basic vocational year and its variants, such as the co-operative year, has been an awareness of the limitations of the traditional system.

Since 1970 the education system, with its traditional division into Hauptschule, Realschule and Gymnasium, has been complemented from the tenth grade onwards by a vocationally oriented full-time alternative channel, starting with the Fachoberschulen, which go from the eleventh to twelfth grade, and which often lead on to the Fachhochschulen, which offer advanced training. Admission to a Fachhochschule can be on the basis of graduation from a Fachoberschule. Young people who have completed an apprenticeship may be admitted to the twelfth grade of a Fachoberschule.

The doubling of places in the Realschulen and the Gymnasia plus the introduction of the Fachoberschulen mean that there has been a marked upgrading of the level of educational attainment in Germany. More and proportionately more young people now go on to higher education; more go on to professional, technical and advanced training; more get apprenticeships in the traditional dual system; and more are receiving basic vocational education in the tenth year at school. The only decline has been among those leaving school straight for work, mainly the unskilled. Even this roughly 10 per cent of the age group, rather more than half of them girls, are obliged by law to undertake part-time vocational education; although it must be said that truancy rates among this group are high and the law is often honoured in the breach rather than in the observance. These unqualified or minimally qualified youngsters are, of course, the most liable to be unemployed. Here too, however, Germany can claim improvement. The proportion of Hauptschule pupils leaving without a certificate fell from 17.4 per cent in 1970 to 11.1 per cent in 1979.

This shift in the educational pattern is illustrated by the jump in the numbers gaining Realschule certificates from 143,900 in 1970 to 310,800 in 1979, and in Gymnasium graduates (Abiturienten) from 83,500 to 134,600. Together they contribute an increase of almost 100 per cent compared with the increase of only 26 per cent in the age-group 15 and 16, and of only 20 per cent in those aged 17 and 18. Forty per cent of German children were in these two types of school in 1978.

In 1978 only 3 per cent of German children were in comprehensive schools. German public opinion has not so far supported a major reform of secondary education on comprehensive, non-selective lines as in Sweden or the United Kingdom. The introduction of comprehensive education has been slow and half-hearted other than in West Berlin. The only other Land to have a large comprehensive school element is Hesse, where 40 per cent of children between 10 and 15 years of age are in comprehensive schools (Gesamtschulen). The reform is still highly controversial there. Elsewhere, as in North Rhine-Westphalia, there are a few experimental comprehensive schools, vitiated by co-existing with selective schools which "cream" the academically able children.

Attempts at less drastic reform have been more successful. There is a movement in certain Laender to lengthen the period in the primary school (Grundschule) to six years, the last two years being broadly based "orientation years" providing time for the child to learn about the kinds of career open to him or her.

The Tenth Year and its Effect on the Dual System

More significant still has been the development of a tenth year of either general schooling or basic vocational education (Berufs-grundbildungsjahr, BGJ). In the mid-1970s, political pressure for a tenth year was particularly strong because of rising youth unemployment and the emergence of significant unemployment among teachers, although that appeared mainly in the primary schools (Grundschulen) as the large age cohorts passed through. Most Laender now offer a tenth year, either in school or in vocational schools. Several Laender (West-Berlin, Hesse, Saarland, North Rhine-Westphalia) make it compulsory for those not continuing with full-time education. In 1979 about 76 per cent of the 15- to 16-year-olds had undertaken a tenth full-time year of education.

The content of the tenth year varies greatly among and within the Laender. Ten of the eleven Laender offer a year of full-time vocational schooling (Berufsgrundschuljahr, BGJ/s) as tenth year. West Berlin provides for ten years of compulsory general education, so that full-time vocational schooling is offered only in the eleventh year. Eight Laender have at present a co-operative year (BGJ/k) for certain regions or occupational fields, which is implemented in the firm on the basis of a training contract and therefore leads directly on to dual training. In the BGJ/s and the BGJ/k the teaching content of the first year of training covers several related trades in an occupational sector with a view to providing comprehensive basic vocational training. There are other variants such as the vocational preparatory year (Berufsvorbereitungsjahr, BVJ) for children who are not ready to enter an apprenticeship, or who have come from special

schools for handicapped children (<u>Sonderschulen</u>), or who have left
the basic secondary school (Hauptschule) without a certificate.

The argument, however, rages on about what that tenth year
should be, and it is an intensely political one. The trade unions
and certain SPD elements informed us that they wanted to see a full-
time school-based tenth year, devoted to general education and pre-
vocational studies, putting off entry to a trade or occupation until
the eleventh year, that is to say 16 or 17. The employers' organisations and CDU/CSU spokesmen and women much preferred the traditional
dual system, or vocationally oriented versions of the basic vocational
education year (BGJ) like the co-operative year (periods of full-time
vocational education interspersed with periods of practical training)
recently adopted by trade unions and employers in the metal trades.
Their attitude to the full-time basic vocational education school
year was at most one of reluctant acceptance. It was felt to be too
broad and general to be an effective substitute for the traditional
apprenticeship's first year. Employers are compelled by federal
regulation to take apprentices for only two years if they have successfully completed a basic vocational school year in the occupational
sector in which they are to be trained. However, employers partially
torpedoed the basic vocational education year by refusing to train
apprentices entitled to such a shorter training time. At first they
even refused to accept its equivalence to the first six months of
apprenticeship but they have now agreed to give half a year's credit
for the basic vocational education year if it is taken in a Realschule.
The employers clearly believe there is no substitute for real workplace experience, or perhaps for real young workers able to produce
marketable goods and services. The employers' reluctance is recipro-
cated to some extent by the young people: if they cannot get credit
for the basic vocational education year to reduce the required period
of apprenticeship, nor, in some Laender, academic credit leading to
a Hauptschule or Realschule certificate, nor even a training allowance, then the BGJ at school becomes a mug's game.

Indeed, the Conference of Education Ministers proved much too
optimistic about the acceptability of the basic vocational education
year. Whereas they had planned for 200,000 young people in 1976 the
actual enrolments are far below target (Table 14).

Traditional places in the dual system expanded faster than
Education Ministers could have expected. In the General Plan for
Education currently being brought up to date by the federal and
Laender governments it is assumed that the percentage of young people
aged 15 in their first year under the dual system who are not receiving comprehensive basic vocational training, and those attending
compulsory vocational school only part-time, will fall from 21 per
cent in 1980 to 6 per cent in 1985 and to 5 per cent in 1990. These

Table 14

ENROLMENTS IN THE BASIC VOCATIONAL EDUCATION YEAR
(thousands)

	In Schools	Co-operative Form	Total
1975-76	16.2	0.9	17.1
1977-78	20.1	1.4	21.5
1979-80	57.0	10.3	67.3

Source: Federal Training Institute.

targets seem most unlikely to be met even though the year has been
recast to meet some of the employers' objections that it was too
broad and too theoretical.

Yet there is a case, and a strong one, for the basic vocational
education year. It is much more broadly based than training in a
traditional apprenticeship. It allows the young men and women to
"taste" a number of related occupations in a broad field before
making an irrevocable choice. It offers better quality theoretical
and general education than the traditional part-time vocational
schools (Berufsschulen) are able to provide. Furthermore, it is, or
should be more responsive to the development of new technologies and
to demands for new skills and techniques than the traditional dual
system.

So, perhaps in recognition that the old order is likely to change
even if they might prefer it not to, the employers and the conservative political forces are beginning to adapt to the basic vocational
education year. Whatever its shortcomings, it is not as unacceptable
to them as a tenth year of general education.

Some Laender, notably North Rhine-Westphalia, are moving towards
a system of options for the tenth year between a tenth year in school,
the basic vocational education year, the co-operative year, or the
pre-vocational preparatory year for handicapped children and slow
learners. There are considerable attractions in offering a range of
provision of this kind, though there are bound to be continuing
battles among the protagonists of one form or another. The struggle
is made worse by the rigid distinctions between teachers' qualifications. Put simply, the position is that teachers are trained in
Germany to teach in a particular kind of school such as a Grundschule,
Hauptschule, Realschule or Gymnasium. The requirements are all different, except for teachers in the Gymnasium and the general teachers
in the vocational school or in the basic vocational education year
whose qualifications are the same. The various professional organisations and trade unions of teachers also tend to be different, members joining the one appropriate to their qualifications. This makes

movements of teachers among schools difficult; it is ill-adapted to comprehensive schools, and it creates conflicting pressures on Laender governments and political parties about which types of institution should be expanded or changed, pressures which are not necessarily related to valid educational objectives. In the battle over what happens to the tenth year, the role of interest groups inside education and outside it should not be underestimated.

Higher Education

The growth of higher education, from the 410,000 students of 1971 to the 950,000 of 1979 also has its impact on the scale and nature of youth employment. The universities now take in nearly a fifth of each year's age group; and the easing of "numerus clausus" provisions could carry that proportion to a quarter or even beyond, although the proportion of the age-group moving from school to university seems to be falling. The social composition of the student body has changed. In 1978, 17.4 per cent of university entrants came from manual workers' homes, twice the proportion of 1971. But compared to the social composition of American university students, or even British and Scandinavian ones, Germany still has a long way to go. Already there are signs of a tighter labour market for graduates. Some young people undertake training after the Abitur, rather than going on to university. Others take post-graduate technical training. A third group is coming to university via the Fachhochschulen, already well grounded in an occupation.

There is considerable disquiet, especially among employers, about the possibility of a major further expansion of university places. Graduates in specialised fields within such popular subjects as architecture, economics and social science find it difficult to get jobs in these fields. The public services, which have been recruiting over half Germany's new graduates, are no longer expanding. Teaching is a shrinking profession as child numbers decline. So university graduates are accepting lower status jobs, and others, qualified by their Abitur or Realschule certificate for higher education, go into apprenticeships abbreviated by credit for that certificate.

The core of the employers' fears is that a further growth of university and other full-time further education could destroy the traditional dual system of apprenticeship; and so indeed it could, in three ways. First, employers do not regard the university degree course as an appropriate qualification for many jobs in industry: they much prefer to control the preparation and training of their new recruits themselves. University education was criticised by many of those we met for being too abstract and theoretical, too far removed from the daily realities of making and selling. Second, those with higher educational qualifications could displace those with lower

qualifications in the competition for jobs. The child without a
Hauptschule certificate is very hard to place now, and in some of the
more favoured trades, even those with Hauptschule certificates may
not be able to get places. Third, the dual system may simply be bypassed by other, more sophisticated forms of training and education,
loosening the employers' hold over vocational education and training.
Professor Lutz, Director of the Institute for Social Science Research
in Munich, told us that in his view a further major expansion of
higher education might kill the apprenticeship system. It is not
without significance that universities are politically powerful in
Germany: each Land has a minister for the universities. In contrast,
the responsibility for vocational education and training is divided
between the Land and the federal government, and also within each of
the Laender and among different ministries of the federal government.

Social Structure and Opportunity

No discussion of education and of the related training system in
Germany would be complete without reference to the social structure
it reflects. Social structures remain in many ways conservative,
strangely at odds with the modern economy. Children's educational
destinies are still largely determined by their parents' occupations
and education. Of course that is true everywhere, but it is notably
true of Germany. Children whose parents completed their Abitur will
be very likely indeed to attend a Gymnasium. Children whose parents
attended a Hauptschule may find their way to a Gymnasium or Realschule,
but most of them will follow their parents' footsteps. Since a
child's certificate will largely determine what occupation he enters,
the most desirable occupations going to those with the certificate
from the Gymnasium (Abitur) or at least the certificate from the
Realschule, there is a close link between the kind of secondary
school attended and a person's life chances. The ladder of academic
achievement is duplicated by the ladder of occupations and trades.
In several of the OECD countries apprentices tend to come from a
limited social situation and to be prepared for work of a recognised
social status. In Britain they are the elite of manual workers.
In France they are mainly trained for lower level skills. But in
Germany there is also a marked social differentiation within the dual
system, training for some occupations like insurance or banking being
much more highly regarded than others, and leading to a career progression. This is reinforced by early vocational guidance and hence
the child's own expectations of his future career. Reimut Jochimsen,
now Minister of Economics in North Rhine-Westphalia, summed this up
in 1977 when he was the Permanent Secretary to the Federal Ministry
of Education: "... there is a complicated, elaborate and highly differentiated, but within that differentiation, also very rigid linkage,

between formal qualifications obtained in education on the one hand, and admission to vocational or professional positions and careers on the other".(1) We recognise, of course, that there is much greater flexibility now within the education system, and that routes to promotion are not barred to those without the Abitur or university degrees as they once were. Nevertheless, life chances still seem to us to be often determined by a child's background, and in particular by his parents' occupation and educational attainment.

Vocational Counselling

Vocational or occupational counselling provides the essential link between the education system and the training system. It smoothes out the inevitable discrepancies between children's aspirations and the training opportunities actually available. It is a sophisticated system, and without it the dual system would work much less well. But it raises large questions about how far it fashions the foot to fit the shoe, when the shoe should fit the foot.

Vocational counselling by the Federal Institute for Employment starts early and is thorough. The Laender Education Ministers, on the other hand, are responsible for educational counselling in the schools. Children are tested, diagnosed for aptitude and then counselled on their future careers. There are vocational conferences for schoolchildren and meetings for parents. There is a supporting psychological service which undertakes testing, especially of children with difficulties, and there is a technical advisory service to assist employers with organisational and ergonomic suggestions for the equipment of training and work places for the disabled. The Federal Institute for Employment has a monopoly of occupational counselling in Germany. It has a network of local offices which also offer vocational guidance, and employs over 5,000 careers officers, who between them manage a thorough interview with every school-leaver.

In Germany information and counselling is provided against a background of instruction in school about working life (Arbeitslehre). This is given in the basic secondary school (Hauptschule) and in some of the experimental comprehensive schools (Gesamtschulen), mainly in grades seven to nine. Children in the general and the academic secondary schools (the Realschulen and the Gymnasia) receive an introduction to political, social and economic systems.

There is a strong emphasis in Germany on helping young people find out for themselves what happens at work. A movement started thirty years ago by teachers in the Land of Hamburg to arrange periods

---

1) R. Jochimsen: Aims and Objectives of German Vocational and Professional Education in the Present European Context. Conference on Education and Work Life of the London Goethe Institute, April 1977.

of work observation in enterprises (Betriebspraktikum) for their
pupils has spread to all but one of the Laender. Children taking
part spend a minimum of 20 hours' preparation in class; three weeks
in an enterprise doing simple tasks associated with an occupation and
observing more complex ones; and another 20 hours in class reviewing
their experience. A student usually sees only one occupation, so the
time spent in the enterprise helps him decide whether or not to continue with the occupation he or she initially chose. It seems that
about one-third of participants apply for training in the occupation
they first chose, one-third apply for a similar occupation, and one-
third choose something else. These periods have the support of unions
and employers. The role of the Laender governments has been to pay
for the extension of school accident insurance to cover the time in
the enterprise. It is striking that very few children in the Gymnasia
have opportunities for work observation, as is illustrated in the
case of Hamburg (Table 15).

Table 15

WORK OBSERVATION IN HAMBURG

PROPORTIONS OF CHILDREN PARTICIPATING

1973-1976

(percentages)

Hauptschulen	75
Realschulen	60
Sonderschulen	80
Gesamtschulen	90
Gymnasia	1

Source: Peter Friedrich, Abhandlungen zur Theorie und Praxis des
Technikunterrichts und der Arbeitslehre, Verlag Barbara
Fransbecker, Bad Salzdetfurth, 1977.

Nevertheless, other OECD countries could learn much from German experience with work observation.

Germany is starting on an ambitious programme to build a network of counselling centres (Berufsinformationszentrum) across the
country. We saw a little of the vocational information available to
school-leavers in Nuremberg and in Dortmund. We were impressed by
the attractive range of magazines and brochures on careers, the use
of television, films and other aids, by the ready availability of
careers counselling, and by the attempts to help as many young people
as possible seek information for themselves. We would like to see
all boys and girls encouraged to become familiar with the range of
opportunities and careers available to them so that they could ex-
press an informed preference for a future occupation.

There is, as always, some divergence between theory and practice,
and the divergence on vocational counselling is wide in the schools.

The schools are very short of careers teachers, and those they do have lack knowledge of industry. As for school counsellors, only five Laender have them, and the target of one counsellor for every 3,000 pupils in North Rhine-Westphalia originally set in 1975 has still not been achieved. Industry is not sufficiently involved, and firms are reluctant to add schools visits and work observation to the existing burdens of training and work experience. Perhaps German schools could consider local links with firms, managers and trade union officials; describing what they do could be a useful complement to school-based vocational guidance.

The fundamental question is whether vocational guidance in Germany is too definitive and starts too young. In few other advanced Western countries are choices of career made as young as they are in Germany. By 14 or 15, even before compulsory schooling ends, a child's future is in many cases set. Yet any child of 14 or 15 is likely to be influenced much more by his parents' wishes than by his own. Their expectations, their values and their conventional wisdom will shape the child's future. But his or her aspirations may outrun that of the parents, or take a different direction. The German system, efficient though it is, leaves little room for divergence between the generations, and does not do enough to encourage more equal opportunity. Furthermore, busy careers officers are bound to be influenced by current training vacancies rather than long-term prospects or the possible, but uncertain evolution of new types of occupations; and the children they advise will be in no position to argue with them. The careers officer has to match training places with applicants. His job is often to persuade a school-leaver and his or her parents to accept a second or third best place, perhaps in training for an occupation the child does not really want. The effort to match training and individuals, and to make the maximum use of available training places, is bound to predominate over the wishes of some individuals, especially of the least confident young people. And careers officers may well have conventional views about the appropriateness of the occupation to the child's academic level or sex.

The present system of early placement has a further disadvantage. The hierarchy of occupations strongly reflects the assumptions of the previous generation, which may not be the best guide for the next. German parents appear to regard being a baker or a butcher as a good secure occupation. Hence Germany has thousands of qualified bakers and butchers who will never practice their trades. Older generation attitudes constrain girls to a limited traditional range of occupations, to staying at home or to a "social year" which does little to help them find a permanent place in the labour market.

It has been said to us that later vocational guidance would make the system too expensive. We doubt if that is the real objection: it might simply break down. For young people of 17 and 18 nowadays have views of their own. They may not want to slot into a traditional structure, or to copy their parents' lives. Some want to pursue un-orthodox ways of earning a living and indeed may not want to conform to conventional employment patterns at all. The German vocational counselling system chronologically precedes the natural period of rebellion and independence during adolescence. But for how much longer? The coming of the tenth year of basic vocational education as a normal pattern is likely to cause tensions for the occupational counselling system, and will demand imagination and flexibility from careers officers. Boys and girls of 16 and 17 are likely to be more determined than 15 year-olds to get what they want.

The tenth year will also pose problems for the dual system if the present period of apprenticeship of three to three-and-a-half years is not shortened by an equivalent length of time. We were told that the prolongation of schooling can lead to young people abandon-ing their apprenticeship before completion, in the second or third year. Since these young people will be 19 or 20 years old, they are likely to want to earn more than an apprentice's allowance; and some of them may have domestic responsibilities, spouses and children, as well. The drop-out apprentice becomes part of the underclass in the labour market, along with school drop-outs and others who are un-qualified.

The traditional dual system is, it seems, all of a piece. To work effectively, it must recruit young people of 15 or 16. Occupa-tional counselling at this young age minimises any mismatch between training places available and young people seeking them. It provides a steady flow of young entrants, many of whom pay for part of the cost of their training by the work they do. It also allows the ma-jority of firms who do not train anyone to benefit from the supply of skilled people by those who do. Attempts to alter parts of the dual system by prolonging compulsory schooling, thus delaying occu-pational choice, could start a process of wholesale destruction. The German public and the German government will have to decide whether to sustain the existing system or to reform it, for instance on the lines set out at the end of Chapter II. The middle path of modifying by changes of detail may no longer be open.

IV

THE MANAGEMENT OF THE TRAINING SYSTEM

The Responsibility for Training

In Germany the dual training system, which has developed over a long period, is much larger than in other OECD countries. Only Austria and Switzerland have apprenticeship systems that are comparable in relation to the number of young people in the population.

The system is quite complex, and the responsibility for policy and for the organisation, financing, management and control of the system is shared among the federal, Laender and municipal governments, employers and unions. It is shared at the level of both the federal government and the Laender among the ministries responsible for finance, labour and education. It is exercised by employers both individually and also collectively through the Chambers of Industry and Trade (**Figure 4**).

Germany being a federal state, there is no single central agency responsible for training policy, or for financing, management and control. Instead, overall policy for the provision of training and its management evolves through continuing discussion among the different interests. This takes place partly through a set of special arrangements for co-ordination in which the unions and the employers are represented.[1] It also takes place through open public debate about the vital issues, in which the political parties take an active part.

The Organisation of Practical Training

The effort made by each partner differs. Each makes its own contribution to the provision of training as well as to total expenditure (Figure 4). Apprentices are given their practical training by enterprises, either in their own workshops, or in the inter-enterprise workshops run by the Chambers of Industry and Trade or in other special inter-enterprise training workshops. Employers have no obligation to provide training places, nor do young people have any obligation to apply for apprenticeships, although strong pressures are exerted by society on both of them. In practice, enterprises are

1) See pp. 142-3, "The participation of employers and employees".

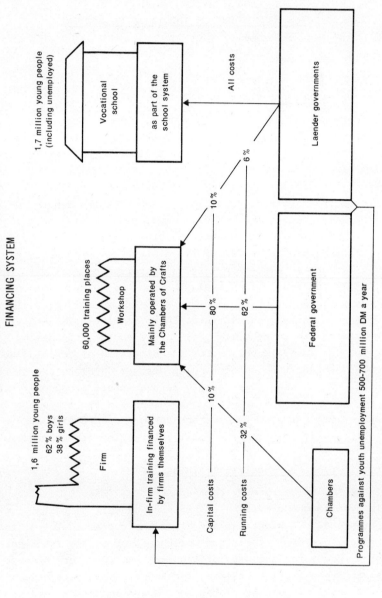

Figure 4

VOCATIONAL EDUCATION AND TRAINING IN GERMANY

FINANCING SYSTEM

1,7 million young people
(including unemployed)

Vocational school

as part of the school system

All costs

Laender governments

60,000 training places

Workshop

Mainly operated by
the Chambers of Crafts

10 %

6 %

80 %

62 %

Federal government

1,6 million young people
62 % boys
38 % girls

Firm

In-firm training financed
by firms themselves

Capital costs   10 %

Running costs   32 %

Chambers

Programmes against youth unemployment 500-700 million DM a year

Source : Federal Training Institute.

willing to provide training, either on their own premises or collectively through the Chambers of Industry and Trade. The public authorities take no part in fixing enterprise expenditures: it is for employers to decide for themselves what effort they are prepared to
make. Moreover, it is accepted that enterprises can provide training
without jeopardising vocational education in institutions. Those
enterprises which do provide training have in effect to compete for
their apprentices, not only with each other, but with institutions
offering full-time training.

Whilst enterprises make training available it is provided
directly mainly by the larger ones. Some of the smaller enterprises
have difficulties in fully providing the training required by law.
For these small enterprises and for the purposes of improving the
quality of training, inter-enterprise training workshops are operated
by the appropriate Chamber of Industry and Trade. Up to 90 per cent
of the capital costs of equipping these workshops may be paid by the
federal Ministry of Education and Science, through the Federal Training Institute. Current costs are borne by the enterprises. Those
enterprises whose apprentices are trained in the workshop pay a fee
to the Chamber, but since these fees do not usually cover all costs
the remainder is shared among the other enterprises belonging to the
Chamber, including those which provide no training. Member enterprises pay a subscription which varies according to their size. In
the case of craft courses the federal and Laender governments pay
grants towards current costs. In exceptional cases the federal
Ministry of Education and Science may also subsidise the current costs
of a new inter-enterprise training workshop if the Chamber concerned
and the enterprises cannot meet them and there is a danger of losing
training places. The aim is to provide some 63,500 new places in
inter-enterprise workshops in 1980.

Finance

Finance for training comes from several sources: the federal
government; the Laender; the municipalities; the Chambers of
Industry and Trade; and enterprises, most of which belong to the
private sector. Private non-profit-making bodies also participate.
It has been estimated that in 1978 the federal, Laender and municipal
governments contributed DM.8.4 billion and enterprises some DM.9
billion, which together represented nearly 1.4 per cent of the GNP.
In addition, apprentices make a contribution in the form of the work
they do. The Edding Commission estimated that in 1971 the value of
apprentices' work could be as much as 40 to 50 per cent of the cost of
their training. Since then training costs have risen and training requirements have become more strict.

i) Expenditure by the Federal Government

Expenditure by the federal government on special programmes, including inter-enterprise training centres, amounted in 1979 to DM.484
million. Financial assistance for the initial or further training of
young people and adults paid directly to the persons concerned or to
training institutions amounted in 1979 to about DM.2.3 billion. In
addition, enterprises which provide training are indirectly assisted
by the federal government through the tax relief they can claim on
their training expenditures. Grants for additional training places
do not have to be included in the statement of a company's income for
tax purposes.

The Federal Training Institute is responsible for the management
of federal funds devoted to occupational training. It has a financial department consisting of two divisions: one responsible for
studying occupational training costs in the private sector, the other
responsible for managing federal resources and allocating them by way
of direct finance or as subsidies.

Within this framework, the federal government's intervention
takes two forms.

The first concerns the financing of training workshops. These
consist primarily of craft centres coming under the Chambers of
Trade (1) and, to a lesser degree, centres run by the Chambers of
Industry.(2) The federal government provides subsidies covering 80
per cent of the theoretical costs. They are not calculated in a
systematic way, but by reference to regional prices. Nor is the
subsidisation automatic. The overall budget is allocated partly in
response to requests made by the Chambers of Commerce and Trades
taking into account the results of checks made by the Institute concerning the location of the centres, their costs and their quantitative and qualitative training capabilities. The budget allocation is
made for the nation as a whole and is apportioned among the various
Laender by arbitration among them. Between 1973 and 1982 it will
have amounted to about DM.1,000 million.

Secondly, the federal government can intervene in the operation
of the centres, usually those run by the Chambers of Trade. The
federal government may provide assistance representing up to 50 per
cent of the operating deficit of a centre. This arrangement has
existed on a provisional basis since 1975, and is likely to be continued. Yet none of the officials concerned can be unaware of the

1) All firms on the register of trades are considered to be craft
   enterprises. The distinction between a craft enterprise and a
   business enterprise is not a matter of the size of the enterprise
   but of the type of activity.
2) 40 per cent of apprentices are in the craft trades, 45 per cent
   in industry and commerce, and 15 per cent in agriculture and the
   liberal professions.

possibility of the Chambers of Trades asking their members for a contribution that is lower than normal, thereby widening the operating
deficit and then requesting a larger subsidy from the federal government to cover its half-share.

ii) Expenditure by the Laender

Expenditure on education is borne by the Laender. In 1978 the
total expenditure on education was DM.61.3 billion, a little less
than three-fourths of this amount being provided by the Laender. No
detailed breakdown exists of the Laender's expenditure on in-school
occupational training. It is estimated that a young person receiving
full-time training for one year or two years in a school (vocational
training school or technical training school, etc.) costs the Laender
DM.6,046 a year, compared to DM.1,758 a year for a young worker
attending classes at a part-time vocational school one or two days
a week for three years.

In addition, the Laender have, on their own initiative, been
organising special programmes for the creation of training places.
This additional effort cost DM.439 million in 1979.

Finally, the Laender provide 10 per cent of the finance for the
inter-enterprise training workshops which come under the Chambers of
Industry and Trade.

iii) Expenditure by the Municipalities

We have seen vocational schools financed by the municipalities,
but no data exist on the expenditure of the municipalities in respect
of these schools. In 1976 they covered 17.4 per cent of total expenditure on education.

iv) Expenditure by the Chambers of Industry and Trade

In 1972, expenditure by the Chambers of Industry and Trade on
training in workshops amounted to DM.132 million. More recent figures
are not available. The Chambers meet 10 per cent of the capital costs
of these training workshops. They assume responsibility for operating them and may have to bear 50 per cent of any deficit that arises.
If they have any financial problems, they can borrow from the federal
government. As a general rule, the funds handled by the Chambers
come from contributions paid by their members. All member enterprises
pay an ordinary contribution that varies according to the size and
revenue of the enterprise. Those who send apprentices to the workshop pay a special contribution for each apprentice. When there is
a deficit on operating expenses all members pay exceptional contributions to cover 50 per cent of it.

v) Expenditure by Enterprises

The Edding Commission estimated that in 1972 enterprises covered 94.1 per cent of overall training expenditure. This, we may repeat, constitutes a "voluntary" contribution: the enterprise undertakes to take young people for training and to bear the financial costs of it, including the remuneration of apprentices, which in 1979 was equivalent on average to DM.450 per month. Enterprises could not easily answer questions about the scale of their participation. During our discussions at the German employers' organisation, one of the representatives explained that an estimate could only be approximate: thus, for 1979 the finance provided by enterprises probably amounted to DM.20 billion, of which DM.16 billion was for occupational training and DM.4 billion for further training.(1)

The annual cost per trainee to the participating firms average some DM.6,000. But some of the major firms that have undertaken the lion's share of the total training responsibilities have spent much more. For example, the Association of German Chambers of Industry and Commerce reports that Siemens, which had 10,800 apprentices in training in 1980, estimated that it spent DM.44,000 on the three years' training given to each trainee; Volkswagen estimated that it spent DM.20,000 to 25,000 a year on each trainee; and the BASF estimated that it spent DM.18,000 a year per trainee. The Edding Commission calculated that expenditure per trainee by enterprises with over 1,000 employees was 17 per cent higher than for smaller ones.

Enterprises may deduct all or part of their training expenditure from their gross revenues when calculating profits for tax purposes. The rate of profits tax varies from 22 per cent to 56 per cent according to the amount of taxable revenues. Thus the tax exemption that enterprises receive is equivalent to a disguised subsidy of 22 per cent to 56 per cent of their training costs. Moreover, this subsidisation is not related to the training activities undertaken but to the taxable revenues of the enterprise. Since it was made clear to us that most apprentices are trained in small enterprises with 50 employees at most, it seems that most of the tax exemptions lie towards the bottom of the 22 per cent to 56 per cent range. However, the value of the work done by apprentices is included in the gross revenues of the enterprise, and is therefore taxed, reducing the effective subsidy to roughly 13-28 per cent. Taking into account both the value of work done by apprentices and the net tax relief,

---

1) By way of example, we were told by BASF at Ludwigshafen that its total training expenditure amounted in 1978 to DM.86.5 million and that for 1979 they had come to close on DM.100 million. These costs were made up as follows:
   - 23 per cent for equipment and operation;
   - 25 per cent for salaries of training staff;
   - 41 per cent for apprentices' remuneration (DM.483 per month in the first year, DM.555 second year, DM.673 the third year, and DM.795 the fourth year);
   - 11 per cent for costs specific to the enterprise.

the net cost of training to enterprises lies in the range of roughly a quarter to a half their gross expenditure on it. In addition, enterprises benefit from the theoretical teaching given in the vocational education schools especially in the second and third years.

Financial Management

In Germany, several bodies are responsible for determining overall financial requirements and their allocation to vocational education and training in relation to the other sectors of education and specific issues concerning training under the dual system, such as decisions about the basic vocational education year. At present, the federal government does not consider it necessary to establish other central boards in addition to those already existing.

The Federal Training Institute is responsible for the management of federal funds devoted to training workshops. It has a governing committee on which employers, employees and the Laender are represented. The Institute determines costs which serve as a basis for the federal government's contributions. It also exercises control by setting standards for new training workshops and the payment of subsidies, and by checking new workshops before they are opened to ensure that they conform to these standards.

Besides the Federal Training Institute there is the Federal-Laender Commission for Educational Planning and Research Promotion (Bund-Länder-Kommission für Bildungsplanung und Forschungsförderung, BLK). The BLK representatives of the federal and Laender governments have elaborated and approved plans for the vocational education sector which serve as guidelines for the development of vocational education in the Laender and also by the federal government, for example in the development of inter-enterprise training workshops. These plans comprise a phased plan in 1975 for the development of vocational education, and a programme in 1976 for implementing priority measures designed to reduce the employment risks encountered by adolescents which was brought up to date in 1977. Vocational education as a whole also formed part of the 1973 General Plan for Education, a new version of which is currently being prepared for the period up to 1990.

The Debate about Financing

The dual system was examined by the Commission on the Cost and Financing of Training (the Edding Commission), which was set up by Parliament in 1970, in view of the expected increase in the number of young people coming onto the labour market between 1970 and 1980. The Commission was composed of economists and members of the teaching profession. The law setting up the Commission stipulated that it should determine the financial consequences of the various projects for the reform of training and propose new methods of financing that would guarantee that the training given in the various enterprises reached a uniform minimum standard.

One of the Edding Commission's most important findings concerned the unequal distribution of the costs and benefits of training among enterprises. As only 16 per cent of firms (1) provided training and nearly half the employees moved to another firm in the year following their training, enterprises not providing training benefited from that given by the others. Moreover, the Commission considered that because of this unequal distribution of training costs, the number of young people trained was less than it could be.

In order to redistribute costs in a more equitable way, the Edding Commission recommended that all enterprises should pay a special tax so as to subsidise the cost of training in those firms that provided it. Accordingly, in 1975, the federal government made a proposal to introduce a training tax which generated a prolonged debate. The vast majority of employers did not conceal their hostility to the proposed system, which they considered to be an unnecessary burden and constraint, since the "voluntary" system worked adequately. They argued that private enterprises were better placed than government to decide the quality and requirements of training, and they protested against this government intervention in the training they provided. They also pointed out that enterprises providing training were the ones that paid some 80 per cent of the total wage bill. Trade union representatives, on the other hand, liked the idea of setting up a fund based on contributions from firms. They thought that it would allow a fairer distribution of training efforts in all professional sectors and a better chance of controlling the vast sums that were provided for training each year. The debate was not limited to the social partners, but reached the political arena. The SPD, the major party in the coalition then in power, did not conceal its interest in the suggestion.

Eventually in 1976 the Training Places Promotion Act was passed by the federal Parliament (Ausbildungsplatzfoerderungsgesetz, APIFG). It provided for a levy-grant system which could be brought into effect if the number of training places was insufficient. Specifically, it provided that the levy-grant system could be implemented if the total number of apprentice training places offered by employers in the private and public sectors did not exceed by 12.5 per cent or more the number of places sought by young people, and if no improvement in the situation were expected during the current year. The

1) 10 per cent of the largest industrial and commercial enterprises and 25 per cent of craft enterprises.

excess of 12.5 per cent was intended to cover regional differences between the numbers of places offered and sought, and to give young people some degree of choice of the occupation for which they would seek training. The levy, if brought into force, would be a maximum of 0.25 per cent of the annual wage bill in enterprises where it exceeds DM.400,000; and the proceeds would be paid to the enterprises that provided training.

So far the federal government has not considered it necessary to invoke the levy-grant mechanism of the 1976 law, even though the number of training places in enterprises has not yet exceeded applications by the required 12.5 per cent. The employers' objections, supported by the minority party in the SPD/FDP coalition government, were strong enough to dissuade the government from doing so, but only on condition that they undertook to increase significantly the number of places available. A considerable increase was in fact realised, the number of places rising by 180,000 from 460,000 in 1975 to a total in 1980 of about 640,000 places.

A levy-grant system is however in operation in the construction industry, in roofing, stone masonry and stone cutting crafts and in horticulture by agreement between the Trade Unions and the Employers' Associations.

Controlling the Quality of Training

The quality of the dual training system within enterprises providing training and in inter-enterprise training centres is safeguarded by regulatory, organisation, and control mechanisms set up under the Vocational Training Act of 1969.

To adapt training to technical, economic, and social requirements and developments, the content of training for a recognised apprenticeable occupation is governed by statutory training regulations (Verordnung). They are issued by the federal minister responsible (the federal Minister of Economics, for example, is responsible for crafts and for industrial and commercial occupations) in agreement with the federal Minister of Education and Science. These training regulations are prepared on the instruction of the federal minister concerned by the Federal Training Institute in close consultation with specialists representing the employers and the employed. The Ministers of Education and Culture of the Laender simultaneously prepare the corresponding skeleton curriculum of the part-time vocational school for the apprenticeable occupation or group of occupations in the federal government's training regulations. The federal ministers and the Ministers for Education and Culture of the Laender co-ordinate these training regulations and skeleton curricula. This procedure is perhaps somewhat complicated, but it is a necessary consequence of Germany's federal Constitution which assigns to the federal government responsibility for the practical side of training in enterprise and inter-enterprise workshops within the dual system, and to the Laender responsibility for the schoolroom side of dual training.

Since 1969, 95 sets of training regulations have been issued for 129 recognised apprenticeable occupations. By 1978, approximately 700,000 apprentices, roughly 45 per cent of all trainees in the dual system, were being trained in these newly regulated occupations. In occupations for which recent training regulations have not yet been issued, training and examinations have not been limited by the old regulations. Statutory training regulations contain only minimum requirements, and in practice enterprises providing training continuously adapt training to modern demands. This is especially true of the metal-working occupations, which in 1978 had some 170,000 apprentices, for which the introduction of new training regulations has been delayed by differences of opinion between the employers and workers about the length of training: the workers want it to be longer and the employers prefer it to be shorter.

The statutory training regulations contain requirements which cannot be met by all small and medium-sized enterprises, some of which are very specialised. These requirements can be met in the inter-enterprise training workshops which are generally operated by the Chambers of Industry and Trade.

The requirements laid down by the federal government concern the suitability of enterprise and of inter-enterprise training workshops as well as the professional, teaching and personal qualifications of the instructors. An instructor in crafts must be qualified as a crafts master, i.e. must have proved his knowledge and skills in his profession; be able to teach to professional standards and working methods; and also be qualified in economic and legal fields on a crafts master level. Instructors are certified after an appropriate examination regulated and held by the government. In principle, this also applies to agriculture and home economics. In other fields, not only personal suitability but also a minimum age of 24 years, a completed final examination in the occupation for which training is to be given, as well as proof of the necessary teaching qualification, are required, as a rule, in an examination before an examination board of the responsible body. The responsible bodies provide courses to prepare instructors for their teaching qualifications. Enterprises providing training have to ensure that a sufficient number of such qualified instructors is available. In practice, instructors, especially the full-time ones, have generally attained a higher level of vocational training than that described above, namely as a crafts master in industry or even in engineering.

Compliance with the requirements for training workshops and instructors and the implementation of training in accordance with the

statutory training regulations is supervised by responsible bodies
appointed under the law. In part they are direct government authorities or, to a larger extent, the Chambers of Industry and Trade, which
act as an indirect government administration and are subject to law-
ful supervision by the appropriate Land government. If shortcomings
regarding qualifications are found, the responsible body must demand
corrective measures or, if correction is not possible, report to the
responsible Land authority which must then prohibit sub-standard
training. The responsible body employs training counsellors who have
to advise and supervise the enterprises, instructors and apprentices.
In 1978 there were about 1,000 full-time and about 8,000 part-time
honorary training counsellors.

The results of the intermediate and final examinations for
apprentices which are held by the examination boards of these responsible bodies are a further means of monitoring the quality of
training. Employers, employees and teachers each have an equal number
of representatives on these examination boards. The examination requirements for each occupation are laid down in the statutory training regulations. The examination questions are to an increasing extent being developed at the federal level. The examination results
provide the responsible bodies with important information on the
quality of training and on the suitability of the training workshops.

Despite this impressive set of mechanisms to regulate training,
in practice, equipment, teaching and supervision vary greatly. During
our stay, we had occasion to see training workshops with the most
varied equipment, ranging from the most sophisticated to the most
rudimentary. The same held good for the role of the instructor:
some centres had particularly strict supervision, but in others the
instructor confined himself to demonstrating the essential movements.
The Minister of Education of the Land of North Rhine-Westphalia explained to us that in the vocational schools there was a shortage of
instructors to take charge of general education, so for young persons
in training the usual 12 hours a week in a vocational school are reduced to nine because of this lack of instructors.(1) The main weakness appeared to us to be a lack of enough inspectors in the Chambers
of Industry and Trade. We were not able to obtain overall information
on the number of inspectors, but in the Düsseldorf region, for
example, of the 40,000 enterprises which are members of the Chamber of
Trades, about 19,000 of them gave training to some 48,000 apprentices.
Yet for this region there were at the end of 1979 only eight full-
time inspectors (Ausbildungsberater), which seems to us to be clearly
insufficient.

---

1) An 8-hour minimum is stipulated in the law.

Every confidence therefore seems to be placed in the enterprises.
There seems to be a reliance on self-discipline and on the fact that
it is in the firms' own interest to provide good training. But in
this system of supervision, which mainly depends on the commercial
and trade bodies, there is nothing to guarantee that young people will
not be used as cheap labour. A body of supervisors which depends on
those dispensing training (and particularly one so limited in numbers)
cannot be as independent and thorough as would be necessary for it to
play its full role. The responsible authorities should surely give
their attention to this problem, which concerns the recruitment of
sufficient supervisors and the independence of the profession as a
whole.

The Participation of Employers and Employees

The participation of employees and employers in the various
bodies that manage vocational training is an important monitoring
instrument.

At the enterprise level (in those with at least five employees)
the employees' representatives on the Works Council have a right to
co-determination in the implementation of training in accordance with
the 1972 Works Constitution law. If an enterprise employs five or
more young people, they must elect a youth representative.

In the Chambers of Trade and Industry there is a training committee consisting of six representatives of employers, an equal number of employees' representatives and six teachers from vocational
training schools. The committee has to be informed about and heard
in all important questions concerning training. It adopts the legal
regulations of the responsible body for the implementation of training such as examination procedures, arrangements for further training,
or special regulations for disabled apprentices.

At the Land level there is a training committee consisting of
an equal number of representatives of employers, employees and the
Land authorities. It advises the Land government on training, must
work towards co-operation between full-time school and dual training,
and has to ensure that training is taken into consideration in any
adjustment or development of the school system.

At the federal level delegates of the employers, the employees,
and Land and the federal governments are represented with equal votes
in the Main Committee of the Federal Training Institute. The Main
Committee participates in all important tasks of the Federal Training
Institute. These are: preparing the legal training regulations to be
issued by the responsible federal Ministers; preparing the annual
Report on Vocational Education of the federal Minister of Education
and Science; compiling statistics on training; the planning, setting
up and developing inter-enterprise training workshops; advising the

federal government; and conducting research in training. In the work of the Main Committee the role of employers' representatives and of the unions has, in the opinion of the people we interviewed, increased since 1976. In financial matters although each side has only one-quarter of the votes, it has a right of veto. On technical questions covering the preparation of legislation both sides have to be unanimous for a text to become a parliamentary Bill. The federal government has decided that it will not pass training regulations unless they have been agreed by both employers' and workers' representatives.

Views of Government, Labour and Management

In some of our talks we were reminded of an earlier suggestion that the dual system should be replaced by training coming under the public sector, in other words, entirely carried out in occupational training centres. But the federal and Land ministers stressed their determination to maintain the present system because of the results. Indeed, they reasserted the value of a system based on a normal procedure of negotiation in which the State intervenes only at the highest level and more by way of guidance than compulsion.

The system depends heavily on the voluntary commitment of enterprises to provide practical training. In the words of Mrs. Fuchs, the Federal Secretary of State for Labour, "enterprises recognise that they have a responsibility for training, a responsibility, moreover, which is related more to accepting young people than to financing the system", but this is not "solely a responsibility and a moral obligation: they also find it in their paramount interest". Thus the federal government, like management and, to a slightly lesser degree, the trade unions, is satisfied with a system whose essential quality is that it works.

The representatives of management did not conceal the interest they had in keeping alive the present system, and particularly the proposed system of financing. Those whom we interviewed both from the German Confederation of Chambers of Industry and Commerce (Deutscher Industrie-Handelstag) and the Federation of Employers' Associations (WPA) protested against the idea that the Act of 1976, by operating as a threat, compelled enterprises to train young persons; on the contrary, according to them, it is because they realise their own interests that they provide training. They are well aware of their responsibilities towards young persons, but know that for themselves such training is an investment. These same management representatives are fundamentally against State interventionism, because they consider that enterprises provide training spontaneously. Moreover, any financial intervention in the form of a direct subsidy or aid would have a disincentive effect were it to cease.

The employees' representatives whom we met at the headquarters
of the German Trade Union Federation (DGB), while being more critical
than the management representatives, did not criticise the system out-
right. Their main criticism is that training is unduly dependent on
firms, although they do not think it practicable to change the dual
system at present. Their strongest criticisms concerned finance. In
1968 the DGB proposed a new financing system. The government succeeded in having the Training Places Promotion Act passed but failed
to change the system of voluntary financing. So since 1975 the DGB
has been studying the possibilities of self-financing by enterprises,
without however expecting everything from collective bargaining agreements, since the government has a decision-making role in this particular field. The idea of the DGB with regard to financing is that
(taken up in the Edding Report) of a fund financed in part by a levy
on enterprises and in part by a federal government subsidy. This
fund would be controlled by the Federal Training Institute.

V

WOMEN AND GIRLS, YOUNG FOREIGNERS AND DISADVANTAGED CHILDREN

Women and Girls

For many years the incidence of unemployment has been twice as high among young women aged 20 to 24 and girls aged 15 to 19 as among the corresponding male age-groups (Figure 5). In 1978, the estimated rate of unemployment for adolescent girls was 6.8 per cent compared with 3.5 per cent among boys, and 6.4 per cent for young women against 3.2 for young men. A substantial proportion of girls are not counted in the labour force so the official figures certainly underestimate their rate of unemployment. In September 1979 nearly two-thirds of the unemployed adolescents were girls, and they contributed the same proportion of those who started work without any training.

The conventional wisdom of careers officers and teachers, and the early age of occupational choice in Germany may go some way to explain the parlous situation of girls. The majority of girls are still trained in full-time vocational schools rather than in the dual system, and they continue to train predominantly for traditional women's occupations. We were told that the aspirations of those girls who go into apprenticeships were also limited, and that most of them wanted to go into such traditional women's occupations as hairdressing or the retail trade. Our own observations largely confirmed that.[1] But there is not much encouragement for the ambitious girl. Her parents are likely to accept low horizons for her. And employers show little desire to train girls for non-traditional jobs. We were told that, in the whole of Germany, only ten substantial and some smaller firms are willing to train girls in technical occupations such as electrical or electronic engineering. Perhaps if a shortage of labour emerges in the late 1980s it will drive German employers to revise their views, but it is not certain, and in any case will not happen soon.

---

1) Of girls who left school before the end of the ninth grade, 63 per cent renounced further training or education, compared with 39 per cent of all children: that is to say, almost all those who renounced were girls. Most of them went into housework or "related economic activities". Given that these children were only 15 or 16 at the time of renouncing further education and training, the responsibility for this dire state of affairs clearly rests with their parents and their teachers.

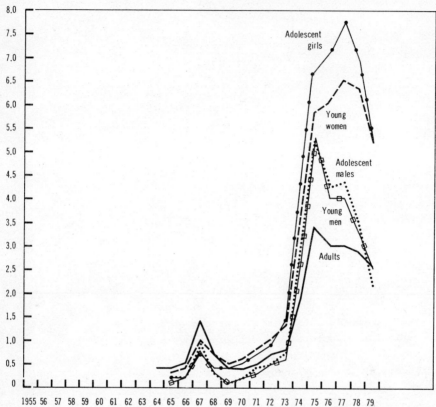

Figure 5

AGE- AND SEX-SPECIFIC UNEMPLOYMENT RATES

Source : OECD, *Youth Unemployment : The Causes and Consequences, op.cit.*

The Federal Ministry of Education, which deserves credit for
pioneering new ideas, has mounted 19 pilot projects to train girls
for non-traditional occupations. Since girls are concentrated almost
entirely in 20 of the 450 listed separate occupations, any efforts of
this kind deserve applause. Eight Laender have followed the federal
lead. North Rhine-Westphalia, for instance, offers a special subsidy
of DM.300 a month to firms willing to train girls in non-traditional
occupations, and the Land government will also finance the necessary
additional facilities such as lavatories, washrooms, etc. Yet the
number of girls training for non-traditional occupations remains
stubbornly small.

Some 6,000 girls go into the "social year", a year of community
service after leaving school, which looks surprisingly like a cosmetic
means of dealing with the disproportionately high unemployment among

girls. Students in this social year, 90 per cent of whom are girls, receive a rock-bottom living allowance. It is a maximum of DM.250 a month and is usually less. Yet in the less attractive occupations dominated numerically by men, the training allowances which increase in each year of apprenticeship and are set through collective bargaining are DM.300 to 350, and in attractive male-dominated occupations, as much as DM.700. The discrepancy is only one of many indications that the female sex is still very much a second sex in the eyes of employers, trade unions, parents and girls themselves.

The reasons for discrimination against women, outside certain traditional areas, are rooted in social patterns. Many women leave the labour market when they marry. Few can manage a full-time job once they have children, for the obvious reason that nearly all German schools are open only on a half-day basis. There is only a handful of full-day schools, and in fact less than 3 per cent of German children attend whole-day schools. Hence there is a huge unfilled demand for part-time jobs: 37 per cent of women seeking work want part-time employment.(1) But employers do not welcome workers who want to work part-time, who have lower qualifications and who often have a history of broken employment. So women are caught in a vicious circle: they cannot easily get work on the terms set by their society: and being without work, they cannot easily influence employers or trade unions to alter those terms.

Children of Foreign Workers

If girls are badly served, the children of foreign workers are even worse off. Compared with native-born Germans, young foreign workers experience a much higher rate of unemployment. The proportion of them entering the labour force during the 1980s will increase significantly because of the higher birth rates of the population of foreign workers. By the end of the 1980s about one of every six adolescents entering the labour force will be the offspring of a foreign worker, and his or her preparation for sustained work may be hampered by deficient education and lack of skill. Unless vigorous steps are taken to integrate foreign-born young people as well as their siblings born in Germany, the problems of youth unemployment are likely to be aggravated in the years ahead. A major challenge will be to offer compensatory education and training to the children of foreign workers and to provide them with the opportunity to adjust to labour market demand so that they can compete effectively for sustained employment.

---

1) Few Laender governments try to place people in part-time jobs, but the Rhineland-Palatinate is among the exceptions.

We have already said that the authorities have been ambivalent about foreign young people: the illusion that many will return sooner or later to their countries of origin has until recently inhibited serious proposals to integrate them into society. But the Kühn Report, submitted in September 1979, has already had a marked effect on attitudes at the federal level; and the federal government decisions of 19 March 1980 demonstrate a prompt and comprehensive response to a disturbing report.

In 1978 52.9 per cent of all foreign children attended no kindergarten, the percentage of Turkish children attending no kindergarten being even higher. About 20 per cent of the approximately 485,000 foreign children of school age attend no general education school, and about 50 per cent attend no vocational school. Over 50 per cent of young foreigners do not obtain an upper primary school leaving certificate, and over two-third of foreign school leavers (totalling about 45,000 a year) receive no vocational training.

The Kühn Report listed a number of causes for this situation and we do not dissent from what Herr Kühn has said. We particularly emphasise that we do not accept the widely-held belief that foreign parents care only for money, that they want their children to earn as quickly as possible. Whilst it is true that some parents may not appreciate the vital importance of schooling and others may not be able to give their children the support they need, we agree with Herr Kühn that even education-minded parents are likely to lose heart because they are unable to understand the school system and because of the difficulties actually encountered by their children at school. In one private charitable vocational school we visited in Cologne, where trouble was taken to contact parents and explain to them what the training was for, the parents took more interest than did indigenous parents, turning up for parents' evenings and showing support for their children. One reason for this favourable response may have been that a Turkish counsellor worked with German counsellors in giving vocational counselling, an idea that seems worth following up. Admittedly, traditions and customs can be hard to alter: Turkish parents obviously find the idea of sending their daughters to school strange and, if the school is co-educational, even alien. So much responsibility falls on the teachers.

Sadly, there are not enough of them. We have pointed out that teachers of general education in vocational schools require the same qualifications as teachers in a Gymnasium. Given the status of the Gymnasium, few teachers opt to work in a vocational school instead. And at senior secondary level, pupil numbers are still increasing, so there is little unemployment among these teachers, as distinct from teachers at the primary level. Consequently, classes for general education, including language and mathematics, are large; teachers can spare little time for contact with parents or counselling children; and the quality of general education in the vocational schools is, we suspect, poor. Yet for these foreign youngsters, general education is perhaps even more vital than vocational education if they are to be employable. Many have had only two or three years of schooling before arriving in Germany. The best hope of remedying their desperately inadequate education is at the level of the Berufsschule. We welcome the emphasis given to this matter in the federal government's response to the Kühn Report.

The federal government recognises that integration policy will only be acceptable to foreigners in Germany if it does not aim at alienating children and young people from their cultures. But this recognition at the federal level is sometimes absent at the Land level. On one occasion we were told that the children of foreigners must completely lose their parents' national identity if there was to be integration. This is not integration in our opinion, and we share the view of the federal government. In view of their responsibility for education, we emphasize the importance of Land and local authorities' responding positively and promptly to the following measures urged by the federal government

   i) at the pre-school stage more places in crèches and kindergartens (especially all-day kindergartens); and the adaptation of kindergartens to the needs of foreign children;

  ii) at the school stage, the inclusion of foreign children in ordinary German schools as soon as they know enough German; instruction in the mother tongue under German school supervision; better staff and equipment for schools with a high proportion of foreign children;

 iii) at the part-time vocational school stage, the provision of special courses, better qualified teachers and better staffing ratios, better equipment, more attention to the special situation of young foreigners and enough full-time school courses to give occupational qualifications to young foreigners without leaving certificates;

  iv) at the further education stage, the conversion and extension of capacity to give the foreign population better access;

   v) information and counselling for young people and their parents about compulsory schooling and education and training facilities.

We note that the federal government will finance (at some DM.19.5 million a year from 1981) experiments with models to encourage the development of the measures listed, and that the federal

government will also expand occupational preparation for young
foreigners without leaving certificates (MBSEs) from 7,000 places
at present to 20,000 in 1982-83.

Some of the other measures put forward by the federal government
on 19 March 1980 are matters entirely within their own field. But
the success of many other measures, and of the programme as a whole,
will depend on active responses and close co-operation from the Land
and local authorities, trade unions, employers and from German society
as a whole.

Disadvantaged Children

The third difficult area of youth employment, that of educationally disadvantaged young people, presents a more encouraging picture.
Of students in the pre-vocational year (Berufsvorbereitungsjahr) 80
per cent are low achievers. Training is offered in five broad vocational areas, and after completing this year about half manage to get
a proper apprenticeship place in the dual system or move on to the
basic vocational education year. For those students who are very
slow learners, there is a lower grade pre-vocational course, Type V,
which provides training in basic skills and socialisation; but it
leads only to unskilled jobs. Pre-vocational courses including
courses Type V are financed by the Federal Institute for Employment
and the vocational counselling officers select the children who go on
them. The medium-term aim is that the Laender should take over this
task. Given the strained state of the education budgets in several
Laender, it is not clear how soon this can be done or whether it
should even be attempted.

In 1975-76 there were 40,000 young people on pre-vocational
courses. The Ministry would like to see a tenth year for all young
people unable to take up a training place for reasons of educational
inadequacy. North Rhine-Westphalia already makes provision for
children who have neither a job nor a training place, 27,500 of them
in 1979. Young people completing the course may then go on to a
traditional apprenticeship or a job or a subsidised apprenticeship.
This programme, with a considerable emphasis on general education,
including language, mathematics and economics, is much more successful than most pre-vocational courses.

One reason for the success of the programme in North Rhine-
Westphalia may be the emphasis on getting training places, if necessary via a subsidy. Children who already are doing badly in school
rarely respond to more and more of it. They are "school-tired".
Practical training and practical work are most likely to elicit
interest and motivation in them. The idea of short initial training
followed by a training place in a group training scheme or workshop

may also prove fruitful. We would not rule out job creation for these hard-to-place youngsters. The rigid relationship between examination success and vocational opportunities in the traditional system leaves little room for them in present labour market conditions.

VI

Germany has made an impressive attempt to deal with the unemployment of young people, both adolescents and young adults. It seems clear that the rate of unemployment among adolescents is under-estimated: but even allowing for this, and the tendency in many other countries to underestimate unemployment, there is no doubt that the burden of unemployment falls much less heavily on adolescents in Germany than in most other OECD countries.

We suggest that the German authorities should review the way they measure the unemployment of adolescents. The rate is under-estimated by the current practice of including them in the measured labour force (the denominator) and excluding them from the measured unemployed (the numerator) if they are seeking only an apprentice-ship. The official view is that apprentices are in full-time educa-tion and do not work. If statistical practice were compatible with this view, apprentices would not be counted in the labour force.

The relatively low level of unemployment among German adoles-cents which has existed for many years can largely be ascribed to a well-established system of education and training which keeps adoles-cents out of the regular labour market. In addition, the recent sharp increase in the number of adolescents has been absorbed by a rapid expansion of full-time education into a tenth year and of the number of training places provided by employers. At the same time, there was some reduction in unemployment during 1978 due to the in-crease in output. Germany has mainly relied on expanding education and training measures to prevent unemployment among young people and has made relatively little use of subsidies to create new jobs.

A strategy for dealing with the unemployment of young people which gives pride of place to vocational education and training seems to us to be eminently sensible. It is preventive rather than remedial. It is extended to some two-thirds of each generation of adolescents rather than merely to the unemployed. It enables young people to use their time constructively in preparing them to enter the labour market. We also recognise that in Germany it is an effort which mobilises the responsibility and concerted efforts of all levels of government, the employers and the trade unions.

We think that Germany has yet to face the problem of absorbing
the recent increase in the number of young people into the labour market when they become young adults. The official view is optimistic:
it holds that unemployment is due to lack of education and training
and that the efforts made to provide training to a majority of young
people will help them compete for work. Nevertheless, it would be
wise to plan for the downside risk that during the next few years a
larger than usual influx of young people will be looking for work at
a time when the rate of growth of output could be slow, when the
scope for further reductions in the labour force, especially foreign
workers, will be much less than in the recent past, and when the effects of technology are uncertain.

The German dual system provides opportunities for a larger proportion of young people than in any other OECD country to work and receive an income, make the transition from school to working life and
receive skill training.

We have noted great variations in apprentices' allowances.
Allowances are very low in some occupations and regions. Because of
their concentration in traditional female occupations, average girls'
allowances are lower than those for young men. Moreover, training
allowances as a proportion of the wages paid to newly qualified
craftsmen progress only slowly from the first to the last year of
training. Serious study could be given to raising allowances at a
fast rate each year, not only for equity reasons but in line with the
recognition in Germany of the importance of work.

One cannot fail to be impressed by the efforts made in Germany
during compulsory education and then in the dual system to help young
people learn about the realities of the working life, and to do so at
first hand. This part of vocational education is at least as important as skill training. We believe a closer relationship between
firms and schools could similarly bring a new realism to vocational
counselling.

Whilst there is much to learn about the world of work during
training we question the need for three or more years of training in
the lower-skilled occupations, although we have been told that the
technical content is being raised. Consideration might be given to
shortening training in some occupations during the 1980s when the
supply of trainees diminishes.

Some of the specific skill training is wasted when trainees
cannot find jobs in the occupations in which they have been trained,
although we recognise that some skills can in practice be applied in
several kinds of work. We do however believe that fast changing
technologies will require a multi-skilled man or woman in future,
rather than one trained for a highly specific skill.

We think that the right answer is a foundation year of basic general-vocational education, followed by a broader-based initial skill training. Germany is certainly moving in this direction, but will need to iron out some of the problems of the tenth year, in particular the inadequate number and quality of general subject teachers. If necessary, an improvement in remuneration or in working conditions beyond that accorded to Gymnasium teachers (who at present receive equivalent pay) may have to be considered. Dual training could become broader-based if there were opportunities for apprentices to move among enterprises and gain knowledge of more than one skill or occupation. The present indenture with a single employer is not immutable. An experiment could be made in a few districts or in a particular industry.

The responsibility for adapting training to new technologies rests primarily with enterprises. The federal government's training regulations are minimum standards. It is only enterprises that can maintain training related to innovations in markets, technology and production.

The introduction of a tenth year of schooling is a particularly important innovation. Ideally it should be generally adopted, with freedom of choice between a tenth year of general education or a year of basic vocational education either full-time or of the co-operative kind. Children who are school-tired or not suited to academic studies may do better in a work-related course, e.g. the BGJ or co-operative year. This has been the English experience of raising the school-leaving age to sixteen; and efforts are being made to get more vocational courses into the schools. But the basic vocational education year should be broad and not narrowed down to training in a few occupational groups.

A tenth year would delay occupational choice, and so it should. Vocational choice made as early as it is in Germany may be based on lots of information and guidance, but it cannot be the choice of the child concerned. Hence each generation reflects the aspirations of the previous generation rather than its own. This is particularly hard on girls and foreign children.

Preparation in school for working life is relatively well-developed in Germany, but it should be extended to all pupils in all types of school, especially opportunities for work exploration or observation in enterprises for students in the Gymnasia. This should be linked to a reform of counselling with the aim of helping children widen the range of their occupational choice.

The shortage of career teachers and vocational guidance counsellors is serious, especially for disadvantaged children. Even more serious for these children is the shortage of teachers in general education in vocational schools since unqualified children have little choice of a decent occupation. The vocational school is at present the last chance to remedy educational gaps for many of these children. It is particularly important that opportunities should exist in all post-compulsory institutions, such as the basic vocational education year, the vocational schools, etc., to take and pass the _Hauptschule_ certificate.

We were impressed by the way in which the complex financial arrangement and the management of the system operate by consensus among the governments, employers and the unions.

Despite the sensible approach in training curricula intended to help apprentices be flexible and mobile, there nevertheless seems a need in overall training policy for a longer-term perspective with the aim of preparing young people for the technical and social changes that will appear during the 1980s. This should not entail planning based on manpower forecasting which Germany has so far wisely resisted. Consideration might be given to the possibility of using additional federal and Laender financial inducements to encourage training in selected sectors, regions or occupations where there is an evident need. Possible examples are training for the wider use of new technologies and for the entry of girls into traditional male occupations.

The quality of training is well controlled in respect of prior planning, regulation and curriculum development and in subsequent examination of apprentices. It seems weak during the course of training for lack of sufficient inspection. We would like to see a corps of training inspectors professionally independent of employers and trade unions. Indeed we would like to see such a corps employed by the federal or possibly, Land governments with its own career structure, separate from the regular civil service. Inspectors in Britain and inspectors of apprenticeship in France enjoy independence and perform a valuable role in encouraging good pedagogic and technical practices in vocational schools. We commend the idea to the German authorities for their consideration.

The federal government should expand its pilot training schemes for girls outside traditional occupations, and should try to persuade firms, if necessary by subsidising training places, to offer apprenticeships in non-traditional trades. Efforts should be made to increase the number of part-time jobs, for instance by "pairing" two employees to undertake one full-time job. Although it is not within our brief, we recognise that the provision of more whole-day schools, so that at least the option exists, would help many women. Single parents are likely to increase in number if Germany follows precedent elsewhere, and the part-day school does not meet their needs.

The provision made for foreign children is so sparse as to constitute a potential social danger. Hundreds of thousands of foreign children are going to grow up to live permanently in Germany; many

will be unqualified and untrained in all but their expectations of
material prosperity which they will share with their German fellow
citizens. Their disillusionment could be disturbing. The federal
and Laender governments should rapidly improve the provisions they are
beginning to introduce by offering language courses and special training schemes with a large element of general education and social
training. If necessary, they should be willing to bear the full cost
of training places and to create some public service jobs open to the
foreign community. Joint counselling in which a foreign adviser works
in collaboration with a German adviser is likely to be more acceptable
to Auslaender children. Liaison with parents, again ideally with
joint counsellors, is of the first importance.

The current necessary focus on training disadvantaged young people
for low level occupations, which is essential for humanitarian and
social reasons, should not divert attention from Germany's economic
need for a supply of manpower with high and rising technical qualifications. Opportunities should be created for young people trained at
lower levels to be trained for and employed in higher level occupations.

Annex I

STATISTICAL TABLES

Table 1

UNEMPLOYMENT BY AGE GROUPS
1973-1979, MAY AND SEPTEMBER

	All Unemployed	Age Group				
		Under 20	20-24	25-34	35-44	45 and over
		Numbers				
1973 Sept.	219,105	20.960	30,041	49,560	36,559	81,985
1974 May	456,603	38,706	66,753	115,066	95,288	140,790
1974 Sept.	556,876	69,793	88,258	140,062	107,154	151,609
1975 May	1,017,903	86,052	167,659	281,439	221,380	261,373
1975 Sept.	1,006,554	115,753	171,620	267,237	198,953	252,991
1976 May	954,150	84,963	159,694	252,934	191,965	264,594
1976 Sept.	898,314	102,649	154,456	229,371	167,350	244,488
1977 May	946,491	87,342	164,077	248,400	187,546	259,126
1977 Sept.	911,257	105,949	161,873	231,840	169,067	242,528
1978 May	913,034	76,980	157,120	239,481	178,868	260,585
1978 Sept.	864,243	92,030	153,931	217,461	156,931	243,890
1979 May	775,548	57,537	127,004	199,431	144,351	247,225
1979 Sept.	736,690	68,593	123,709	180,758	129,144	234,486
		Proportion of All Unemployed				
1973 Sept.	100	9.6	13.7	22.6	16.7	27.4
1974 May	100	8.5	14.6	25.2	20.9	30.8
1974 Sept.	100	12.5	15.9	25.2	19.2	27.2
1975 May	100	8.5	16.4	27.6	21.7	25.7
1975 Sept.	100	11.5	17.1	26.5	19.8	25.1
1976 May	100	8.9	16.7	26.5	20.1	27.7
1976 Sept.	100	11.4	17.2	25.5	18.6	27.2
1977 May	100	9.2	17.3	26.2	19.8	27.4
1977 Sept.	100	11.6	17.8	25.4	18.6	26.6
1978 May	100	8.4	17.2	26.2	19.6	28.5
1978 Sept.	100	10.6	17.8	25.2	18.2	28.2
1979 May	100	7.4	16.4	25.7	18.6	31.9
1979 Sept.	100	9.3	16.8	24.5	17.5	31.8
		Unemployment Rate				
1973 Sept.	1.0	1.1	2.5	0.9	0.7	1.2
1974 May	2.0	2.0	2.5	2.1	1.7	2.1
1974 Sept.	2.4	3.6	3.3	2.5	2.0	2.3
1975 May	4.4	4.6	6.4	5.0	3.9	3.8
1975 Sept.	4.4	6.2	6.5	4.8	3.5	3.7
1976 May	4.2	3.8	6.2	4.6	3.4	4.0
1976 Sept.	3.9	4.6	6.0	4.2	2.9	3.7
1977 May	4.2	4.1	6.3	4.7	3.2	3.9
1977 Sept.	4.0	5.0	6.2	4.3	2.9	3.7
1978 May	4.0	3.6	5.9	4.5	3.0	3.9
1978 Sept.	3.8	4.4	5.8	4.1	2.6	3.7
1979 May	3.4	2.6	4.6	3.8	2.4	3.7
1979 Sept.	3.2	3.1	4.5	3.4	2.1	3.6

Source: Amtliche Nachrichten der Bundesanstalt für Arbeit.

Table 2

UNEMPLOYED YOUNG PEOPLE,(1) MAJOR CHARACTERISTICS

	September 1974	September 1975	September 1976	September 1977	September 1978	September 1979
Number of cases (= 100%)	69,800	115,800	102,600	105,900	92,000	68,593
a) Foreigners	10.8	9.1	6.8	7.7	8.8	10.4
b) Men	46.1	48.5	40.3	39.3	37.8	38.5
Women	53.9	51.5	59.7	60.7	62.2	66.5
c) Age						
15 years	10.1	5.7	4.5	3.4	2.7	2.2
16 years	15.9	13.6	13.7	10.9	9.4	8.7
17 years	22.2	19.9	21.7	20.1	17.9	17.7
18 years	24.8	27.3	28.2	31.5	32.8	32.3
19 years	27.1	33.5	32.0	34.1	37.1	39.0
d) Level of education and training						
1. Without complete vocational training/ed.	69.8	67.4(2)	62.6(2)	67.6	71.0	72.5
2. Of which without basic science diploma	32.2		26.3	27.9	28.1	
3. With basic school diploma	28.4		27.1	26.4	28.0	
4. With higher diploma	3.2		7.4(2)	11.6	13.1	
Semi-skilled	3.2					
With complete training in enterprise	25.9	30.5	34.2	28.9	25.3	
With complete vocational education in school	1.3	2.1	3.2	3.6	3.7	
e) Professional activity						
Without	23.6	18.9	22.4	29.4	29.5	29.5
With	76.4	81.1	77.6	70.6	70.5	70.5
f) Participation in vocational courses (BA)	0.9	2.2	2.9	2.8	1.6	
Of which: Basic training courses(3)	0.1	0.9	1.4	1.2		
Supporting courses(4)	0.4	0.8	0.8	1.0		
Insertion courses(5)	0.4	0.7	0.7	0.6		
g) Desire for training/ed. of unemployed youth without complete voc. training/education						
Yes	14.3	8.5	12.0	15.0	20.3	
No	85.2	10.5	88.0	85.0	29.7	
h) Health problems	8.2	7.1	8.4	9.5	10.6	12.8
i) Duration of unemployment						
Less than 1 month	38.2	26.8	30.8	27.9	28.2	31.8
1 to less than 3 months	41.2	36.4	40.1	41.0	41.4	40.9
3 to less than 6 months	12.5	19.1	14.3	15.3	14.9	14.2
6 to less than 12 months	7.4	14.6	10.7	11.7	10.9	9.3
12 months and more	0.7	3.1	4.0	4.0	4.7	3.8

1) Aged less than 20; 2) Including semi-skilled; 3) Grundausbildungslehrgang; 4) Förderungslehrgang; 5) Eingliederungslehrgang.
Source: "Jugendliche beim Uebergang in Ausbildung und Beruf" Beiträge aus der Arbeitsmarkt und Berufsforschung, Bd. 43, p. 36.

Table 3

REGIONAL DISTRIBUTION OF UNEMPLOYED YOUNG PEOPLE

(September 1979)

Laender Districts	Number of unemployed		Per cent of total unemployed		Rate of unemployment(1)		
	Under 20 years	20-25 %	Under 20 years %	20-25 %	Under 20 years %	20-25 %	All age groups %
Schleswig-Holstein-Hamburg	4,851	13,405	9.3	25.8	5.7	6.8	3.9
Niedersachsen-Bremen	11,367	30,672	10.1	27.3	5.8	7.0	4.6
Nordrhein-Westfalen	20,352	63,902	8.1	25.3	4.5	7.3	4.6
Hessen	4,604	12,672	9.2	25.3	4.1	4.9	3.1
Rheinland-Pfalz-Saarland	8,279	20,166	13.4	32.5	5.9	6.5	4.4
Baden-Württemberg	6,599	17,669	9.9	26.6	2.8	3.2	2.2
Nordbayern	5,959	15,728	10.3	27.1	4.1	6.1	3.9
Südbayern	4,723	13,356	8.4	23.7	2.8	4.1	2.9
Berlin (West)	1,859	4,732	6.9	17.6	7.8	4.7	3.9
FRG	68,593	192,302	9.3	26.1	4.4	5.8	3.8

1) Denominator refers to dependent active persons (excluding armed forces) of the previous year.

Source: BA, Strukturanalyse September 1978 (ANBA 3/1979).

Table 4

SCHOOL LEAVERS BY TYPE OF SCHOOL 1970/71 TO 1984/85

Year	After obligatory enrolment		With Diploma from Secondary Middle School & Equivalent	With Entrance Diploma for Higher Education	Total
	Without Basic(2) School Diploma	With Basic School Diploma			
1970-71	139,394	350,856	153,560	86,264	730,064
1971-72	144,241	364,939	162,549	93,514	765,243
1972-73	141,725	369,109	186,914	101,417	799,165
1973-74	135,099	371,572	210,592	114,171	831,334
1974-75	114,576	347,060	234,030	118,125	813,791
1975-76	114,884	351,647	225,146	135,769	827,446
1976-77	123,900	403,257	248,652	149,035	924,844
1977-78(1)	130,540	414,720	287,670	160,920	993,850
1978-79(1)	128,620	414,650	309,370	132,080	984,720
1979-80(1)	125,460	400,650	323,960	160,200	1,020,270
1980-81(1)	119,360	365,310	327,240	192,360	1,004,270
1981-82(1)	119,020	379,190	329,980	205,980	1,033,390
1982-83(1)	113,100	368,080	329,840	207,610	1,018,630
1983-84(1)	106,210	348,970	321,890	206,540	983,610
1984-85(1)	97,840	317,950	305,420	202,300	923,510

1) Previsions;   2) Including Special Schools.

Source: Statistische Veröffentlichungen der Kultusministerkonferenz, H.55 (1977), H.56 (1978), H.60 (1978).

Table 5

POPULATION AGED 15-17 BY TYPE OF LABOUR FORCE ACTIVITY

	Resident population aged 15-17 000s	Apprentices in the Dual System		Employed(1) "Young Workers"		Unemployed or outside the labour force	
		000s	%	000s	%	000s	%
1962	1947	1315.3	67.6	277.2	14.2	21.6	1.1
1965	2368	1450.2	61.2	311.7	13.2	18.2(2)	0.8
1970	2412	1360.4	56.4	215.0	8.9	17.8(2)	0.7
1976	2915	1354.4	46.5	163.8	5.6	68.8(3)	2.4

1) Including young persons helping parents; in Germany "young workers" are a special category in the labour force statistics separate from apprentices.
2) Between 1965 and 1970 the peak unemployment level was 28.4 thousand in 1967.
3) Unemployed was 52.9 and 70.0 thousand in 1974 and 1975 respectively.

Source: Jugendliche ohne Ausbildungsverträge, MAGS Nordrhein-Westfalen, in Arbeit & Beruf, No.24, p. 25.

Table 6

ATTENDANCE AT VOCATIONAL SCHOOLS

Year	Total	Without training contract	With training contract	Per cent of non-qualified youth %
1950 (1)	1,563,260	533,002	1,010,258	35.4
1951 (2)	1,877,891	655,847	1,222,044	34.9
1952 (2)	2,053,775	743,229	1,310,546	36.4
1953 (2)	2,126,979	757,947	1,369,032	35.6
1954 (2)	2,244,293	751,522	1,492,771	33.5
1955 (2)	2,301,873	736,466	1,565,407	32.0
1956 (2)	2,269,275	642,528	1,626,745	28.3
1957	2,131,100	550,138	1,580,962	25.8
1958	2,009,017	452,248	1,556,769	22.5
1959	1,830,187	380,273	1,449,914	20.8
1960	1,661,911	321,045	1,340,866	19.3
1961	1,135,695	222,970	912,725	19.6
1962	1,614,035	298,754	1,315,281	18.5
1963 (3)	1,699,002	321,973	1,377,029	18.9
1964	1,741,889	324,328	1,417,561	18.6
1965	1,780,044	329,876	1,450,168	18.5
1966	1,747,444	309,365	1,438,079	17.7
1967	1,780,205	291,188	1,489,017	16.4
1968	1,754,765	269,963	1,484,802	15.4
1969	1,631,920	244,483	1,387,437	15.0
1970	1,593,207	232,815	1,360,392	14.6
1971	1,570,270	221,395	1,348,844	14.1
1972	1,611,654	226,561	1,385,093	14.1
1973	1,623,432	226,883	1,396,549	14.0
1974	1,621,856	243,374	1,378,482	15.0
1975	1,610,557	243,731	1,366,826	15.1
1976	1,586,801	236,687	1,350,114	14.9

1) Excluding Hessen and Saarland.   2) Excluding Saarland.
3) Excluding Nordrhein-Westfalen.

Source: K. Schweikert, Fehlstart ins Berufsleben, Schriften zur
        Bildungsforschung No. 55, BIBB, p. 6.

Table 7

SCHOOL LEAVERS INTENDING TO START AN APPRENTICESHIP IN THE DUAL SYSTEM(1)(2)

(as % of students in the various classes)

| Year | General Education Schools | | | | | | | Vocational Education Schools |
| | Basic School | | Middle School Class 9/10 | Gymnasium Class 9/12 | Special School | Comprehensive School Class 7/12 | Total | |
	Class 7/8	Class 9/10						
1977	59.7	66.1	67.7	52.3	38.9	60.5	63.5	71.4
1978	62.5	66.5	67.8	49.0	47.1	65.0	64.4	72.1

1) Survey of the KMK (Kultusministerkonferenz).
2) School leavers with a diploma for universities or special higher education institutions are not included in this survey. The annual survey of the Federal Statistical Office shows however that the part of "Abiturienten" who do not want to go on to level III institutions grew from 4.1 per cent in 1972 to 12.3 in 1978, whereas those who were hesitating increased from 6.2 per cent to 18.4 per cent. About 8 per cent of the 1976 Abiturienten concluded training contracts in the same year and an additional 6 per cent of them concluded such a contract in 1977 (i.e. 12 per cent of the 1976 Abiturienten were in dual training in December 1977).

Source: Berufsbildungsbericht, (BBB) 1979, p. 20.

Table 8

TRANSFERS TO DIFFERENT SCHOOLS OR TRAINING PROGRAMMES

(percentage)

Graduate of	Academic or professional career	Vocational full-time schools	Training in firms	Other federal defence	Other miscellaneous	Total
Basic schools or special schools	0.0	10.8	64.3	1.6	23.3	100.0
Modern secondary schools - intermediate degree	0.0	23.5	66.7	1.9	8.0	100.0
Gymnasium or other institutions - matriculation examination	89.2	2.5	5.8	2.5	0.0	100.0

Source: Kühlewind, Mertens and Tessaring, 1975.

Table 9

NEWLY-ESTABLISHED TRAINING CONTRACTS BY LAENDER

	Newly-established contracts 1978	Training places offered as per cent of places demanded		Changes from 1977 to 1978 in %	unoccupied registered training places 30.9.78 (in %)
		1977	1978		
FRG	602,063	99.7	99.3	-0.4	5.8*
Schleswig-Holstein + (Hamburg)	42,592	99.7	98.9	-0.8	4.7(3.7)
Niedersachsen + (Bremen)	80,768	100.3	99.7	-0.6	7.4(1.6)
Nordrhein-Westfalen	161,956	102.0	99.4	-2.6	4.0
Hessen	51,087	99.8	99.3	-0.5	5.0
Rheinland-Pfalz + (Saarland)	49,838	96.6	95.4	-1.2	5.3(3.1)
Baden-Württemberg	89,719	100.3	101.6	+1.2	6.4
Bayern	112,255	99.5	99.8	+2.4	9.0
West Berlin	13,848	97.9	95.3	-2.6	3.0

* The number of registered unoccupied training places decreased by 12.5 per cent between 30.9.1977 and 30.9.1978.

Source: BBB.79 Table 8, p. 76, Table 6, p. 73 and Table 9, p. 22.

Table 10

OFFER AND DEMAND FOR TRAINING PLACES(1)

Year	Places offered(2)	Places demanded(2)	Offer compared to demand	
			abs.	%
1972	637,990	466,000	+171,990	+36.9
1973	551,169	465,341	+ 85,828	+18.4
1974	478,992	470,312	+ 8,680	+ 1.8
1975	480,198	485,559	- 5,361	- 1.1
1976	516,874	526,512	- 9,638	- 1.9
1977	584,327	585,909	- 1,582	- 0.3
1978	624,346	628,445(3)	- 4,099	- 0.7

1) According to paragraph 5 of the Training Places Promotion Act.
2) About 61 per cent of the total places offered and approximately 74 per cent of the total places demanded are estimated to be registered in 1978.
3) Excluding unsuccessful demanders who have indicated their desire for dual training in the KMF Survey but have then renounced this desire for a variety of reasons including resignation. "Young workers" who left school in earlier years and who now wish to start dual training are also excluded.

Source: Beiträge 43, p. 79.

163

Table 11

APPRENTICES ACCORDING TO SECTOR OF ACTIVITY, 1970-77

Year	Total		Industry and Commerce		Crafts		Agriculture		Public Service(1)		Domestic Service		Liberal Professions, Merchant Navy	
	abs.	%	abs.	%	abs.	%	abs.	%	abs.	%	abs.	%	abs.	%
1970	1,270.120	100.0	724,898	57.1	420,936	33.1	38,133	3.0	20,172	1.6	7,191	0.6	58,790	4.6
1971	1,273,078	100.0	729,636	57.3	406,629	31.9	28,929	2.3	23,081	1.8	6,804	0.5	76,999	6.0
1972	1,302,751	100.0	722,173	55.4	434,130	33.3	27,786	2.1	30,557	2.3	6,436	0.5	81,669	6.3
1973	1,330,801	100.0	694,068	52.2	464,996	34.9	25,651	1.9	49,659	3.7	6,438	0.5	89,989	6.8
1974	1,330,768	100.0	664,554	49.9	486,531	36.6	27,404	2.1	47,189	3.5	7,110	0.5	97,980	7.4
1975	1,320,906	100.0	633,958	47.7	504,662	38.0	32,954	2.5	45,953	3.5	7,319	0.6	104,061	7.8
1976	1,316,562	100.0	611,173	46.4	510,356	38.8	37,361	2.8	43,850	3.3	6,797	0.5	107,025	8.1
1977	1,397,429	100.0	643,817	46.1	556,088	39.8	41,003	2.9	44,841	3.2	7,215	0.5	104,465	7.5

1) Without those apprentices whose training professions according to the Vocational Training Act are registered with other authorities (Chambers).

Source: Stat. Bundesamt (Hrsg.), Fachserie 11, Reihe 3, Berufliche Bildung 1977, S.10.

Table 12

STUDENTS IN THE FIRST YEAR OF VOCATIONAL SCHOOLS 1975-1982 (1)

Year	All students	(2)	Basic vocational educ.year (BGJ)			Special forms of the BGJ	(3)	(4)
			Total	full-time	co-operative form (1)			
1975	100.0	58.7	3.3	3.1	0.2	1.1	12.7	24.2
1976	100.0	60.6	4.0	3.6	0.4	2.7	8.1	24.6
1977	100.0	58.6	5.7	5.2	0.5	4.9	6.2	24.6
1978	100.0	56.0	8.7	8.2	0.5	4.6	6.7	24.0
1979	100.0	55.7	9.6	9.0	0.6	4.8	6.7	23.3
1980	100.0	55.3	10.5	9.9	0.6	5.0	6.4	22.8
1981	100.0	54.9	11.6	11.0	0.6	5.3	6.1	22.1
1982	100.0	54.3	12.9	12.2	0.7	5.6	5.7	21.5

1) From 1977 projections are according to the programme of the BLK (i.e. target figures).
2) Apprentices in the traditional dual system.
3) Young workers and other students without training contract.
4) Students in full-time vocational schools (Berufsfachschule).

Source: BLK-Programme, 5.12.77, p. 80.

Table 13

TRAINING PLACES NEEDED IN ENTERPRISES (1)

(in thousands)

Year	First year of training(3)	Second year of training	Third year of training	Fourth year of training	Total
1975	411.9(2)	451.0	371.8	95.0	1,329.7
1976	423.0	459.6	360.3	73.8	1,316.7
1977(4)	444.0	474.3	367.7	72.2	1,358.2
1978	452.8	507.3	379.4	73.5	1,413.0
1979	459.6	546.9	405.8	75.9	1,488.2
1980	459.6	562.2	437.5	81.2	1,540.5
1981	450.0	569.7	449.8	87.5	1,557.0
1982	436.2	566.9	455.8	90.1	1,549.0

1) Excluding applicants from the previous year who re-apply.
2) According to BMBW.
3) Including the co-operative Berufsgrundbildungsjahr.
4) From 1977 projections according to the BLK-Programme.

Source: BLK - Programme 5.12.1977, p. 84.

Annex II

THE LEGAL AND INSTITUTIONAL FRAMEWORK

The legal framework for policy measures against youth unemployment in Germany is determined by three major laws:

  i) The Employment Promotion Act of 25 June 1969, and
     its fifth amendment of 1 August 1979
     (Arbeitsförderungsgesetz, AFG);
 ii) The Vocational Training Act of 14 August 1969
     (Berufsbildungsgesetz);
iii) The Training Places Promotion Act of 7 September 1976
     (Ausbildungsplatzförderungsgesetz).

The Employment Promotion Act, 1969

The Act represents the basic instrument for the federal government's labour market policy. According to this law and in the framework of the federal government's social and economic policy, the Federal Labour Office (1) is in charge of the following tasks:

  - vocational counselling;
  - placement;
  - encouraging retraining;
  - facilitating and promoting insertion into work;
  - vocational and work promotion or "rehabilitation" of
    the handicapped;
  - subsidies to enterprises for the preservation and the
    creation of work places;
  - income subsidies to individual workers.

Vocational counselling is proposed to young people and adults who have questions concerning their professional choice, the change of profession and vocational training and education.

Insertion into work is facilitated by financial aid to workers, especially in order to increase their geographical mobility. Financial aid to employers is to increase the chances of the hard to place.

---

1) Note that the Federal Labour Office is a tripartite institution, administered by employers, unions and government representatives.

The promotion of retraining is particularly important for the employment of young people. It includes financial aid for those who cannot afford to participate in training and/or education otherwise.

Initial vocational education and training. Young people and adults can get aid for training in enterprises or in inter-enterprise workshops and for the participation in different courses and measures for vocational preparation proposed by the Federal Labour Office. This aid may take the form of subsidy or of loans. The applicant must be "suited to the envisaged profession", and his training must be "useful with respect to the situation on and the evolution of the labour market". The amount of financial aid depends on the income of parents or the spouse if this income is higher than a certain "free amount" and in any case on the eventual income of the applicant himself.

Further training and retraining for a different occupation. Financial aid can be given in order to maintain or enlarge professional capacities, or to adapt them to technological development or to make professional advancement possible. The applicant must either have completed vocational training plus three years of professional work, or he must have worked for at least six years. The applicant must have paid unemployment insurance contributions for at least two years during the previous three years.

There may be exceptions to these rules for applicants who have not paid employment insurance if they consent to work for at least three of the following four years in a job submitted to unemployment insurance contributions. However, these applicants must be registered as unemployed, or be threatened by unemployment, or have no complete vocational qualification, or want to learn a profession in a field where there is a lack of qualified labour and be obliged to work for material reasons.(1)

No one can get financial aid for enrolment in general education schools. Participants in full-time courses (or other "measures") receive 80 per cent of their previous net income if they are unemployed, threatened by unemployment, have no complete vocational qualification or want to take up a profession with a lack of qualified labour. Otherwise financial aid amounts to 58 per cent of the previous or of the "probable" income.(2)

Besides these income subsidies aid can be given for the cost of courses, learning material, travelling, work clothes, insurance and additional living costs caused by necessary geographical displacements.

Besides these aids to individual workers, the Federal Labour Office can provide help to employers who:

---

1) Leitfaden zum Arbeitsförderungsgesetz, August 1979, para. 44.
2) Ibid.

- recruit "hard-to-employ" persons (generally up to
  60 per cent of the normal wage for one year,
  exceptionally up to 80 per cent for two years);
- recruit persons for jobs which necessitate prolonged
  training on the job (up to 80 per cent of the normal
  wage for one year). The training must last longer
  than four weeks and the trainee must have worked before
  for at least six months;
- recruit older persons for economically useful work
  (50 to 80 per cent of the wage as a long-term subsidy);
- create an additional work place which is of public
  interest (at least 60 per cent of the wage - mainly in
  public service).

The Federal Labour Office can also give support to employers who
continue activity in spite of bad seasonal conditions (especially
construction in winter) and pay "short working time money" (Kurz-
arbeitergeld) to workers if an enterprise is forced to lay off workers
on a part-time basis.

The Vocational Training Act, 1969

This Act organises the responsibilities for training in the enterprise on the level of:

- the enterprise;
- professional bodies of self-administration (Chambers of
  Industry and Trade, Chamber of Crafts), which must
  create a Vocational Training Committee composed of
  representatives of employers and unions and (with
  counselling voice only) of vocational school teachers;
- the State, where tripartite State Committees for
  Vocational Training with representatives from employers
  unions and state governments must be created.

On the federal level the Committee for Vocational Training and
the Federal Institute for Research in Vocational Training, which had
been established by the 1969 law were replaced by the Federal Institute for Vocational Training through the Training Places Promotion
Act in 1976.(1)

The Training Places Promotion Act, 1976

According to this law the Vocational Training Levy (Berufs-
bildungsabgabe) is to be paid by enterprises with a gross wage sum

---

1) The content of this Act concerns mainly the quality of training
   in the enterprise. The Federal Minister for Education and Science
   has published an English version of this law.

of more than DM.400,000/year if the annual Vocational Training Report (Berufsbildungsbericht) established by the Federal Institute for Vocational Training states that the overhang of training places offered with respect to demand is less than 12.5 per cent for Germany as a whole.

The law also regulates the collection of statistics on vocational education (Berufsbildungsstatistik).

It finally indicates the structure and the tasks of the Federal Institute for Vocational Training which depends directly on the Federal Minister of Education and Science. Its administrative board (Hauptausschuss) is composed of: representatives of employers, unions and the Laender governments (11 representatives each) plus five representatives of the federal government (who also have 11 votes). There is finally a "Laender-Commission" (Laender-Ausschuss) with representatives from the Laender (11), employers (3), unions (3) and the federal government (3) which is charged with promoting the co-ordination of the vocational school education programme regulations elaborated by the Institute.

Annex III

RESUME OF THE EDDING REPORT ON THE
COSTS AND FINANCING OF TRAINING

The following are the main findings of the Final Report on the
Costs and Financing of Training by a commission of experts under the
Chairmanship of Professor Friedrich Edding, which reported in 1974
to the German Bundestag (Federal Parliament).

Whilst all enterprises have a strong continuing interest in
having a well-trained workforce, only a minority of them (10 per cent
of the larger industrial and trading enterprises and 25 per cent of
small industrial enterprises) are actually providing training.

Training given inside enterprises in line with the generally
recognised objectives of the 1969 Vocational Education Act (Berufs-
bildungsgesetz) usually involves considerable net expenditure (cost
of the training less the returns from it) which under the existing
financing system is a direct burden on the enterprises. These net
costs ranged in 1972 from DM.2,582 for trainees in one of the crafts
to DM.6,692 for trainees in large enterprises. They are probably
totalling at present from about DM.7,000 to about DM.10,000 per
trainee per year, depending on the trade and the size of the firm.

As a result of these costs the competition is distorted to the
disadvantage of firms providing training to the extent that they cannot pass on all or a sizeable part of the training costs, i.e. re-
coup them in the price of their products or services. This would be
acceptable if, after completion of training, the resulting returns
accrued to the firms which provided it, but that is not what happens.
Owing to the fluctuations of employees between enterprises the costs
of training are often met by one enterprise while the benefits from
it accrue to another.

Due to the raising of standards of the quality of training
which is considered desirable and necessary, training costs will increase, which, it is feared, will eventually lead enterprises to
abandon formal training programmes under the dual system.

Training costs and the returns from them vary widely among different occupations. This creates a tendency to train more or fewer
young people than are actually required for a particular occupation,
so that after training some of them have to switch over to other occupations.

Young people living in the less industrialised areas usually find a smaller range of trades open to them than young people living in cities or areas of industrial concentration. The Committee found these regional disparities disquieting inasfar as young people start their training at the age of 15 or 16 when their regional mobility is still very restricted.

The present way of financing training has an impact also on the contents of training. The experts assumed that enterprises have the tendency to train primarily for the specific skills needed in the enterprise concerned while neglecting more general aspects relating to overall problems of the world of work and society as a whole.

Fewer training places were provided during recessions than in boom periods by enterprises offering training in occupations which are attractive on account of their career prospects, or offering special high quality training. In both these cases the demand from young people for training places regularly exceeds the supply, so that the enterprises can decide themselves what numbers of trainees to take. In these cases, the availability of training places follows business cycles. The recruitment of trainees in other enterprises is counter-cyclical. This is true especially for trades which are less attractive to young people and for enterprises which, in the opinion of many young people and their parents, do not provide good quality training.

The quality and the range of training available is not the same for both sexes. The supply of training places for girls covers fewer trades and areas and is concentrated on many less demanding trades, because the expert Commission believed enterprises will only accept long-term net expenditure on training if they can expect such invest-ment to pay off during the further employment of the trainees con-cerned in their service. As the expected term of employment in an enterprise is shorter for girls than for male trainees, it is assumed that these economic considerations lead to inequality of opportunity as between female and male trainees.

After studying the features and effects of the present system of financing training, the Commission of experts concluded that present-day demands for training were on the whole not being met satisfac-torily. Having examined a number of alternative financing methods the Commission advocated a system of collective financing, i.e. the establishment of a corporate or trust fund fed mainly by contributions from firms and enterprises. It was strongly of the opinion that training standards could only be raised and be co-ordinated with general education if responsibility for financing it were transferred to the State or to a corporate fund. However, the Commission pointed out several possible inconveniences and shortcomings of a financing system from several public revenues and favoured, therefore, a central corporate fund to be financed by levies from enterprises on the basis of the wage bill.

Part Four

A REVIEW OF YOUTH EMPLOYMENT POLICIES
IN THE UNITED STATES

THE OECD EXAMINERS

The Rt. Hon. Mrs. Shirley Williams, P.C.
Chairman

    Senior Research Fellow at the Policy Studies Institute
(formerly Secretary of State for Education and Science),
the United Kingdom

Mr. Allan Larsson

    Editor in Chief, "Vi" Magazine (formerly Under Secretary
of State, Ministry of Labour), Sweden

Professor Fritz Scharpf

    Director, International Institute of Management,
Wissenschaftszentrum, Berlin

INTRODUCTION

The turbulent 1970s have brought with them new problems, especially for the young as they enter the world of work. Consequently, in recent years much of the OECD concern in the field of manpower and education has been directed to tackle the human, social and economic problem represented by youth unemployment, believing that it is not only a challenge to our social values and economic institutions - but also to our political will and foresight.

Our report is derived from a number of sources of information: a) The Background Report prepared by the United States Department of Labor and the Vice-Presidential Task Force on Youth Employment; b) some of the many studies commissioned by the Department of Labor and the legislative documents; c) research reports from independent institutes in the United States; d) meetings with federal representatives in the Departments of Labor, Health, Education and Welfare, the Office of Management and Budget and members of the Domestic Policy staff of the White House; e) meetings with a wide range of interested groups including employers and labour unions, academic researchers, pressure groups and community-based organisations; f) meetings with members of the Congress and their staff; g) field visits to a limited number of projects and discussions with representatives at state and local level; h) some limited discussion with young people themselves.

Our team visited the United States for an intensive programme which lasted two weeks in the summer of 1979 and completed our report in March 1980.(1) Although the team visited Washington, Boston, Detroit, Baltimore and New York, interviewed many people and looked at a number of projects, we are only too aware of how much was missed in a country of such diversity. Before setting out to report the outcomes of this review, we feel it important to define our role, given the conditions under which we have conducted our study and the limited time available.

The review has been largely conducted at a policy level, with all the limitations which stem from such an approach. This report does not involve original research or new data collection, although

---

1) Some subsequent statistical revision has been carried out; the cut-off date for information contained in this report was December 1980.

many people with whom we talked were involved in impressive programmes of original research and evaluation. Our review has concentrated on the programmes provided under the Comprehensive Employment and Training Act (CETA), 1973, especially as they relate to youth, and the Youth Employment and Demonstration Projects Act (YEDPA), 1977. Our examination has only briefly looked at the United States education system which is so evidently an important part of the picture and of the problem.

Before proceeding we would remark on our respect for the honesty and frankness with which the problems of youth unemployment were discussed with the team during the visit. Many of the problems find similar parallels in European countries which make exercises such as this particularly important. Our task has been to raise issues, to participate in the development of an overall policy for youth in this area and to offer fresh perspectives from those unconstrained by established political influences or vested interests. Whilst there are many limitations to our report, there are certain advantages in approaching the problems of another country with a fresh approach, looking at them from different perspectives and bringing the insights and experiences from our own countries to bear on the problems. We hope that our comments, our criticism and our praise will be seen in that light by those who read this report.

I

THE ECONOMIC AND SOCIAL SETTING

The United States is a country of immense and creative diversity about which it is dangerous to generalise. While this chapter attempts to state the economic and social setting against which anybody looking at the youth employment programmes has to make a judgement, we recognise that many of these generalisations will be untrue of certain parts of the country, or of particular states, cities or districts. As we travelled from one area to another, we noticed wide variations in the particular approaches different jurisdictions, or prime-sponsors, were taking to the CETA legislation; we suspect there are also wide variations in the standards of these programmes and in the competence with which they are administered. That would be unsurprising in a country as large and as varied as the United States. It has to be borne in mind in any assessment that is made of these, or for that matter of other, decentralised or devolved programmes.

Congress decided at the time of the passage of the major comprehensive education and training legislation in 1973 that it should be administered through a system of prime-sponsors. These prime-sponsors may be individual municipalities, consortia of counties or what are sometimes called "balance of state" areas, particularly in less densely settled rural states. They range from the very large to the very small and from cities with major and sophisticated administrations to counties with a skeletal staff. There are prime-sponsors with substantial political standing in their state and others with much less influence. Throughout everything that is said later in this report about the youth employment programmes and about employment programmes more generally, this variegated and widely differentiated structure needs to be borne in mind.

The CETA prime-sponsor system interacts, in respect of youth employment programmes, with an equally diverse but totally separate school system. It is crucial in assessing the CETA system to look at its relationship with the public school system, because so much of the problem of youth unemployment is concentrated upon the under-qualified and the under-educated, and therefore the answer to that problem must lie within the school system as well as within the employment and manpower programmes. The United States school system

175

is based upon 50 states, but its heart lies in the 16,000 school districts which are normally administered by a superintendent. A school district may be run by an elected school board which is often also an independent taxing authority. But this is not true of all jurisdictions. In some, for example Baltimore, the school board is not elected, it is appointed by the mayor. Generally, there is a separate administrative structure for schools and for the local authority, or, as it is called in the CETA programme, the prime-sponsor. These totally separate administrative structures are not conducive to co-operation; indeed sometimes they are conducive to the very opposite. Bridges are being built between the two systems, and in later parts of this report, ways in which those bridges can be widened and strengthened are discussed.

The American public high school system has been one of the nation's builders. The concept of the common school to which all children in the neighbourhood should go has been a crucial element in the structure of the Federal State and in particular in the gradual acculturation of the many separate ethnic groups that over the generations have come to create the United States. Unlike European school systems the American school system has not been characterised by either selection or division. The central concept has been that all children should be educated together. Nowadays this means that they are at school throughout twelve grades from the age of 6 to the age of 18 or 19 or even later. The American high school system has long been a justified object of pride in the United States and has been believed to be the key to individual progress and self-fulfilment.

In the last decade, however, the American public school system has come under increasing attack. One representative of a prime-sponsor said to us, "the American public school system is still lodged in the last century". We heard a great deal of criticism which, to those of us who have been involved in education in Western European countries, is not wholly unfamiliar and much of which echoed what we had heard in our own countries. Perhaps partly because in the United States high school education often represents little more than the ability of the young man or woman concerned to live through twelve years or more of education, there has been a strong movement in the United States towards competency testing and the careful grading of children's achievements. The growth in private schools and the alternative school movement are both further indications of loss of faith in the traditional public school system.

For the education authorities, there is something of a dilemma. They can either take steps to strengthen the public school system by coercing or pressurising young people to stay in it, or they can undertake a more substantial reform in order to encourage them to do so voluntarily. The CETA legislation bases some of its programmes on

176

the insistence that boys and girls should stay in school and attend
regularly and then, in return, they will be offered work experience
paid at the federal minimum wage for the work they undertake. It
might be characterised as a system of outdoor relief for the schools
but we have some doubts about the wisdom of trying to compel boys and
girls to return to a school out of which they have voluntarily dropped.
Perhaps it should also be said that the public school systems, especially in the inner cities, have not had an easy time where funds
have been in the forefront of the move towards desegregation.

We have noticed that the period of adolescence, or, if one prefers,
the transition from school to a full-time stable job in the adult
economy, is very much longer in the United States than in most of our
own countries. The phrase that has often been used to describe this
extended youth by many of those interviewed, has been "milling around".
It is characteristic of this extended period that there is a mixture
of education and work. This of course has been true for many years of
the American system at rather earlier ages when children are still in
high school. Indeed the American system encourages young people to
take part-time jobs from quite early in their school careers, especially in the long summer vacations. This then widens out to something of a movement to and fro between work and school in the late
teens and early 20s. It is a system which has its attractions without
a doubt, but which, unstructured as it is, may be more difficult for
disadvantaged young people to cope with than for those who have the
advantages of a reasonably good education and some financial support,
if necessary, from their families.

While the great majority of American boys and girls graduate
from high school, some 25 per cent drop out of high school without
graduating, a figure that rises to as much as 50 per cent in some of
the inner cities. Incidentally, the national dropout figure has
shown little variation for over a decade; in 1964, 76.3 per cent
graduated, much the same as in 1976-77. There are many opportunities
to return to school or college. The system of community colleges
largely devoted to the education and training of adults is an open-
ended system which allows people to continue their education at any
stage in their lives. Nevertheless, we suspect that among high
school dropouts many never return to education and are also lost to
the formal economic process, as they move outside society as a result
of having missed the crucial qualification of high school graduation
or its equivalent outside the schools, the general education diploma.
Indeed, we were told more than once that as many as 700,000 minority
youth (1) had virtually "disappeared" from the system, being registered

1) Vice-Presidential Task Force on Youth Employment, "Background
   Report on U.S. Youth Programs prepared for the OECD Review Team",
   (mimeo, U.S. Department of Labor, Washington, D.C., 17 July
   1979). The Bureau of Labor Statistics collects data on the age,
   sex and race of persons of working age who are out of the labour
   force, i.e. neither employed nor unemployed.

neither as employed nor unemployed. It is open to speculation how
they live; on the proceeds of crime, within the unofficial economy
of spare time work and odd jobs, or on whatever other members of the
family can scrape together?

In the ten years up to 1979 the United States population grew by
17.4 million, an increase of 8.5 per cent over the 1969 figure. The
number of young people between the ages of 16 and 24 has grown much
more rapidly, by 6.4 million, i.e. 20.6 per cent. The population
under 25 years of age in 1979 was almost 42 per cent of the total
population, but declining. The number of young people between the
ages of 16 and 19 increased to 16.8 million in 1979 and is now falling,
but the number of young people between the ages of 20 and 24 will continue to increase up to the end of 1981 and is projected to decline
in subsequent years. The youth population (16-24) will now decline
quite rapidly to an estimated figure of 34.8 million by 1985.(1)   In
addition to the population figures we have outlined here there are
estimated to be between 4-12 million illegal immigrants, most of them
from Mexico, and the flow continues. Therefore, the projection of
population we have given above for 1985 would need to be increased by
a figure nobody can precisely calculate. We have been unable to get
a more exact figure for this illegal immigration. Over the past ten
years there has been some decline in the participation of young people
in the labour market for social reasons, although this has not been
particularly statistically significant. However, among young married
women there has been a considerable increase in labour market participation in the past decade.

Fortunately, the United States has been remarkably successful in
creating jobs. It is estimated that between 1975 and 1979 no less
than 12 million new jobs were created outside of the agricultural
sector,(2) well above the 8 or 9 million that were expected to be the
maximum that could be attained. However, 90 per cent of these new
jobs were in the tertiary sector, both in private and public employment. Over the four years since 1975 employment in manufacturing industries has declined, as it has done in the primary sectors of agriculture and mining. The creation of new jobs has been more substantial in the so-called "Sunbelt" than in the "Frostbelt"; that is to
say, in the south and south-west of the United States, rather than
in the older industrial areas of the north-east and the middle west.
It is above all in the older cities - and among racial minorities in
the cities - that youth unemployment is concentrated. Indeed the
lack of jobs for inner city young people lies at the heart of the
United States unemployment problem. Union membership is much higher

1) U.S. Bureau of Census, Current Population Reports, Population
   Estimates and Projections, Series P-25. Nos. 704 and 708.
2) U.S. Department of Labor, Employment and Earnings, November 1980.

in the traditional industrial areas of the north-east and the industrial middle west, and it is therefore not surprising that there has
been a gradual slow fall in the national level of union organisation.
Union membership is estimated to be not more than 25 per cent of the
employed workers of the United States, and we suspect that this may
well be a rather high estimate. What is certain is that union organisation is extremely patchy, being very nearly 100 per cent in some
occupations in eastern and middle-west cities but hardly existing in
substantial parts of the south and south-west.

The figures given above tell a paradoxical story: in the United
States both employment and unemployment have risen over the past five
years. Despite that fact, the United States has been more successful
than most European countries in the proportionate rise of employment
over the last four years. This is not entirely due to the various
public service and other employment programmes that have been operated,
but owes a good deal to the vigorous expansion of the United States
economy. Indeed, given the United States system of registering unemployment, which is based on the number of people looking for a job
as distinct from the number registered for unemployment benefit, as in
the United Kingdom, it might be argued that the level of American unemployment (which at the time of our examination in 1979 was 5.7 per
cent) is not disturbingly high. This argument is stronger if one
measures it against the concept of many American economists, including
the Council of Economic Advisers, that a figure of 5.5 per cent constitutes the lower level of unemployment at which the economy can be run
without engendering dangerous inflationary pressures.[1] It is argued
that in the case of the United States the level of unemployment at
which an economy can be run safely is bound to be higher than it is
for many western European industrial countries. The United States is
a much more mobile society in which both geographical and occupational
mobility is more marked and consequently there is bound to be a rather
high figure for frictional unemployment. A group of United States
economists with whom we discussed the matter argued that a 2 per cent
unemployment rate can be attributed to frictional unemployment, twice
as high as the estimation usually given in Europe. Indeed the rate of
job change is substantially higher in the United States than in
Western Europe. The average duration of unemployment among adults is
shorter. We are, however, a little dubious about the argument that
the economy could not run safely with a level of unemployment lower
than 5.5 per cent, although we recognise that there are features of
American society that might make this benchmark figure rather higher
than would be characteristic of our own economies. But, it is as much

1) Sometimes referred to as the "Non-Accelerating Inflation Rate of
   Unemployment": Economic Report of the President, January 1979.

the pattern of unemployment as its level that disturbs us. This is
described in detail in Chapter II.

The additional employment arising from the 12 million jobs
created between 1975 and 1979 was not correspondingly reflected in a
fall in unemployment. This was not only because of the population
increase, but also because some of these new jobs were filled by those
who were previously outside the labour market and not therefore
registered as seeking employment. The truth of the matter is that
there has been a dramatic rise in the employment of married women and
of women family heads in the United States over recent years, many of
whom were not previously in the labour market. Partly as a result of
changing social expectations, the pressures of inflation and the anti-
discrimination legislation in favour of women, there has been a marked
rise in labour market participation rates for all ages of American
women. Amongst women over 20, labour market participation is now
estimated at over 50 per cent in the United States, second only to
Sweden among OECD countries. Between 1978 and 1979, there was an addition of 2.5 million to the number of people employed in the United
States, yet the numbers unemployed declined by only 100,000. The
balance of 2.4 million is believed to be largely accounted for by
married women returning to the labour force whose participation rate
has been increasing by 1.5 per cent or more each year. Indeed, it
has been argued to us by some that minority groups may have suffered
in terms of employment opportunities because of the recent move to
economic equality on the part of women.

At the time of our visit there were many indications of a recession on the way. While the unemployment rate was not rising,
there was reason to believe that employers were hoarding labour as
the decline in productivity indicated; we therefore expected there
to be a tendency for employers to lay off existing employees as the
economy moves further into recession. Already in some of the more
exposed and vulnerable areas of the country, unemployment was disturbingly high. In addition to that, there had been a substantial
cut in the budget for public service jobs funded under the Public
Service Employment (PSE) programmes at a time when states and cities
are under great pressure to reduce expenditure and to cut back their
budgets. They were unlikely to be able to compensate for the decline
in the federal funding of this programme. Consequently, to the recession in the private sector we expected austerity in the public
sector to be added, and this seemed likely to adversely affect the
level of employment.

It would be impossible to end a chapter concerned with setting
the scene against which employment programmes should be considered
without making some reference to the very complicated institutional
structures of the United States. Legislation in the employment field,

as in all other fields where the federal government is involved, is
drawn up in intricate dialogue between the Administration and Congress;
between the federal government and the states; and between the states
and the municipalities or local jurisdictions. At each level there
are inevitably political pressures and political considerations.
Thus, Congress frequently amends or adds to the Administration's
proposals or it may refuse or reduce appropriations for existing programmes. The recent fragmentation of the old party structures and the
reform of the seniority system in Congressional committees, whatever
their other merits, have made this process even more hazardous, uncertain and untidy. To get legislation enacted, an administration has
to make it attractive to a majority of individual representatives
from states and districts with very different economic structures and
very different problems. An administration may have to agree to
amendments and additions which may complicate the legislation or even
be largely irrelevant to it. Further, Congress is more likely than
it once was to make frequent changes, to start or stop programmes or
only to appropriate finance for short periods. A senior Senatorial
aide said to us: "It is impossible to prevent the legislature from
legislating", and we can but agree.

It is not possible in a democracy, nor would it be right, to try
to remove all political considerations from the administration of programmes which spend large sums of money. As long as there are poli-
tics in the system there will be diversity, but sometimes there will
be bias and the improper use of influence. We note that in the attempt
to deal with this situation there tends to be a proliferation of precise goals set by Congress, efforts to assess exactly how programmes
are working and a very large number of federal regulations. We have
to say that sometimes this can be self-defeating. It can become part
of a system of goal-setting based upon numbers which necessarily gives
little weight to either the quality or the depth of the programmes
it measures. We hope that those concerned will bear in mind that
regulations based upon the counting of so-called successful placements,
or successful terminations, put a premium on trying to reach these
goals, rather than trying to build up effective and lasting programmes.
We would hope that, in future, consideration can be given to a rather
different balance between quality and quantity.

Finally, there is the institutional aspect that concerns the relationship between federal programmes generally and the individual
citizen. We recognise that for the reasons set out above, federal
programmes may be excessively complicated and hard to understand.
The amount of change to which they are subject means that even those
who understand the programmes at any one time will rapidly find that
their knowledge is out of date. This means that only the most sophisticated local managers of programmes really understand the system that

181

they are trying to work and that the individual citizen, especially
if she or he is disadvantaged, has virtually no chance at all of doing
so. Therefore the question of communication channels between those
who run the programmes and are responsible for them on the one side,
and those who are supposed to benefit from them on the other becomes
crucial. It is to this complex aspect of modern administration that
we devote some attention in a later chapter.

II

THE PROBLEMS OF YOUTH IN THE LABOUR MARKET

A report such as ours cannot be expected to provide a definite analysis of the youth unemployment problem. Indeed, the review team members were struck by the extent of disagreement between the academic economists with whom they met. Whilst the team suffered from no lack of statistics, they were constantly made aware of the inherent limitations of the statistics and the dangers of drawing too rigid interpretations from them. Our report is of course a report in time; the understanding we offer of the youth employment problem reflects this in the statistics which have been quoted.

Given that our review has been conducted at a policy level, we have felt it necessary to describe what the problems are, as well as to give some indication of the historical context in which the problems have developed. We would stress that this is not a definitive picture: it is heavily influenced by our perceptions of problems which we have formed in discussion with American experts and those working most closely in the field, rather than from original research.

Given the generally unfavourable macro-economic environment of the past two years, it is not surprising that for the OECD as a whole (excluding Turkey) the youth unemployment rate increased to 11.3 per cent in 1979 compared to 10.4 per cent in 1976. The United States represented one of the few exceptions to this trend: youth unemployment fell from a yearly average of 14.0 per cent in 1976 to 11.2 per cent in 1979. However, at the time of our visit there were some indications from recent youth unemployment figures which suggested that this favourable trend may have been reversing. Further, our discussions with American economists revealed an almost universal expectation of economic recession some time in 1980, with the probability of its bringing increased employment problems for the young. Our fears were borne out in that the youth unemployment rate averaged 13.3 per cent over the first eleven months of 1980.

The United States has performed exceptionally well with regard to general unemployment between 1975 and 1979. The review team were therefore especially interested in movements in the ratio of youth to adult unemployment rates rather than movements in the overall level of youth unemployment. Whilst in some OECD countries the ratio had declined, it is noteworthy that this was not the case in the United States where the decline in the adult rate of unemployment had been

Table 1

MILLIONS   THE YOUTH POPULATION, AGES 14-24 BY RACE, 1950-2000

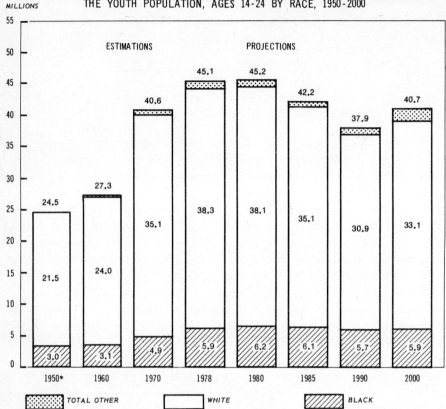

ESTIMATIONS   PROJECTIONS

* In 1950, the number of black youth includes other nonwhite races.

Source : «Background report on US Youth Programs» *op.cit.*

more rapid than in the youth rate (the ratio of youth to adult employment rates has increased in the United States from 2.6 in 1976 to 2.9
in 1979).(1) Despite this, employment opportunities for young workers
are highly sensitive to the state of the labour market, i.e. generally
improving disproportionately in times of rising employment and deteriorating more rapidly than for adults in times of increasing unemployment.

As has been pointed out in Chapter I, the youth population falls
after 1980. However, the decline in the youth population over the
next decade will occur primarily among white youth. The decline in
the birth rate in the late 1960s and early 1970s for the black population was considerably slower and less dramatic than for the white
population. The black youth population is expected to remain broadly

1) OECD, Youth Unemployment: The Causes and Consequences, Paris,
   1980. However, as the recession got under way in 1980, the youth-
   adult unemployment ratio has declined somewhat to 2.7 (average of
   eleven months).

Table 2

TOTAL POPULATION OF PERSONS 14-24 YEARS OF AGE BY RACE AND SEX: 1950-1978

(numbers in thousands)

Ages 14-24	1950	1960		1970		1978	
	Number	Number	Per cent change over preceding period	Number	Per cent change over preceding period	Number	Per cent change over preceding period
Population	24,519	27,347	11.5	40,597	48.5	45,055	11.0
Male	12,277	13,776	12.2	20,538	49.1	22,798	11.0
Female	12,242	13,570	10.8	20,059	47.8	22,257	11.0
White	21,556	24,008	11.4	35,129	46.3	38,359	9.2
Male	10,851	12,143	11.9	17,841	46.9	19,485	9.2
Female	10,706	11,865	10.8	17,288	45.7	18,873	9.2
Black	2,964	3,072	3.6	4,914	60.0	5,893	19.9
Male	1,428	1,496	4.8	2,419	61.7	2,909	20.3
Female	1,536	1,576	2.6	2,495	58.3	2,986	19.7

Source: U.S. Bureau of Census, Current Population Reports, Series P25, Numbers 311, 519, 721, 800.

Table 3

TOTAL POPULATION OF PERSONS 14-24 YEARS OF AGE BY RACE AND SEX: PROJECTIONS 1980-2000

(numbers in thousands)

Ages 14-24	1980 projection		1985 projection		1990 projection		2000 projection	
	Number	Per cent change over preceding period	Number	Per cent change over preceding period	Number	Per cent change over preceding period	Number	Per cent change over preceding period
Population	45,225	11.4	42,245	-6.6	37,920	-10.2	40,698	7.3
Male	22,873	11.4	21,374	-6.6	19,212	-10.1	20,693	7.7
Female	22,352	11.4	20,871	-6.6	18,708	-10.4	20,005	6.9
White	38,086	8.4	35,078	-7.9	30,912	-11.9	33,106	7.1
Male	19,333	8.4	17,811	-7.9	15,712	-11.8	16,871	7.4
Female	18,754	8.5	17,267	-7.9	15,200	-12.0	16,234	6.8
Black	6,191	26.0	6,063	-2.1	5,720	-5.7	5,881	2.8
Male	3,062	26.6	3,005	-1.9	2,846	-5.3	2,947	3.5
Female	3,129	25.4	3,059	-2.2	2,975	-6.0	2,934	2.1

Source: U.S. Bureau of Census, Current Population Reports, Series P25, Numbers 311, 519, 721, 800.

stable until 1985 and will then decline from 1985 to 1990 but at a
rate much slower than for white youth. The number and proportion of
other non-white youth is expected to increase during the next two
decades. Tables 1, 2 and 3 set out the figures in greater detail for
the 14-24 age range by sex and race.

Demographic swings in the United States have been severe. For
example, in 1976 young people aged 16 to 24 accounted for just over
24 per cent of the labour force compared with the lowest post-war
figure of 14.9 per cent in 1954.(1) The United States economy has
absorbed this considerable change in the age structure of the population with comparative success. But whilst there has been an enormous
increase in the young working population, there remains a substantial
residue of youth unemployment, unevenly distributed by age, race and
location. In 1979 one in every nine young people in the labour force
was unemployed. In 1980, it was more than one in eight. These
figures, however, do little to reveal the composition of the problem
or to provide any insight into the causes of youth unemployment which
is concentrated upon racial minorities, those who are economically
or educationally disadvantaged and those living in the inner cities.
Clearly there is a good deal of overlap among these categories and
therefore we are to some extent looking at the same phenomenon from
different angles.

The burden of youth unemployment has been distributed unevenly
by race with average rates of black youth unemployment running at
approximately twice that of white youth unemployment. Further, the
growth in the differential between black and white youth unemployment
has been substantial. In 1954, 25 years before we made our examination
of youth unemployment in the United States, their rates of unemployment were roughly equal, whereas today there is a difference of over
2 to 1. These statistics are however not wholly convincing since the
massive movement of black people from the agricultural economy of the
south to the industrial and service economy of the north has increased their rate of recorded labour force participation and hence
their recorded rate of unemployment. The rate of unemployment among
the Hispanic group is also disproportionately higher than for whites.
The published figures, however, do not take account of an estimated
700,000 minority youth (2) who seem to have virtually disappeared from
the system, who are not at work, not looking for work and not in education. This group represents a social phenomenon in itself, of which
we shall say more later in this report. Graphs A and B give the

---

1) For an analysis of the impact of the changing age composition of
   the population on age- and sex-specific unemployment rates among
   young people see OECD, Youth Unemployment: The Causes and
   Consequences, op.cit.
2) "Background Report on U.S. Youth Programs", prepared for the OECD
   Review Team, op.cit.

unemployment rates for males and females by age and race between 1954
and 1979 and Graph C gives unemployment rates by ethnic group for
1954-1979.

Whilst race is the area where youth unemployment differentials
are most marked, the unemployed youth population is also disproportionately composed of young people from economically disadvantaged
households. This is both a compounding and a complementary part of
the problem because minorities are over-represented in this classifi-
cation. Table 4 indicates the distribution of employment and unemployment, by age and race, for economically disadvantaged youth.
This shows, for example, that white males (16-17) from economically
disadvantaged households have an unemployment rate 98 per cent higher
than the same youth from non-economically disadvantaged households
and for white males between 22 and 24 years of age reveals a rate of
unemployment 197 per cent higher. Similar comparison for non-white
males shows a much smaller differential at 16-17 years of age (28.3
per cent). However, it rises by 166 per cent for the 22-24-year-old
age group. Whilst there is a broadly comparable position for white
females to that of white males, the position for non-white females is
markedly different. Unemployment among female minorities who are not
economically disadvantaged (16-17) is actually 20 per cent higher than
for non-white females from economically disadvantaged households.
However, this pattern changes with age; among 22-24-year-olds, the
non-economically disadvantaged minority women are nine times less
likely to be unemployed than those from disadvantaged minority
families. Table 4 gives the picture in greater detail.

The area of distribution of youth unemployment in July 1979 shows
that the problem is most severe in urban areas and least severe in
non-metropolitan areas.

	Urban Areas	Suburban Areas	Non-Metropolitan Areas
Youth as a percentage of population	27%	40%	33%
Youth as a percentage of total unemployment	34%	37%	29%

At first there seems to be no major disparity between these
areas in terms of shares of unemployed youth, although there is some
doubt about how accurately official figures reflect the problem. For
example, the National Urban League has developed an unofficial index
of black youth unemployment which suggests much higher levels of
youth unemployment than those recorded in official statistics. As
black youth tend to be concentrated in urban areas, this may well

Graph A

UNEMPLOYMENT RATE FOR MALES BY RACE AND AGE : 1954-1979

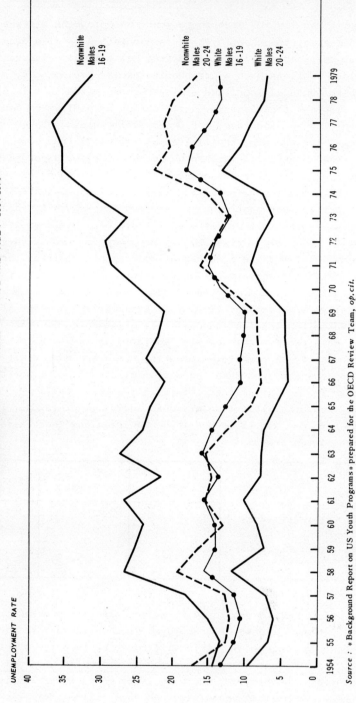

Source : « Background Report on US Youth Programs » prepared for the OECD Review Team, *op. cit.*

Graph B

UNEMPLOYMENT RATE FOR FEMALES BY RACE AND AGE : 1954-1979

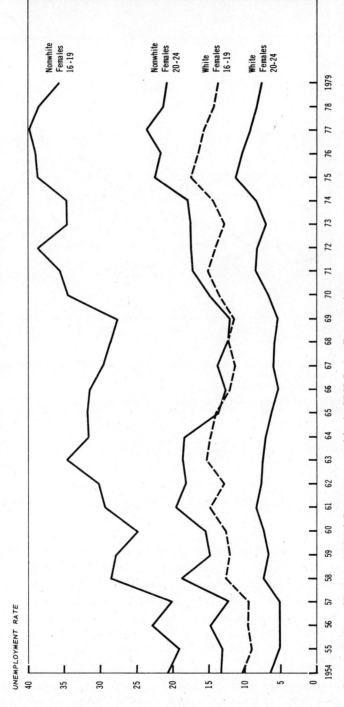

Source : « Background Report on US Youth Programs» prepared for the OECD Review Team, op.cit.

189

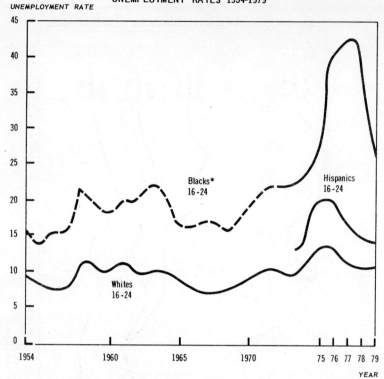

Graph C

UNEMPLOYMENT RATES 1954-1979

UNEMPLOYMENT RATE

Blacks*
16-24

Hispanics
16-24

Whites
16-24

YEAR

* *Note :* Due to changes in reporting procedures, data prior to 1972 are available only for
Blacks and other races. From 1972 through 1979, the graph reflects data for Blacks alone.
Hispanic data were not available until 1973.

Source : The Vice-President's Task Force on Youth Employment, *A Summary Report,*
Washington D.C., 1980.

significantly affect the area-distribution of the unemployed. Much
more striking differences emerge when individual towns, cities or
areas of cities are considered. For example, the level of youth unemployment is estimated at 60 per cent in the Watts district of Los
Angeles, and at 40 per cent in the inner parts of Detroit.

The Department of Labor has developed a form of analysis of
youth unemployment statistics which allows for examination of the
stock of unemployment, as well as flows into and out of the unemployed.
Using this form of analysis they estimate that a great deal of the
total stock of youth unemployment is accounted for by young people
who remain unemployed for over 15 weeks. This group is relatively
small in comparison with the total numbers who experience unemployment.
Again, this analysis suggests that the distribution of unemployment by
duration is not even, and that minority youth and those concentrated
in depressed inner-urban or isolated rural areas disproportionately
suffer from longer-duration unemployment. Table 5 gives some illus-
tration of the absolute pattern of duration of youth unemployment in
the United States.

Table 4

EMPLOYMENT STATUS OF YOUTH, MARCH 1978, BY FAMILY INCOME
STATUS IN 1977, BY AGE, RACE, AND SEX

	Disadvantaged Youth			Non-Disadvantaged Youth		
	Population in 000's	Employment Population Ratio	Unemployment Rate	Population in 000's	Employment Population Ratio	Unemployment Rate
White Males:						
16-17	550	.28	31.5	1,856	.44	15.9
18-19	411	.56	24.1	1,987	.62	9.9
20-21	365	.59	20.1	2,015	.72	8.4
22-24	554	.64	21.4	2,738	.84	7.2
Non-White Males:						
16-17	296	.11	61.1	136	.11	47.6
18-19	239	.32	39.7	111	.42	29.9
20-21	166	.45	32.8	159	.69	20.7
22-24	194	.49	29.8	245	.79	11.2
White Females:						
16-17	569	.22	28.4	1,697	.41	16.4
18-19	546	.40	25.5	1,847	.58	9.0
20-21	594	.40	19.1	1,852	.67	7.0
22-24	750	.34	21.6	2,635	.75	5.7
Non-White Females:						
16-17	336	.11	37.1	104	.15	44.6
18-19	301	.14	54.6	127	.40	31.3
20-21	271	.21	49.9	113	.63	10.9
20-24	371	.30	37.7	223	.84	4.0

Source: "Background Report on U.S. Youth Programs" prepared for the OECD Review Team, op.cit.

Table 5

DURATION OF UNEMPLOYMENT FOR PERSONS ENROLLED IN SCHOOL, HIGH SCHOOL GRADUATES NOT
IN COLLEGE AND SCHOOL DROPOUTS, BY AGE, SEX AND RACE.   OCTOBER 1978
(per cent distribution of persons 16 to 24 years old)

	Total		Duration of Unemployment				
					15 weeks or more		
	Number (in thousands)	Per cent	1 to 4 weeks	5 to 14 weeks	Total	15 to 26 weeks	27 weeks or more
Both Sexes							
Enrolled in school, 16-24 y.	937	100.0	56.9	36.3	8.8	6.1	2.7
16-19 years	776	100.0	57.3	34.5	8.0	5.7	2.3
20-24 years	161	100.0	42.9	44.7	12.4	5.1	4.3
High-school graduates not in college	1,051	100.0	50.9	31.7	17.5	10.5	7.0
Dropouts	635	100.0	52.6	30.8	16.6	8.0	8.6
Men							
Enrolled in school, 16-24 y.	507	100.0	56.2	34.5	9.1	6.1	3.0
16-19 years	425	100.0	60.0	32.7	7.3	4.9	2.4
20-24 years	81	100.0	37.5	43.8	18.8	11.2	7.5
High-school graduates not in college	451	100.0	50.3	29.3	20.0	12.0	8.0
Dropouts	374	100.0	48.4	33.5	18.1	8.2	9.8
Women							
Enrolled in school, 16-24 y.	431	100.0	52.9	39.0	8.4	6.0	2.3
16-19 years	351	100.0	54.4	37.0	8.5	6.3	2.3
20-24 years	80	100.0	48.1	46.8	5.1	3.8	1.3
High-school graduates not in college	600	100.0	50.9	33.4	15.6	9.3	6.3
Dropouts	261	100.0	58.6	26.8	14.6	7.7	6.9
White							
Enrolled in school	713	100.0	58.5	34.4	7.2	5.4	1.3
High-school graduates not in college	756	100.0	54.3	31.1	14.6	10.5	4.1
Dropouts	462	100.0	56.6	29.1	14.3	7.6	6.7
Black							
Enrolled in school	188	100.0	40.3	44.6	15.1	9.7	5.4
High-school graduates not in college	272	100.0	39.1	34.7	26.2	11.1	15.1
Dropouts	165	100.0	41.5	34.8	23.8	9.1	14.6

Source: U.S. Department of Labor. Bureau of Labor Statistics: per cent not shown where base is
less than 75,000.

We would lay special stress on the problem of under-educated youth. The widespread reports from employers and labour unions about basic deficiencies in numeracy and literacy of young people seem to have been reflected in a reluctance to employ them, in at least some companies. This is a particular problem in a society which is increasingly dependent on the service sector of the economy, where mathematical, reading and writing skills are paramount in a way they are not in some manufacturing jobs. The fact that so many of the schemes which we visited contained a remedial education element confirmed the importance of resolving this problem if young people are to be able to find employment. Longer duration unemployment is much more concentrated amongst those with a lower level of educational attainment. Approximately 12 per cent of high school graduates who do not proceed to college experience unemployment, and of those, 17.5 per cent experience more than 15 weeks' unemployment and 7 per cent experience more than 27 weeks' unemployment. Of high school dropouts, 24 per cent experience unemployment, although only two-thirds of young adult dropouts are in the labour force. Of those in the labour force, 16.6 per cent experience unemployment for more than 15 weeks and 8.6 per cent for more than 27 weeks. The estimated rate of high school dropouts in the United States is 25 per cent. The pattern of youth unemployment by educational attainment for 1976 is illustrated in Graph D.

The review team discussed three possible explanations of the youth unemployment problem:

i) <u>Demand-deficient unemployment</u>
- <u>General demand-deficient unemployment</u> where young people are unable to find employment because of the overall lack of demand.
- <u>Local demand-deficient unemployment</u> where young people, because of the lack of demand in the locality in which they live, are unable to find employment, even though the economy as a whole may be operating at a level approaching full employment compatible with price stability.

ii) <u>Transitional unemployment</u> where young people are unable to find employment because of their relative lack of competitiveness (at given levels of earnings) against other groups seeking employment, and because of employer hiring policies which are biased against youth. Also included are the particular problems of entrance or school-leaver unemployment, unemployment as a result of labour market experimentation, and unemployment of the young who are principally in full-time education.

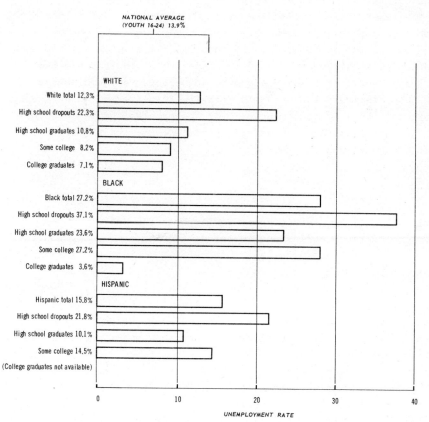

Graph D
YOUTH UNEMPLOYMENT BY EDUCATIONAL ATTAINMENT 1976

NATIONAL AVERAGE
(YOUTH 16-24) 13.9%

WHITE
White total 12.3%
High school dropouts 22.3%
High school graduates 10.8%
Some college 8.2%
College graduates 7.1%

BLACK
Black total 27.2%
High school dropouts 37.1%
High school graduates 23.6%
Some college 27.2%
College graduates 3.6%

HISPANIC
Hispanic total 15.8%
High school dropouts 21.8%
High school graduates 10.1%
Some college 14.5%
(College graduates not available)

0   10   20   30   40

UNEMPLOYMENT RATE

Source : US Bureau of Labor Statistics, *Special Labor Forces Report 200*, «Students, Graduates and Dropouts in the Labor Market, October 1976» and unpublished data cited in National Center for Educational Statistics, *The Condition of Education*, 1978.

iii) <u>Structural unemployment</u> where young people, because
      of inadequate education, race or minority status,
      economic disadvantages or location in chronically
      distressed neighbourhoods, such as the inner city,
      are unable to find employment.

Not surprisingly, we found considerable disagreement as to the weighting and composition of each of the three factors in the composition of the total problem.

We have felt it useful to apply part of the queueing theory (1) to help explain our diagnosis of the United States youth unemployment problem. According to the theory, people seeking work are lined up in queues with the most attractive in employment terms at the front and the least attractive at the rear. Employers hire from the front of the queue backwards down the line. Young people by virtue of their very newness in the labour market, and their lack of skill and work experience, are disproportionately concentrated towards the back of the queue, and consequently are more vulnerable to unemployment in times of relatively low economic activity than are many other groups. Undoubtedly this accounts for part of the problem and measures which are taken to stimulate the United States economy are therefore likely to reduce youth unemployment.

Demand-Deficient Unemployment

The problem of localised demand-deficient unemployment is particularly significant in a country as large as the United States. Given the enormous variations in the United States economy ranging from its cutting-edge areas such as Boston-Cambridge and the "Sunbelt", to the depressed rural areas and declining cities, local demand-deficient unemployment seems almost inevitable. However, this problem is not fully recognised in manpower policy; a point we shall develop later. The particular forms of policy response needed to tackle it might include mobility incentives, the encouragement of regional economic development and the integration of manpower policy into the economic development process. These were areas of policy where the team found less activity than in Western Europe.

The review team heard about some of the initiatives for bringing manpower policy closer to regional or local economic development policy. They are also aware of the initiatives which have been taken following the Area Redevelopment Act in 1961. The review team consider an effective interface between manpower policies and the creation of new jobs in areas or regions where youth unemployment is high a crucial issue. The resolution of the youth unemployment problem

----

1) For a full discussion of queueing theory see Lester C. Thurow,
<u>Generating Inequality</u>, London, Macmillan Press, 1975.

involves bringing jobs to young workers as well as young workers'
moving to jobs. The extent to which government should be involved
in this area is an open question but the CETA delivery system seems
uniquely placed to provide effective training at the local level for
enterprises which are considering relocating in a particular area.
Such an approach to manpower policy would require an economic approach
from prime-sponsors as well as a social and educational one.

Transitional Unemployment

The review team were concerned about the lack of a framework for
skill-training for young people in the United States, and the lack of
a programme for providing apprenticeship training for young people
immediately after school. Given what we have previously said about
the vulnerability of young people because of their lack of skill in
the labour market, it was not surprising that we found considerable
evidence of transitional unemployment in the United States.

As a significant element in the transitional unemployment problem, this lack of skill and mechanisms for providing it have become
institutionalised in corporate hiring policies. Evidence given to
the review team suggested that in some companies there might be collective discrimination against young people in favour of older
workers. A number of leading firms reported that they were unwilling
to hire people under 21 years of age and that they expected young
people to gain work experience, and to develop good working habits
before they would be recruited. The review team felt this to be a
particularly serious phenomenon. This pattern of corporate hiring
policy may well reflect increasingly internalised labour markets,
the high costs of hiring (administrative, training, induction costs,
etc.), as well as the prospect of higher than normal turnover rates
for youth. Collective discrimination against young people may also
be encouraged by the labour unions' insistence on maintaining
seniority systems within companies.

The review team are also concerned that the existing structure
of incentives to employers to provide sufficient training provision
may be inadequate. The training of young workers involves considerable costs to employers, who in times of low economic activity and
excess supply of labour may prefer to hire out of the pool of unemployed and potential workers, or to extend overtime working, rather
than make a longer-term investment in training. In part, this problem reflects the lack of an interface between manpower policy and
economic development policy which was observed during our visit.
The craft-skilled population in the United States seem disproportionately clustered among older workers. This would lend some credi-
bility to the argument that the United States economy could face
serious skill shortages in the 1980s as the number of young people

entering the labour force declines and there is a larger retirement
of older people at the top. Recent projections indicate that persons
older than 55 will decline from 17.5 per cent of the labour force in
1970 to 11.2 per cent in 1990.(1)

The times required to train skilled workers are quite long, and
it is often difficult to deal with skill shortages in periods of
buoyant economic activity. It may be possible for a training programme, related to future economic needs, to be mounted as a counter-
cyclical programme, particularly given the length of economic down-
turns in many OECD countries. It seems unlikely that such a policy
could be mounted unless an adequate structure of incentives, both to
individuals and to companies, was available. We shall say more about
this later in our report, but we should comment that United States
apprenticeship arrangements, which typically involve people in apprenticeship training in their mid- to upper twenties, may be inadequate
as a means of preparing young people for the labour force. They may
however provide a much better system for the upskilling of adult
workers than is found in many other countries.

The problem of transitional unemployment in the United States is
further complicated by a form of adolescence unknown to most of Europe.
It was consistently suggested to us that young people should not expect to enter the mainstream labour market before they are 21 or 22
years of age. One distinguished United States manpower economist set
the figure at 24 years of age. It was suggested that young people
should either remain in education, or that they should actively change
jobs in a process of labour market exploration. Certainly, it seems
that for many young Americans this is the dominant pattern and a significant amount of youth unemployment can be accounted for by job-
changing. In a society as affluent as the United States, such a form
of adolescence is possible and perhaps even desirable. The review
team would however stress that "milling around", as it was called,
could become a living nightmare for under-educated youth living in
chronically stressed inner cities or depressed rural areas. Further,
there are distinct possibilities that this pattern of behaviour may
well result in some young people never being able to make the transition into the primary labour market.

Structural Unemployment

The structural problem of youth unemployment, concentrated
amongst minorities, the under-educated, those from economically disadvantaged backgrounds and often living in the most chronically
stressed neighbourhoods, is the most complex, the most daunting and
the most serious. Whilst youth are generally towards the back of the

1) See Professor D. Quinn Mills, "Human Resources in 1980s", Harvard
   Business Review, August 1979.

queue of those looking for employment, it is possible to see youth as a separate queue, with those affected by structural unemployment concentrated at the back of it. They tend to be concentrated in particular locations, especially the inner urban areas and poor rural communities. In a sense these are doubly disadvantaged areas containing a disproportionate number of young people less attractive to employers, whilst at the same time having industrial and commercial infrastructures which give rise to partial or localised demand deficiency. They are also often areas with declining tax bases and serious revenue problems at the local government and state government level. It is this group at the back of the queue who find it most difficult to enter the labour market successfully, and who are most likely to experience serious problems of unemployment. Before proceeding to give some of our understanding of the problem, we would wish to stress that this is a problem much wider in scope than manpower policy is ever likely to be able to tackle on its own. The labour market problems of this group are often the result of accumulated social, family, educational and economic influences, which have borne on the individual or groups of individuals throughout their entire development from birth to adulthood.

The evidence presented to the review team shows that a large part of the longer-term youth unemployment problem is concentrated in the inner city areas. Major urbanisation and sub-urbanisation of the United States in the post-war period coincided with a massive shift in the geographical distribution of the black population; 80 per cent rural in 1941 and 80 per cent urban today. In many cases, whites have moved out to the suburbs, leaving blacks, other minorities and poor whites in the inner cities. City boundaries are, however, not adjusted because of rigidities in the American system; conurbations commonly spread over a number of jurisdictions (including several states in some cases, e.g. in New York and Washington). The consequence is that cities often have diminishing tax bases but increasing costs, whilst suburbs have sound tax bases with lower costs. This, with related consequences (e.g. rising crime rates) has led to a flight of business and employment from the relatively costly inner cities, although the energy crisis could lead to some reversal. The massive urban renewal projects of the mid-1960s too often led to both an extension, and a deterioration, of ghetto areas. In some inner city areas there has been a significant failure of the school system, because of their inability to meet rising costs and to attract and retain good teachers. This, in turn, has further encouraged a transfer of the skill-based employment out of central areas.

Although not immigrants in the common American pattern, the size and nature of the migration of blacks to the cities makes for some similarities - the inner city concentration, for example. Strong family cohesion was a marked and important feature of most immigrant groups whereas the very nature of slavery and its aftermath had a fracturing effect on black family life, an effect which was accentuated by the pressures of urban life. Blacks fled from rural poverty and rigid segregation in the old south, to find poverty and massive racial discrimination elsewhere. Although the Supreme Court struck at de jure discrimination in 1954, de facto segregation and discrimination was not widely tackled until the mid-1960s. The importance of the demonstration effect cannot be ignored; immigrant groups saw that other such groups had made it; blacks saw that blacks had not, although in reality the other minority groups had taken a long time after their arrival in the cities to achieve success. However, there has been substantial progress since the mid-1960s -- witness the construction industry. In 1960 only 2 per cent of apprentices were black (despite the predominantly urban nature of the industry) and in 1978 the figure had jumped to nearly 20 per cent. But discrimination is still a major factor.

III

THE DEVELOPMENT OF LEGISLATION
IN THE FIELD OF MANPOWER POLICY

The Wagner-Peyser Act of 1933 was the first significant federal
legislation passed in the United States in the manpower area. It
authorised the establishment of an Employment Service co-operatively
operated by the federal and state governments to serve as a labour exchange for employers and job-seekers. Considering the depressed economic conditions of 1933, the legislative intent was to establish an
agency that would refer those looking for work to the emerging New
Deal relief programmes. It was an instrument of public programmes -
not of private labour markets - since the public Employment Service
could hardly be expected to match non-existent jobs to the masses of
the unemployed.

In 1935 the Congress enacted a programme for unemployment insurance under the Social Security Act. The Employment Service was
assigned the task of administering the "work-test"rules to ensure that
recipients of unemployment compensation were "ready, willing and able
to work".

In 1937 the Congress passed legislation which established The
Bureau of Apprenticeship and Training which provided for the regulation of standards of apprenticeship and the protection of apprentices.
The legislation provided for voluntary registration of apprenticeship
places by employers and unions and the establishment of minimum standards for registration (set at federal level). Whilst the Bureau of
Apprenticeship and Training is charged with responsibility for the
development of the systematic training of skilled workers, it does not
operate programmes itself and works essentially in a voluntary manner.

Until the rate of technological change reached some critical
mass in the late 1950s, education took place in schools and training
took place on the job. By 1961, however, the rate of unemployment in
the United States was 6.7 per cent, technology was threatening to
drastically alter the workplace and there was a growing political
concern with eliminating discrimination and poverty. The Congress
responded by enacting The Manpower Development and Training Act in
1962 (MDTA), fundamentally a non-partisan measure under the auspices
of the Department of Labor. This provided for training in vocational

schools as well as "on the job". Between 1962 and 1970, about two-third of the participants were in vocational schools and one-third "on the job". The initial manpower training Bill concentrated on male heads of households with at least three years' experience in the labour market and included other eligibility qualifications which conflicted with the equity aims of Congress. Such limitations curtailed its relevance to youth and the hard-core unemployed. Amendments in latter years relaxed requirements for admission and targeted more funds to youth and the disadvantaged. In 1963 the Youth Employment Act was introduced to improve vocational education for young people which included some of the components of MDTA and applied them specifically to youth.

In contrast to previous legislation MDTA provided for an active operational role for the federal authorities rather than just an intermediary or regulatory role which it had previously played. Whilst MDTA was the principal manpower legislation of the 1960s, Congress passed considerable additional legislation in the manpower field. For example, the Employment Service established under the Wagner-Peyser legislation was assigned responsibility for regulation and enforcement of no less than 22 laws, 14 executive orders and 14 inter-agency services. The movements to eliminate discrimination and poverty was reflected in the Civil Rights Act 1964 which prohibited racial discrimination in employment and established the Equal Employment Opportunity Commission and in The Economic Opportunity Act which established the Neighbourhood Youth Corps and the Job Corps Programmes. The Economic Opportunity Act also authorised the Community Action Programme which gave grass-roots organisations (Community-based organisations, CBOs) the opportunity to co-ordinate services for the poor at the local level. Local grass-roots organisations were also involved in the Work Experience and Training Programme which aimed at upgrading the competitiveness of the unemployed so that they might compete effectively when trying to secure employment.

Two important points should be stressed about these two pieces of legislation. First, that the anti-discrimination legislation related to sex as well as to race and in consequence there was some degree of conflict between affirmative action programmes for women and those for ethnic minorities. Second, the legislation provided a major stimulus to activity by independent grass-roots organisations at the local level. The role which many of these organisations played as both operators and political spokesmen for their client groups was a crucial part of the wider War against Poverty programmes, conceived and operated by the Kennedy/Johnson Administration. Private industry was also involved in the operation of manpower policies for the disadvantaged through the National Alliance for Business, which was formed by leading United States businessmen following a direct approach from President Johnson in 1968. This organisation runs a range of manpower and work experience programmes and also programmes of career preparation in schools.

In January 1968, amendments to Title IV of the Social Security Act authorised the introduction of the Work Incentive (WIN) programme which was designed to move recipients of Aid to Families with Dependent Children (AFDC) from welfare to work. The programme is jointly administered by the Department of Labor and the Department of Health, Education and Welfare. The WIN programme obliges women with children over six, living on AFDC to register for work. As social service offices are partly financed by the size of the reduction in their welfare roles, the pressures on mothers with young children to find employment are strong.

In 1971, faced with a national unemployment rate of 6 per cent, the Congress passed, and the President approved, the Emergency Employment Act. This Act authorised an appropriation of $2.25 billion during 1972-73 to establish a programme of transitional public service jobs for unemployed and underemployed persons, with emphasis on specific population groups, including returning veterans. It was, however, not extended in 1972.

In December 1973 the Comprehensive Employment and Training Act (CETA) was signed into law. It replaced the MDTA and the EOA. The purpose of the Act was to provide training, employment and other services leading to unsubsidised employment for economically disadvantaged, unemployed and underemployed persons. CETA was later amended by the Emergency Jobs and Unemployment Assistance Act 1974 and by the Emergency Jobs Programmes Extension Act 1976. Numerous other revisions have been made to CETA over the last few years. We shall say more about the changes in manpower policy which occurred under CETA in Chapter IV as it remains the substantive legislation under which manpower policy is operated. Details of the various Titles under the CETA legislation, the scope of the regulations and eligibility criteria, are set out in Annex II of this report.

In 1977 the Youth Employment and Demonstration Projects Act (YEDPA) was signed into law. The purpose of the Act was to provide a broad range of co-ordinated employment and training programmes for eligible youth. The goal is to create information for the formulation of policy on youth programmes. YEDFA authorised four new employment programmes and an expansion of Job Corps and the Summer Youth Employment Programme. Full details of this legislation are set out in Annex II and its origins and purpose discussed in Chapter IV. In 1977 the new Carter Administration also introduced a substantial Public Service Employment programme, in the face of an 8 per cent unemployment rate.

In 1978, the <u>Full-Employment and Balanced Growth Act</u> (generally known as the Humphrey-Hawkins Act) was signed into law. This legislation declared that the intent of public policy should be to achieve full employment but heavily qualified the pursuit of this objective with other economic considerations which needed to be borne in mind. Perhaps the most important aspect of the legislation is that it represents a political move to bring employment considerations closer into economic policy. It must, however, be stressed that the legislation is only declaratory.

During 1979 several Bills have been introduced in the Congress aimed at improving or expanding existing youth programmes or to introduce new programmes. The total federal expenditures on employment programmes has increased substantially over the last two decades, also the structure of expenditures has changed from unemployment compensation to active measures for training and job creation. Since 1970 the outlays for training and employment activities have increased from about $3 billion to about $15 billion in 1978, a real increase of approximately 200 per cent. Expenditures have varied at particular points in time, for example the 725,000 Public Service Employment places created under CETA II and VI as part of the President's 1977 Economic Stimulus Package dramatically increased expenditure.

The development of the legislation and the funding of the programmes should be seen in context with the institutional framework and the economic, social and political development.

- The new programmes during the 1960s under the Kennedy and Johnson administrations expressed a new political consciousness of the government's responsibility for stimulating employment opportunities, making increased intervention in the labour market necessary. Those programmes, which formed an important part of the War Against Poverty policy were also a response to the political pressures exercised by the Civil Rights Movement.
- The CETA legislation of the Nixon Administration was an attempt to decentralise employment policy and thereby diminish the political power exercised by the federal government and encourage revenue-sharing.
- The introduction of YEDPA and the expansion of the other youth programmes can be seen as an expression of the fear that a general improvement in the economy is not in itself sufficient to combat youth unemployment. Further, that some of the causes of youth unemployment may require responses which recognise some different underlying reasons for youth as opposed to general unemployment.

IV

THE SHAPE OF THE PRESENT PROGRAMMES

The present programmes represent a continuation and evolution of the initiatives developed in the 1960s. The Comprehensive Employment Training Act (CETA), passed in 1973, was an attempt to bring more coherence into federal manpower policies (a full description of CETA is in Annex I). The Act attempted to consolidate and to decentralise the 10,000 or so fragmented manpower projects which existed across the United States. The legislation established a new institutional structure for United States manpower policy by placing operating responsibility on prime-sponsors, which are generally local government units at city, county, and in some cases, state level. There are more than 450 prime-sponsors operating the CETA programme in the United States.

In August 1977 the President signed the Youth Employment and Demonstration Projects Act (YEDPA) into law (a full description of YEDPA is in Annex II). This legislation is aimed primarily at disadvantaged youth and provides for the continuation of some existing programmes. It also authorises a wide range of experimental projects with accompanying systematic monitoring and evaluation of results. The legislation reflects both uncertainty about what should be done as well as a degree of political compromise between the Administration and the Congress. It is, however, useful to recall the political motivation behind the legislation. President Carter, on signing the Act into law, indicated its importance as follows:

"This bill will take a great stride forward in trying to correct this serious affliction on our nation's economy ... I think all of us realise that if a young person reaches the age of 16, 17, 18 and all the way up to 24 years of age and cannot get a job in the formative years of life, there is a feeling of despair, discouragement, a loss of self-esteem, an alienation from the structure of society, a lashing out against the authorities who are responsible, which can shape that life for years to come. We are trying to address that now in the first major step forward. We will not only provide jobs under this programme, but we will also learn about the best mechanisms for increasing jobs even more in the future."

Structural Changes under CETA

The development of CETA involved changes in the philosophy and approach of government, as well as a movement to greater rationality within manpower programmes. The 1960s had been characterised by the Great Society programmes as American social scientists explored the "other America". With the "War against Poverty" came a mass of federal legislation and large sums of money. Indeed, some have remarked that the answer to problems was seen as "throwing money at the problem until it went away". This approach was also characterised by direct federal interventions and direct federal relations with community-based organisations which bypassed the established "power structure" of state and local government. The late 1960s saw political changes and also a change in approach characterised by a general preference for income transfers rather than social services, for local government responsibility rather than federally administered programmes, and perhaps most important of all, for revenue-sharing rather than categorical grants. While this philosophy was not completely translated into the CETA legislation (particularly with regard to funding), it had important effects on the institutional structure created to administer the legislation.

In contrast to the administration and implementation of anti-poverty programmes through local community-based organisations and of the Manpower Development and Training Act through the Employment Services, CETA was designed to be administered through a system of local "prime-sponsors". These are local government units, which have to have a population of 100,000 or more to receive direct federal funds and to become prime-sponsors. The state Employment Service is supposed to provide services to the CETA prime-sponsors for counselling and recruitment. Each prime-sponsor is meant to provide a comprehensive manpower plan which details the problems of the area, programmes to be mounted and groups to be served.

Three important points should be stressed. In all cases, the functions of the prime-sponsor are directly attached to the elected political representatives and are often carried out by newly-created administrative units directly attached to the Mayor's Office, the County Board, or the Governor's Office. It was this introduction of local political control to which many CBOs objected. The second major departure from previous practice is the attempt to decategorise programmes under CETA. Prime-sponsors receive a substantial part of CETA funds in the form of block grants distributed according to formulas based upon population, unemployment and income criteria. Programme priorities, within the broad purposes specified by the authorising legislation, are determined locally and under limited supervision by the regional officers of the Department of Labor. But third, prime-sponsors have to contract with other agencies to undertake training, education, work experience, etc. These agencies tend to be the very ones that flourished under anti-poverty, civil rights and manpower development programmes, namely CBOs and non-profit foundations, so that the new organisation was not quite as different from the old as it first appeared. There are in practice thousands of contracts with many hundreds of CBOs. This approach also assuaged some of the original political opposition of the CBOs to the prime-sponsor concept.

The CETA legislation also included, in Title VII, a new approach to the private sector. Prime-sponsors were encouraged to set up private industry councils, and could receive financial support from the Department of Labor, providing certain conditions were fulfilled, including a requirement that it must supplement and not supplant on-the-job training and related activities. Title VII was a good idea, and one we believe could be further developed. But it was subjected to so many conditions and regulations that many private sector firms were unwilling to get involved, despite the valiant efforts of several Private Industry Councils. In a few prime-sponsor areas PICs were influential; probably the outstanding example was Baltimore.

Young people can be assisted through various parts of the CETA legislation and by 1977 about 2 million young people had participated in CETA programmes. But the increasing level of youth unemployment produced a demand for additional initiatives to deal with the structural problems faced by disadvantaged youth, especially by school dropouts and the economically disadvantaged. At the same time, it was feared that youth might be squeezed out of existing programmes as general unemployment rose. As a consequence, a great number of legislative initiatives were mounted in the Congress which gained considerable support. Many of these initiatives had to be accommodated by the new White House Administration within its own proposals for youth unemployment, and in consequence the Youth Employment and Demonstration Projects Act is a complicated and fragmented piece of legislation. The President signed the legislation in August 1977. It is primarily administered under the CETA umbrella. However, there was no clear understanding of the underlying causes of youth unemployment and the most effective ways of tackling it, and this was reflected in the many conflicting approaches being proposed in draft legislation in the Congress.

Accordingly, YEDPA:

i) increased the funding of certain existing programmes such as a) the Summer Jobs Programme, b) the Job Corps;

ii) established the Young Adult Conservation Corps based on the concept of the Civilian Conservation Corps of the 1930s; and

iii) provided further funding for certain new programmes.

The principal new departure has been the experimental entitlement programme guaranteeing a part-time job during the school year and a full-time job during the summer to every eligible young person within designated experimental areas, provided that the participant remains enrolled in school or returns to a high school or an alternative school. In addition, YEDPA provided discretionary funds for demonstration projects and experimentation. The Department of Labor had seized these opportunities and indeed attempted to give it some coherence through its "Knowledge Development Plan", which utilised discretionary funds to develop systematic and controlled experiments, with professional standards of monitoring and evaluation, in order to determine the effectiveness of a wide variety of new approaches to deal with problems of youth unemployment. It also aims to obtain a better understanding of the conditions under which different approaches are likely to be effective or ineffective.

What we have found out about the design of the Knowledge Development Plan is impressive. If it is well-executed, one may expect much reliable policy information never before available. But it is regrettable that the present authorisation of the programmes will expire, and new legislation will have to be drafted, at a time when most of the findings to be expected from demonstration projects and evaluation research will not be available, and when many projects will still be in a development stage.

Obviously, the OECD review team would also have profited greatly from the results produced by the Knowledge Development Plan, and from the availability of systematic evaluation studies of ongoing and experimental programmes. Under the circumstances, however, our report must be impressionistic, reflecting the conclusions which we have formed after extensive but necessarily selective discussions. Thus, we do not have the basis for conclusive judgements about the success or failure of CETA and YEDPA programmes aimed at youth unemployment. All we can offer is our understanding of the underlying problems, and of the operation of some of the programmes as they were presented to us, as well as our reflections upon the factors which might facilitate or impede programme success.

V

OPERATIONAL CHARACTERISTICS AND PROBLEMS
OF CETA PROGRAMMES

In Chapter II we distinguished three aspects of the problem of
youth unemployment in the United States: demand-deficient unemployment, transitional unemployment and structural (hard-core) unemployment. We now discuss some of the ongoing CETA programmes and their
relationship to these differing aspects of the unemployment problem.

Demand-Deficient Unemployment

Even though demand deficiency is a characteristic of the general
labour market, it does affect younger job-seekers who are just entering into the labour market to a disproportionate extent. Consequently,
policies generally aimed at counteracting demand deficiency are also
highly relevant for youth employment opportunities. We have been
given to understand that there are now a number of programmes and
initiatives aiming at economically distressed regions and localities
which seek to stimulate private and public investment and, ultimately,
to create new employment opportunities. We have also gained the impression, however, that the United States is not systematically
pursuing regional policy objectives on a large scale at federal level.

The CETA programmes that we have primarily investigated are not
intended, so it seems, to deal with longer-term (i.e. non-cyclical)
deficiencies in the demand for labour. Public service employment
under Title VI of CETA is clearly aimed only at cyclical unemployment;
and the rules limiting the duration of subsidised employment preclude
its use for long-term employment creation in distressed areas.
Public service employment under Title II, part D), while often called
a structural measure, is only aimed at the structural aspect of the
supply side, i.e. attempting to overcome the specific handicaps of
disadvantaged groups in the labour market. Significantly, CETA does
not provide for any long-term employment subsidies in the private
sector which might generally increase overall demand for labour.
Thus, under CETA, measures aimed at demand-deficient unemployment are
concentrated upon the public sector, and public sector employment
itself is used primarily as an instrument to bridge the trough of
cyclical unemployment.

There are, however, problems with public service employment, even if viewed strictly as a counter-cyclical measure. The main problem in the past appears to have been one of fiscal substitutions and the PSE programme has been the subject of a good many press attacks on this subject. Whilst some of the more extreme claims have not been confirmed in an evaluation carried out by the Brookings Institution, the review team were informed of a number of cases where higher paid professional staff in local government were paid out of PSE funds. In trying to prevent public service employers from using the programme to support services which otherwise would have to be financed out of locally raised funds, Congress has recently imposed rigid limits upon the duration of employment and upon the maximum pay that participants in the programme are allowed to receive. It has also set maximum figures for the wage supplements which the employer may add. In many of our interviews, we gained the impression that the rules have been tightened to such an extent that it is now difficult to make use of Public Service Employment programmes, particularly in high-wage areas. This is especially true where union wages for entry-level jobs, to which employers are bound by collective bargaining agreements, may already be higher than the maximum allowed under PSE rules.

Whilst young people are not the main beneficiaries of the PSE programmes, one of its most useful features is that it allows prime-sponsors to recruit the necessary staff to undertake labour-intensive counselling and training activities within other CETA Programmes. The effectiveness of many of the most attractive projects would suffer greatly if restrictive rules on the duration of employment and allowable salaries were to prevent prime-sponsors from putting together complex programme packages which required PSE staff in order to be operated effectively. One example of a project using several funding sources which particularly impressed the review team was the Boston (Cambridge) Urban Arts Project in Deafness which brought together unemployed artists under PSE funding and deaf children under YEDPA funding.

While public service employment is acting upon the demand side of the labour market in a straightforward, though limited, manner, some other CETA programmes may also have indirect effects which encourage demand expansion for labour. Among these we would include all programmes that provide for extensive skill training aimed at employment in the private sector. Such skill training can presently be achieved through on-the-job training under CETA Title II, part B, and Title VII, and through the Youth Incentive Entitlement Pilot Projects under Title IV. In addition, we have also heard that other programmes under Title II and Title IV of CETA have been used for training directly related to specific skill demands in the private sector.

Our expectation that skill training directly related to private sector output may in fact increase overall demand for labour is based upon the following hypothesis (for which we have found some support in some of the projects we have visited). While it is characteristic of the United States labour market that employers will usually provide skill training at their own expense, such training will often be quite expensive. When the aggregate demand for goods and services is strong and certain, it will be profitable for firms to invest in training; but if demand is weak and uncertain (as is presently the case in many branches of the industrial sector), investment in the training of additional labour may appear as a high-risk investment. Under such conditions, firms will search for skilled employees in the labour market and, if they should be unavailable, are likely to accept this as a constraint on their production.

Under such circumstances, a subsidisation of skill training or a government-induced increase in the supply of skilled labour may in fact remove an overall constraint on production and, hence, on employment opportunities. If it were vigorously pursued, an expansion of apprenticeship programmes in order to enlarge the supply of skilled labour in those sectors of the economy which are most likely to grow in the near future might be one of the most promising measures for increasing the total volume of employment opportunities in the private sector. This has indeed been the case in Germany. Clearly, such a programme could not be initiated without the active support of unions and business associations. But given a clear perspective of the likely benefits of such a programme for business and organised labour, we should expect that their support could be obtained. We do not have the impression that this possibility has been fully explored by the policy-makers responsible for manpower programmes in the United States.

There is also a case for a traineeship programme for semi-skilled work below the apprenticeship level but more developed than the work orientation, socialisation and work experience implicit in training courses of 3-4 months or less. Such a scheme could be useful "end-on" following high-school graduation. Employers would need a subsidy to cover the training element, part of which might be off-the-job training in community colleges or vocational schools. Intermediate agencies which deal with form filling, administration, relations with the Department of Labor regional and national offices as well as counselling and support services, could be established in order to increase the attractions of such a scheme to the private sector.

Transitional Unemployment

When demand is low, measures aimed at transitional unemployment of young people (like those directed at hard-core unemployment) are essentially redistributive in the sense that they will only affect the competitiveness of younger versus older job-seekers, without increasing overall employment. However, at times when, and in regions where demand for labour is relatively high, measures to reduce transitional and hard-core unemployment may actually increase total employment. Given the uneven distribution of demand for labour across the regions and localities of the United States, the sectors and branches of the economy and especially across skill groups, there are likely to be many pockets of unfilled demand for labour, even at times of relatively high general unemployment. In such circumstances employment and training measures which help young people to enter the labour market more easily will tend to increase (rather than merely to redistribute) total employment if they are precisely demand-targeted.

Of all the measures which are intended to deal with the difficult transition from school to work, the Summer Youth Employment Programme is the largest, reaching close to one million youngsters each year. It offers disadvantaged youngsters subsidised summer jobs which have generally been available without subsidy to most young people in the United States. The programme does provide income and valuable work experience, and it seems particularly useful when combined with programmes of labour market orientation. The jobs provided are in the public and private "non-profit" sectors which curtails its usefulness as an introduction to work in the private sector.

In many instances, however, the programmes seem beset by administrative problems caused mainly by the late arrival of funds. This is serious because there also seems to be a good deal of competition for summer job openings among the great variety of agencies and organisations offering summer employment. Given that the summer employment of young people is very widespread in the United States, we also suspect that a good deal of substitution by subsidised employment and summer jobs of employment opportunities which would have been available without subsidy is taking place. We were informed of at least one city where employers had been asked to delay filling vacancies with permanent employees until after the summer vacation, in order to enable a summer job vacancy to be offered. However, given that the intent is to favour disadvantaged youth under CETA, such substitution effects may well have to be accepted.

Valuable work experience and labour market orientation is also provided by other employment and training programmes under Title IV, Title VIII, and (when young people are included) Title II of CETA. We have not been able to observe directly the wide variety of programme activities carried out under these titles, and so we restrict our remarks to three points regarding the training effects of some of the programmes that we have observed.

Much of what seems to go on under the label of "training" in all youth programmes appears to be remedial education in one form or another. We fully endorse the point that basic skills in reading, writing and mathematics are an essential precondition of employability in almost all sectors of the labour market. Further, we have been informed time and again that such skills are widely lacking, even in young people who have graduated from high school (and, thus, who would not be included among our original definition of the hard-core disadvantaged groups). However, we were somewhat uneasy to see that, in many instances, remedial education is defined as training or even employment, and paid for at the rate of federal minimum wages. It seems to us worthwhile to explore what effects this practice may have upon the motivation to learn at school (where financial compensation is lacking) as well as upon the motivation to perform jobs where regular work (instead of participation in educational activities) is required. If it is necessary to provide income support to participants in remedial education programmes, perhaps some other form of payment could be provided, such as educational scholarships or maintenance allowances rather than wages.

It is also our impression that, where remedial education is required, pushing youngsters back into the regular high school system, which has failed them in the first place, is not likely to be the most effective solution. This problem may result from the terms of the Youth Entitlement Experiment which requires continuing school enrolment, or a return to school, as a condition of enrolment in the programme. Two cases which we have observed: education at an "alternative school", and computer-based instruction which permits the individual to proceed at his own speed, seemed to offer more effective solutions for those who have been unsuccessful in the regular school system.

Many of the bona fide training activities under CETA appear to be very short-term. They mainly provide work experience or, often, a series of brief work exposures, rather than specific skill training. If young people are actually at a disadvantage in the labour market, we wonder whether such limited programmes are really sufficient. Training in "socialisation", or in making young people familiar with the demands of commerce or industry in terms of behaviour, appearance, punctuality, polite forms of speaking to customers, etc., such short courses certainly have value. But they need to be linked much more effectively than at present with more advanced forms of training, including specific job-related skill training, which would go some way towards equalising labour market opportunities as between young people and more experienced older job-seekers. This is especially true under conditions of high unemployment. Such training will often require the direct involvement of the private sector - which is not easily accomplished under some programmes. We further consider that training is most effective if it is linked to employment on completion and is both systematic and of adequate length. The providing of training, as opposed to subsidised employment, is also likely to produce greater labour union support for programmes. Private employers will want to make their own rules and preferably have participants on their payroll, while accepting a subsidy for the training costs. This leads us to believe that one effective way to do this is to expand apprenticeship programmes, especially outside the traditional area of construction which constitutes at present 60 per cent of the registered schemes. But any expansion would require additional funds, either directly through the prime (1937) legislation, or through Title II of CETA, and also reasonable continuity. Under Title II funds were only made available for one year, fiscal 1979; normally an apprenticeship scheme takes 3-4 years in the United States.

We recognise that registered apprenticeship programmes have shown an encouraging increase in the recruitment of minorities - now over 18 per cent against 4 per cent in 1960. But the record for girls and women is very poor, only 3 per cent. The extension into new areas such as paramedical, computer programming and distribution should improve opportunities for girls. There is a need also to encourage small businesses to train. At present on-the-job training requires an employer to commit himself to a permanent hiring on day one. A short probationary period of say one month, after which the employer commits himself to hiring the young person, may encourage more small business co-operation.

One programme which facilitates some private-sector involvement for part-time work by young people still at school is the experimental Youth Entitlement. While it may be difficult to provide the right to employment in a programme which would apply to the whole country (instead of a few selected experimental sites) the possibility of subsidised work experience in the private sector provided by the experimental programme might well be generalised to other parts of the country. We have observed at least one impressive example in Baltimore where training is provided under a contractual arrangement which obliges the employer to hire all successful participants as skilled workers at the end of the entitlement period. Under such conditions, the demand orientation of skill training is fully assured.

Similar effects can, of course, also be achieved through on-the-job training, under Title II, and we have also been informed about a programme in which intensive skill training is provided under Title IVa, Sub-part 3, upon specification by individual employers who have agreed to hire successful trainees at the end of the training period.

While contractual arrangements between employers and prime-sponsors might be the most direct way of assuring demand orientation

212

for CETA training programmes, we are uncertain how easily the successful examples that we have visited could be replicated. The roots of
the difficulties of CETA/private sector co-operation seem to lie with
both sides. We were often informed that prime sponsors and community-
based organisations have carried into CETA programmes the predominantly
welfare orientation of the "War against Poverty" programmes of the
sixties, and also that they are insufficiently aware, or interested
in, the demand side of the labour market, especially in the private
sector. On the other hand, private employers (and even unions) seem
to have an extraordinary fear of becoming involved with any government programmes (including subsidies) to which strings or red tape
may be attached. Admittedly, the extent and complexity of federal
regulations provide some justification for their attitudes. Unless
non-governmental intermediary organisations are able to absorb many
of these difficulties and to simplify the bureaucratic requirements
for employers, directly demand-related skill training for the private
sector is likely to remain difficult within CETA. The review team
considers that fewer and simpler regulations and fewer changes in
programmes would help bring about a more co-operative attitude from
the private sector where the large majority of permanent jobs are to
be found.

It is perhaps a comment on the remarkable distance which exists
between government and private sector that in two cases of apparently
successful pre-employment training programmes, one sponsored by
industry and one by a labour union, we were told that CETA funds were
not involved and would not be accepted by the sponsors if offered.
We, however, doubt that programmes provided in this way would be able
to provide sufficient coverage across the country.

Structural Unemployment (Hard-core Unemployment)

The dividing line between transitional unemployment and the hard-
core unemployment of under-educated and impoverished minorities in
the inner cities is not a clear one. Many of the CETA programmes are
equally applicable to both aspects of the unemployment problem. As a
result it is generally quite difficult to target programmes precisely
upon the most disadvantaged groups, with the consequence that a certain
degree of "creaming-off" will have to be accepted as inevitable in
all CETA programmes. Nor do we believe that very tight targeting is
desirable if it tends to label the targeted group as "disadvantaged"
or "poor", most acutely in the case where young people on CETA programmes or on compensatory education programmes are segregated from
the rest of their peer group or school-class. We set out in the next
chapter some ways in which we believe the main financial argument for
targeting can be met without severe social consequences.

By an almost universal consensus of opinion, the Job Corps is regarded as the programme with the tightest targeting accuracy, and with the highest rate of success for those participants that complete the programme. Of the 44,921 trainees from the programme in fiscal year 1978, post-programme data are available on 32,340 which shows 68 per cent placed in employment, 20 per cent in education and training programmes and 5 per cent in the Armed Forces. By taking the youngsters out of their ghetto environment and exposing them not only to remedial education and skill training, but also to a rather intensive psychological, motivational and behavioural modification process, the Job Corps seems to be able to break the hold of the culture of poverty and hopelessness over its enrolees. By the same token, however, the Job Corps is an expensive programme (estimated at $15,000 per participant year) and even if much more money could be made available, it is not clear that it could greatly expand its membership to become commensurate with the quantitative dimensions of the problem (1.2 million young people estimated to be eligible in 1979). Indeed, the growth of Job Corps membership from 22,000 to the authorised number of 44,000 slots is taking some time, and it seems that neither staff with the required skills and high dedication, nor applicants with the required motivation are available in very great numbers at the moment. We would be interested to know if the new departure, by which Job Corps are operated by "SER", a community-based organisation for Chicanos, improves the recruitment of the most disadvantaged. We suspect, however, that the Job Corps is likely to remain something of an elite institution — perhaps even more so now that it has extended its educational opportunities to include college education.

For the great majority of seriously disadvantaged young people it appears that remedial education and basic skill training might offer better hopes of success than straightforward employment programmes. While summer jobs, where available, certainly provide valuable working experience, they will not necessarily facilitate entry into the regular labour market if the basic conditions of employability are not met. In an increasingly service-oriented economy, with a shrinking number of manual industrial jobs, a person who is unable to read and write is likely to remain at the fringes of the labour market. This, to be sure, is primarily a problem of the American public school system. While we have not been able to fully grasp the reasons underlying the almost universal scepticism about the possibility of improving the effectiveness of public education in the inner cities, we must accept that remedial education is one of the tasks which CETA programmes have to assume. If that is so, a concentration on programmes which rely on alternative school settings and which use teaching methods that avoid the negative reinforcement of experiences of failure should merit special attention. In particular, we would recommend careful comparative analyses of the cost-effectiveness of the great variety of approaches to remedial education which we have found even within the limited scope of our visit.

Apart from remedial education, subsidised employment in the private sector may also have to be considered as one of the approaches to hard-core unemployment. Subsidies are now provided for on-the-job training as well as for employers hiring disadvantaged persons under the Targeted Tax Credit and Work Incentive Programmes. We have encountered a great number of doubts about the ultimate success of these programmes from many quarters. Apparently, available funds for subsidised employment were not fully used at the end of the 1960s under previous National Alliance of Business schemes, and there are also some doubts whether it will be possible to target such subsidies narrowly enough to really help the hard-core unemployed. Thus, many of the experts we talked to expected that either subsidies would not be taken up or that they would have to be offered on such broad terms that they would substitute for regular employment, without providing much relief for the hard-core unemployed.

It seems to us that the crucial elements in achieving success for subsidised employment are not necessarily the availability and the amount of subsidies (even though they may also be important). First there is a need for adequate career guidance, job preparation and social skill training in industrial habits, language, dress and behaviour in order to allow young people to perform well during interviews for employment. As has already been suggested this could be organised through short industrial courses, combined perhaps with work experience. This could take place whilst the young person is still in school. Second, there is a need for effective outreach services that are able to recruit disadvantaged young people into the programme. Even more, the availability of job development and counselling services which will motivate employers to offer employment for the disadvantaged and provide working arrangements which will facilitate the integration of participants into an ongoing work organisation are crucial. Encouraging examples of private sector initiatives for the hard-to-employ have been collected and published by the Committee for Economic Development, and we should expect that the Private Industry Councils set up under Title VII of CETA will have their major function in this area of job development and counselling.

General Observations

We should like to conclude this chapter with some general remarks about the operating conditions of CETA programmes as they appear to us. In making these remarks, we are very much aware of the fact that we have seen only a very small segment of all CETA activities, and that even across this segment generalisations are of limited value in the light of the great variety among programmes and between local conditions. But this is again the first point of our report.

215

From a European perspective, the most impressive feature of American labour market programmes is their immense variety at the local level. What is going on in one locality seems to have little resemblance to programmes going on elsewhere. This may reflect the differences between local labour markets. More importantly, it seems to reflect the differences in the institutional infrastructure of the community-based organisations and educational institutions with which CETA programmes are dealing, as well as the political and administrative organisation of the prime-sponsor unit itself. Most important of all, measures seem to depend upon the imagination and creativity of the individuals involved in one capacity or another in the design and operation of local programmes and upon their ability to obtain the support (or at least the tolerance) of those federal, state and local agencies and authorities that have control over essential resources.

The most successful and impressive projects that we have seen have all been "packages" combining resources from several parts of the CETA programme (for instance, PSE funding for staff members and entitlement funding for participants) with other state and local, public and private financial and institutional resources. This means that the most successful individual projects could not have been mandated from above, and thus could not be generally prescribed by national legislation or regulations.

The precondition for the successful "packaging" of complex and highly innovative programmes and projects at the local level is, of course, the availability of funds that can be flexibly committed. This was the original intention of CETA with its move towards block grants based upon appropriation formulae. In the meantime, however, YEDPA has reintroduced a much greater degree of categorisation of programmes, and it has also reintroduced a good deal of centralised financial control - especially in the experimental programmes. At the local level, this development is generally deplored, especially when it iş combined with the accelerating rate of legislative and regulatory changes that affect the substance and the formal conditions under which CETA funds are made available.

While we have noticed a good deal of frustration over the apparent return to centralised control at the local level, we have not gained the impression that centralisation has yet become a major obstacle to the achievement of local objectives. As long as the variety of separate programmes remains as large as it is now, and as long as there is a considerable degree of overlap between these programmes, local prime-sponsors are not usually prevented from doing what they really want to do, and they are usually able to finance their preferred activities if not from one source then from another. This is true, for example, in the Entitlement experiment which defines (in order to allow for controlled experiments) strictly limited areas

of geographical coverage. It seems entirely reasonable (though unfortunate from the point of view of experimental design) that prime-
sponsors will concentrate other funds available to them on the
adjacent areas in order to equalise the opportunities, for example,
for summer employment which are available to disadvantaged youngsters
living in disadvantaged neighbourhoods.

From the point of view of central programme responsibility, the
high degree of local flexibility may appear unfortunate. It not only
facilitates the design and execution of highly original programmes
ideally adapted to local conditions, it also allows for a good deal
of local inefficiency and, perhaps, ineffectiveness due to either
incompetence or abuse. We have noted time and again that the CETA
programmes lack stability, are subject to sudden change, are funded
over much too short a period and have great difficulties consequently
in building up either professional expertise or competence among those
responsible for the programmes. One of the difficulties of very
short-term programming is that it puts a premium on the rapid build-
up of complicated systems and it is not therefore surprising that
sometimes maladministration occurs. It is not by any means always
due to the bad intent of those responsible but often to the impossible
conditions that they have to try to meet. Similarly, in the relationship between prime-sponsors and CBOs who are responsible for carrying
out many of the programmes, the prime-sponsors are bound to take into
account their strength at grass roots level, or to put it crudely,
the political clout of a particular CBO. It is not always easy to
alter the pattern and planning of programmes if in consequence an
important CBO is profoundly offended. Indeed over the years the CBOs
have come to expect a certain level of financial support and it is
a bold prime-sponsor who makes major changes at least to the larger
or the more powerful CBOs. Pressed on whether he could alter the
distribution of funds among CBOs, a prominent elected official from
a big industrial city prime-sponsor told us: "You have asked the
right question: that's sheer hell".

On the other hand, it is hard to see how problems of inefficiency
and ineffectiveness could be easily eliminated within the present
structure. The decision to use locally-elected authorities as the
main agents for the implementation of CETA programmes in the early
1970s seems to have been politically motivated and appears now to be
politically irreversible. Even if it were reversible, it would be
hard to develop feasible alternatives at all quickly. The State
Employment Service, which was mainly responsible for the implementation of the Manpower Development and Training Act during the 1960s
has lost almost all its responsibilities for active manpower policy
and much of its personnel. It now seems to lack the organisational
capacity and the political support for reassuming major responsibilities

217

for implementing CETA programmes. Given the continuing responsibility of the Employment Service for manpower information systems and placement services, we consider its present institutional eclipse unfortunate. The continuing functions of the Employment Service clearly deserve to be strengthened and to be much better co-ordinated with the activities of prime-sponsors. We, however, do not foresee the possibility that the Employment Service might actually take control of the major part of CETA activities.

The second alternative to prime-sponsors implementation might be a return to the patterns which prevailed in the anti-poverty programmes of the 1960s: federal grants channelled directly to the local community-based organisation and by-passing the regular institutional structure of state and local governments. Again, the choice of mediating the money flowing into the local CBOs through prime-sponsors in the early 1970s was a political one. Again, it seems unlikely that it could be reversed now. Apart from political reasons, this is also due to the fact that the organisational strength of CBOs seems to vary considerably between different parts of the country and, in particular, between large cities and rural areas. In addition, the recruitment of young people by CBOs appears to be selective, each of them concentrating upon a specific population. Significant groups among those eligible for CETA programmes might not be easily reached through an implementation structure which would be exclusively CBO based. Thus, in the absence of a comprehensive system of federal manpower administration at the local level (which would have its own disadvantages) there is no obvious alternative to prime-sponsor implementation of CETA programmes which we could recommend.

Still, it is conceivable that federal direction and supervision of prime-sponsor activities could be considerably intensified beyond the level of present practice. Any such effort is likely, however, to be confronted with the following dilemma:

- On the one hand, the diversity of local labour market conditions, as well as the diversity of local prime-sponsors and of the infrastructure of local CBOs and other institutions, would frustrate any attempt at imposing nationally uniform patterns of standardised programme design through even more detailed federal regulations. Efforts to tighten the conditions under which CETA funds are made available, even if they were not frustrated by the wide availability of alternative sources of funding, would be likely to be counterproductive. Uniform practice is unlikely to be uniformly "good practice", given the immense variety of local conditions under which CETA programmes operate.

- On the other hand, the staff in the regional offices of the Federal Department of Labor, who are charged with supervising the

programme activities of local prime-sponsors are not systematically
acquainted with a wide variety of local operating conditions. They
are often assigned to the regional office fairly early in their career,
hoping to move upward on the Department of Labor career ladder as soon
as an opportunity presents itself. Therefore, in order to effectively
monitor and evaluate the performance of local prime-sponsors under
their supervision, the present staff of DOL regional offices would
very much depend upon the availability of operational (and, therefore,
standardised) criteria of acceptable practice. The number of federal
representatives is small, only 350, and many do not stay long enough
to become familiar with what are complex programmes. At the prime-
sponsor level, monitoring of programmes conducted by CBOs or other
non-profit agencies is rarely conducted by experienced, qualified
people. In short, CETA lacks a permanent core of professional evaluators, monitors and technical advisers.

The dilemma could be avoided if it were possible to define standard criteria of performance instead of standard criteria of practice.
However, even if this were to be possible in principle, we are not
aware of available models which measure the relative successes of manpower agencies tackling labour market problems of different quality
and different orders of magnitude, and drawing upon financial and
institutional resources which differ so widely. Thus, we would not
base our recommendations upon the hope that a system of "objective"
indicators of performance could be devised for the evaluation of prime-
sponsor activities within the near future. Indeed, as we have already
pointed out in Chapter I, efforts to evaluate programmes by purely
quantitative criteria may be self-defeating; such obvious measure-
ments as the number of placements and of successful terminations cover
a wide range of definitions which cannot be distinguished quantitatively
and in which the real value of programmes may be concealed. Instead,
we would place more hope upon the qualitative judgement of a corps of
professional permanent evaluators modelled after the British School
Inspectorate.(1) Such a corps of inspectors would not have to be
very large in order to be effective. But it would have to offer
career opportunities within the organisation itself, and it would have
to provide for the systematic rotation of its members among the various
labour market areas of the country. Such a group of professional
examiners, with provision for the easy communication of experiences
and of professional standards among its members and with opportunity
to promote good practice, might provide a system of federal control
which allows as much as possible for local diversity while still being
able to distinguish "good practice" from inefficiency or downright ineffectiveness. The effectiveness of such an Inspectorate would, in

1) Known as Her Majesty's Inspectorate of Schools, HMIs are independent of the Department of Education and Science and directly accountable to the Secretary of State.

the end, depend upon the willingness and the ability of the national political leadership to back up its professional judgement with effective sanctions, even in those cases where the criticised actions of local prime-sponsors had considerable political support.

We realise that this recommendation would imply major changes in the present pattern of national-local relations within CETA. We are convinced, however, that the actual political and programme costs of our recommendations would be lower than are the costs of responding to allegations of local abuse or mismanagement with very frequent changes in the enabling legislation and in the substance of federal regulations. What local prime-sponsors need most is a degree of continuity in CETA programmes, as well as a degree of effective supervision by critical but competent federal officers who are willing to consider the variety of local conditions and opportunities as well as the imperatives of federal programme goals.

Even with the wide margin for discretionary activities available to prime-sponsors under CETA, we think we have noticed some tendencies towards programme routinisation and even rigidity at the local level. In some jurisdictions, at least, prime-sponsors are under considerable pressure to provide a steady and predictable flow of funds to the several CBOs, educational institutions and other organisations operating CETA programmes. Given the need to recruit, train and maintain qualified staffs, the need to develop effective communications networks with potential employers and with client groups, and the requirement of capital investments, the tendency of frontline organisations towards greater routinisation and stability cannot be criticised. It may even be necessary for successful programme performance. But the routine of established programmes at the local level has a tendency to limit the responsiveness of CETA to new developments in the labour market and to new opportunities of dealing with labour market problems. This is true in principle.

On the sites which we have visited, however, we have found the actual consequences of this dilemma mitigated by the coexistence of decentralised CETA programmes within the responsibility of prime-sponsors with experimental projects which are managed directly from the national headquarters (and their various agents among the multitude of commercial and private non-profit companies). At first we felt that the coexistence of both decentralised and centrally managed parts of the CETA programme only added to the overall confusion which seemed to prevail in United States manpower policy. Upon reflection, however, we now tend to regard centrally managed experimental programmes as an essential corrective for the risks inherent in any nationally funded, but locally administered and loosely controlled manpower programme. The availability of uncommitted funds which can be obtained only upon specific application provides incentives for local initiatives and creativity which might quickly be lost under an entirely decentralised management system. If applied properly, we feel that the availability of discretionary funds for experimental projects is an essential antidote to the dangers of routinisation and rigidity inherent in a CETA programme which is locally administered but centrally accountable.

The full benefits of the experimental programme, however, can be obtained only if the impressive present emphasis upon systematic experimental design and upon professional-quality project evaluation can be maintained. Only if there is reliable knowledge of what works and what does not work can one consider discretionary funds to have been well spent. Only if this knowledge is systematically and widely disseminated can one expect that all jurisdictions will be confronted with information about successful alternative approaches to youth unemployment which may challenge their present routines. In consequence, we would strongly urge upon United States policy-makers that the essential features of the experimental approach should be maintained until the final evaluation and research can be completed; and that in any event, funds for experimentation and demonstration should be continued in the future as an element of CETA programming.

As a final point, we should like to remark upon a problem which necessarily seems to result from the overall pattern of manpower policies in the United States. The immense variety of programmes with varying eligibility criteria, administrative procedures, and organisational responsibility seems to have contributed to the overall creativity of problem-solving in the United States. But, by the same token, these features also contribute to a large degree of bewilderment, confusion and ignorance on the part of those disadvantaged groups who are supposed to benefit from CETA programmes. To a lesser, but important extent we believe that this confusion also exists among community-based organisations at the local level. This is particularly so if they do not have direct political links with "City Hall" or are not part of a politically powerful and professionally sophisticated national organisation. In short, we believe that CETA programmes have considerable difficulties in reaching their intended target populations and in mobilising the services of intermediary organisations which may be close to those target populations.

We are encouraged by the fact that many of the people we have talked to are aware of the problems of "outreach" and "intake" which arise with CETA programmes. In many cases, however, we feel that their almost exclusive reliance upon the outreach capacities of local CBOs is slightly over-optimistic. We should like to see a very careful analysis of the patterns of selection made by differing local intake facilities, and of the effectiveness of central intake, consultation and placement facilities for unemployed youth of the kind which seem to be provided, for instance, in Baltimore. Certainly, the best-designed programmes will be ineffective if they do not develop effective services for reaching, informing, motivating, recruiting and counselling members of their target populations among the disadvantaged, under-educated, uninformed and disaffected. At the very least, information should be available in schools, community colleges, public libraries and other public institutions about youth employment programmes, so that young people will have some idea of what is available and where to go, even if they have no personal connection with a CBO.

VI

RELATIONSHIPS BETWEEN EMPLOYMENT, EDUCATION AND
WELFARE PROGRAMMES

In Chapter I we argued that the role of the education system is
a crucial one in any assessment of what can be done about unemployment among young people. It is difficult for those without skills or
qualifications to get jobs. It is almost impossible for those who
lack even the basic educational requirements of literacy and numeracy.
And changes in the pattern of the United States labour market compound
that difficulty; there is a decline in job opportunities in agriculture and manufacturing, where lack of the basic educational skills was
less of a handicap than it is in the fast-growing service and professional sectors. Employees in these sectors are likely to have to
deal with members of the public; so not only literacy and numeracy,
but acceptable behaviour, appearance and manner become essential for
successful employment.

Taking our three approaches to the problem of youth unemployment
in the United States, demand deficiency, transitional unemployment and
structural unemployment, we do not need to further consider here the
impact of the education system on the first. But both with regard to
transitional unemployment and to structural unemployment, the role of
the education system is significant.

Before we consider the interaction of educational and CETA programmes in these two respects, however, we should make a few prelimi-
nary remarks on the somewhat strained relationships that have undoubtedly existed both at national and local levels between the education system and those responsible for employment policy. There are
aspects of CETA legislation that the schools dislike, such as the
divisive effects of targeting youth programmes on boys and girls from
families with low incomes, and the pressure for sometimes meagre
"training" courses to be given academic credit. Nor was the strain
eased by the failure of those responsible for the YEDPA legislation,
both in the administration and elsewhere, to consult educational
interests, despite their intimate involvement in the Youth Incentive
Entitlement Pilot Projects (YIEPP) and Youth Employment and Training
Programmes (YETP). Co-operation at the administrative level is made
more complex because of the difference in the financial years of the

223

two systems; schools work either on the basis of a calendar year, or of a July/June academic year, CETA programmes on the basis of the fiscal year (October/September). But the passage of the "Javits amendment" to the YEDPA Act of 1977, under which 22 per cent of the money appropriated for the YETP programme (some $500 million in Fiscal Year 1979-80) must be spent in accordance with agreements reached between prime-sponsors and the education authorities, has given a real and valuable incentive to closer co-operation. There are now numerous instances of co-operation between state and local school boards on the one hand, and prime-sponsors or CBOs on the other. There are also still localities where there is little communication or goodwill between the two sides.

Turning first to the problems of the transition from school to work, and the unemployment often associated with this period in a young person's life, we believe that the links between the schools and the world of work could be much improved. The United States has a great asset in its tradition of school pupils and college students working part time, in vacations but also often throughout the year. Working your way through college or university has been and remains an honourable and accepted means of financing the cost of a higher education. Familiarity with work, including manual and clerical work, among boys and girls from a very wide range of backgrounds, including these destined to go on to professional, executive and academic careers, creates an atmosphere of easy mobility between education and industry which many European countries might envy. Ivory towers in the United States are not so hermetically sealed as they are in many European academic circles.

But this major asset has not been exploited as fully as it might be because of a notable lack of links between the school system and the local business community. Even at the federal level, the recently established Joint Interagency Policy Panel, set up to bring together departments concerned with education and welfare and with employment and manpower, has met only twice in the first six months of its existence. Whether informal and personal links between HEW, DOL and the other departments compensate for this somewhat sketchy formal structure we of course do not know.

Similarly at local level, links could be improved. We understand that state education authorities are represented on some, but by no means all the planning councils set up by prime-sponsors to oversee youth employment programmes. Every possible step should be taken by DOL's regional offices to encourage prime-sponsors to invite such representation. Similarly, state or where appropriate, local school boards should be represented on the Private Industry Councils being established under Title VII of CETA.

It would be helpful if school boards were in turn to have rep-resentation from local industry and labour unions. Where these boards are appointed by the mayor, he or she can easily appoint such people after consultation with the appropriate local organisations. Where, as more often occurs, the board is elected, the possibility of co-opting one or more people from industry might be explored.

We were impressed by a local example of co-operation between schools and industry, the "Adopt-a-School" project in Baltimore, under which young executives from a local firm spent half a day each week with high school ninth and tenth graders, talking to them about work and careers. The scheme extended to the offer of three hours' work a week for four weeks, so that pupils could get some work experience. Obviously such a scheme could include work visits and observations, and participation by those from industry in careers study. Such schemes can also be usefully extended to teachers, many of whom are unfamiliar with the world of industry and commerce, and who might welcome opportunities for work observation or even short periods of secondment. In Britain, there is a useful project for seconding science and mathematics teachers to a major technology-based firm (ICI in Teeside) to enable them to see and work on the latest developments in the field.

We would agree with our OECD colleagues who recently completed a report on compensatory education in the United States (1) that a more structured approach to careers teaching and career-tasting might ease the transition from school or college to work. We understand that the Employment Service was building co-operation in this field with the schools in the early 1960s, but that a change of policy brought this initiative to an end. We feel that the Employment Service, which has some 2,400 local offices, could make a useful contribution to careers education in co-operation with the schools, though the steady decline in its funding in constant terms, and the ceiling on staffing, would need to be reconsidered if it were called upon to undertake this task. Meanwhile, within the schools, we learned that over 9,000 school districts now have careers preparation of some kind. Our own experience in Western Europe would lead us to suggest that it is important to timetable careers lessons from eighth or ninth grade on, and to specify a teacher or teachers as having a responsibility for the subject in each school.

Careers lessons should include job preparation, and what is sometimes called, unfortunately, "socialisation". We understand this to mean assisting young people to get jobs by showing them how to conduct themselves in an interview, how to write a letter of application for a job, and the kind of clothes, manners and behaviour that will appeal to a potential employer. This kind of preparation can be essential for a boy or girl whose own background provides no knowledge or awareness of what may be expected from them.

1) OECD, Reviews of National Policies for Education - United States: Federal Policies for Education for the Disadvantaged, Paris, 1981.

Ideally, careers teaching should be linked to work experience and where appropriate to vocational education in the broad areas of the pupil's own interests. A clear interconnection between educational attainment, work experience and an intended career or permanent job can do much to motivate restless and dissatisfied youngsters who may otherwise drop out of school.

We have noted that there has been a substantial expansion of vocational education in the United States in the past ten years, with the number of students doubling between 1970 and 1978, to a figure of over 16 million, over 11 million being in schools. Vocational education, which is federally funded only to the extent of about 8 per cent, was for a long time the orphan sister of the education system, regarded as at best second rate. But there has been notable progress in some districts, and vocational education has a good track record when it comes to young people who complete their vocational courses getting jobs; we were told that over 85 per cent succeed in getting employment, mainly in a related field. Vocational education has played an important part in the CETA programmes, especially in the YETP and YIEPP programmes, and vocational schools, both in the public and private sectors, have offered training, work experience and vocational counselling to CETA participants.

The term vocational education does of course cover a very wide range of courses. Over a quarter of all vocational courses are in home economics and another quarter are in the clerical field. So the term, like the numbers involved, can be misleading to those unfamiliar with the field. In many European countries, domestic science and commercial studies are part of the normal school syllabus, compulsory or optional, and would not be separately characterised as vocational education. We suspect also that the quality of vocational education varies very widely indeed, from genuine well-based pre-apprenticeship courses to an afternoon's typing in a school classroom. Once again, the quantitative measure can hide as much as illuminate. We have some reservations, too, about so much of the training element in the CETA programmes being based within schools. Quite apart from the limitations on the necessary equipment and machinery imposed by school finances, the atmosphere of a school is very different from that of an office or a factory. We believe that training courses if based on school should wherever possible include an element of work experience outside the school.

The Structural Problem

A good deal of what we have already said in this chapter is relevant to the structural unemployment problem among young people as well as to the transitional problem. But there are specially intractable employment problems for those who are poor, whose environments may be culturally deprived, who may live in an atmosphere of despair, and who may lack the emotional support that only a mature parent or parent-substitute can give.

We were told over and over again of young people, some with high school diplomas, who were unable to read, write or calculate, or who could do so at only the most primitive level. One employer in Maryland told us that, of the 17-week training course he was operating, 16 weeks had to be given up to remedial education in the three Rs. Obviously many CETA programmes are inevitably involved in remedial education and in encouraging boys and girls to complete their education. The mainspring of the YEDPA legislation and in particular of the YIEPP programme, is here. Obviously it would be better if remedial education could be undertaken in the schools and not through CETA programmes in the later teen years. But we encountered a good deal of scepticism about the possibility of improving the effectiveness and the standard of achievement in the public schools, especially in the inner cities.

It is not our task to comment on the United States education system. We did, however, read with interest and with sympathy the conclusions of our OECD colleagues in their recent examination of compensatory education in the United States.(1) They congratulated the United States government and preceding administrations on the colossal efforts made to compensate disadvantaged children educationally, and to create more equal educational opportunities. They pointed out that the wide variations in the level of resources made available as between different states and different school districts made this latter task almost impossible of achievement. They were impressed by the various federal programmes, such as Head Start, but pointed out that the episodic nature of United States compensatory education programmes, concentrated as they are on the earliest two or three grades and then reappearing in the senior grades of high school, meant that often early gains made by children were simply lost in the succeeding years. Targeting on individual children could mean, they said, that when a child achieved a fairly minimal level of educational competence, it was withdrawn from the compensatory programme. The same can be true for an individual school, and hence there are certain obvious penalties against those who succeed, often against the odds, in achieving a reasonable educational standard. We share their view that it might be better to target on school districts, and to sustain the help to such districts or to individual schools over several years. Schools and school districts need a certain amount of flexibility in the way they spend this extra money. We would commend the suggestion for targeted programmes, whether CETA

1) Reviews of National Policies for Education. United States: Federal Policies for Education for the Disadvantaged, op.cit.

programmes or compensatory education programmes, that there is much to be said for "thickening up", i.e. the gradual concentration of more teaching time, more equipment, more resources for counselling and other supportive services for disadvantaged young people instead of a sharp delineation between those within and those outside programmes, which can easily become divisive and even painful. Children and young people do not like to be singled out as "poor" or even the euphemism for poor, "disadvantaged". A good school or college will try to avoid making, let alone emphasizing, such distinctions. The funds provided under YETP for experimental programmes involving young people above the normal qualifying income limits for the programme is an encouraging move towards greater flexibility.

Turning to the youth employment programmes, we have already expressed some concern (in Chapters I and V) about relying so heavily under YIEPP and YETP on young people returning to school. It is true that there has been a remarkable and encouraging improvement in high school enrolment among minorities, and especially among the black minority. In October 1977, 88.7 per cent of black male 17-year-olds were still in school, as were 84.5 per cent of black female 17-year-olds. At 18, the figures were 62.0 for men and 58.5 per cent for women. Figures for white youngsters in the same year were 84.6 per cent for 17-year-old males, and 82.5 per cent for females; and for 18-year-olds, 54.2 per cent and 50.1 per cent respectively. It remains true that fewer minority youngsters complete four years of high school, and fewer graduate than is the case among whites, but the trend is encouraging and the motive to learn is obviously strong. Ten years ago the proportion of older black teenagers enrolled in school was considerably lower than for whites.

Nevertheless, we doubt whether the school atmosphere is the best one for young men and women who feel themselves to be adults, or who may even have dropped out. We note that only 6 per cent of the estimated school dropouts have returned under YIEPP, despite the attractions of the federal minimum wage for the part-time job they will be guaranteed until they complete high school. Admittedly most states now have alternative schools, which satisfy the programmes of eligibility criteria providing the student gets permission to attend. Alternative schools have grown fast in recent years; we understand that in Mississippi there were none until the YEDPA programmes became available, and then they sprang up almost overnight.

Many alternative schools are new and experimental, and some may find it difficult to survive in the harsh financial climate at state and local level, where measures to compel balanced budgets or reduce property taxes have a particularly severe effect on education. It might be wise to explore further possibilities: for instance, entitlement programmes might be based on attendance at vocational

centres or community colleges (for those over 18) as well as in school.
Furthermore, there need be no reason then why a young person should
lose his entitlement as soon as he left school. Among the good YIEPP
programmes we saw were those combining education and work experience
in a regular pattern, e.g. two weeks at work, two weeks at an alternative school in Baltimore, over a 16- to 18-week cycle; one week at
an alternative school in Boston with a special emphasis on energy and
one week in an energy-related job, for a total period of six months;
and a similar community college based scheme for four weeks' work, one
week college in California that we did not see but were told about.
It might also be worth experimenting with work-based traineeships and
pre-apprenticeship schemes end-on with leaving high school. We have
outlined these schemes in Chapter VI; the educational element can be
conducted in a community college or a vocational training centre.
Many older young people might find such a framework more acceptable,
and this might encourage them to add to their qualifications.

On the question of granting educational credit, we wonder if the
Office of Education might be able to take the initiative by indicating
a range of course content and an appropriate level of achievement for
the granting of credit. We recognise that it is for state boards to
decide, but the federal government might be able to influence state
and local school boards in finding an appropriate balance between
maintaining educational standards and yet genuinely encouraging young
people to learn and to train. The corps of CETA professional evaluators we have proposed in Chapter V could help in establishing that
reasonable standards were being attained, and perhaps some staff from
the education division of HEW might be seconded to work with them.
Joint monitoring of educational and training courses at local level
between school boards and prime-sponsors would also be very valuable.

There is one aspect at least of CETA programmes - and for that
matter of education programmes also - that involves the co-operation
of the welfare departments. We are informed that many teenage girls
are already themselves mothers before they complete their high school;
in Washington DC the statistic we were given was that 35 per cent of
girls under the age of 19 were mothers, many of them unmarried. It
is clearly important to help these girls to complete their education,
so that the cycle of deprivation will not continue or even worsen.
We think that girls at school or on CETA programmes should be given
some priority for day care for their children. Often family or
neighbourhood arrangements break down, with disastrous effects where
a course, quite properly, has attendance and educational competency
requirements. We would like to see much closer co-operation between
CETA prime-sponsors and CETA contractors with local welfare offices,
so that reasonable provision can be made.

Some of us were able to see several Work Incentive Projects (WIN),
training mothers on welfare and displaced homemakers for work. We

were impressed by the way in which women were being trained for such traditionally male occupations as truck driving. We can see the advantages of giving women on welfare the means to achieve economic independence and self-respect, and thereby the opportunity to come off the welfare rolls. But we do have reservations about the requirement that mothers of children still in elementary school must register for work. We recognise of course that in some welfare offices a requirement to register is certainly not seen as synonymous with a requirement to work. But given the inadequate, indeed sometimes non-existent, provision for after-school or vacation care for young children, and the absence of extended school days for children whose parent(s) is(are) at work, obliging mothers of young children to return to work may simply add another turn to the cycle of deprivation. And, of course, young mothers made to return to work compete directly with disadvantaged young people often in the same depressed labour market. We believe that training or remedial education on a part-time basis might be a valuable alternative to full-time work for these mothers; at least the choice should be for them to make.

In concluding this chapter on the interrelations between employment, education and welfare programmes, we cannot pretend that the problem of structural youth unemployment is one of poverty, inadequate education and a deprived background alone. The factor of race - and in particular what one distinguished American academic called "the pathology of the black male" - is inescapable. All things being equal - and they rarely are - it will be harder for a black young man to get a job than for a white young man. We admire and applaud the brave and imaginative efforts many Americans, black, white and of other colours too, have made to destroy the scourge of racism. Few countries have tackled racism with so much determination and with so little hypocrisy. What we have proposed in this report might, we hope, narrow a little further the gap between employment opportunities for the young in comparison with the rest of the community, and for the young black people in particular. Many of their disadvantages are economic and environmental. But not all. And it is beyond the scope of this report to recommend how to eradicate the prejudice and hatred that still lurks in the human psyche.

VII

Prime-sponsors should be encouraged to develop an economic outlook as well as a social and educational one when developing and operating programmes.

Emphasis should be placed on developing manpower policies in the context of regional policies for those regions and localities which are economically distressed.

The rules on the duration of employment and allowable salaries on Public Service Employment programmes should remain as flexible as possible in order to allow complex programme packages to be operated effectively.

Consideration should be given to the expansion of the apprenticeship, traineeship and retraining programmes in order to enlarge the supply of skilled labour in those sectors of the economy which are likely to grow in the near future.

If it is necessary to provide income support for youth participating in remedial programmes, educational and maintenance allowances rather than wages should be considered.

Consideration should be given to enabling non-governmental intermediary agencies to simplify the bureaucratic requirements of private sector involvement in government programmes.

There should be a careful comparative analysis of the cost-effectiveness of the great variety of approaches to remedial education within CETA programmes.

It should be recognised that the crucial element in success for subsidised employment is not so much the availability and the amount of subsidies as the effectiveness of outreach services to recruit disadvantaged young people and the availability of job development and counselling services to motivate employers to offer employment to the disadvantaged.

The continuing manpower functions of the Employment Services should be strengthened and better co-ordinated with the activities of prime-sponsors.

A corps of professional evaluators of good practice should be established.

Whilst the present institutional structure of CETA programmes should remain, centrally-managed experimental programmes are essential correctives for the risks inherent in any locally administered and locally controlled manpower programme.

There should be a careful analysis of the patterns of selection of differing local intake facilities, and of the effectiveness of central intake, consultation and placement facilities for unemployed youth.

Special attention should be paid to a concentration on programmes which rely on alternative school settings, work-based programmes and community colleges for over-18s, rather than, for example, the Youth Entitlement insistence on school enrolment.

DOL regional offices should strongly encourage prime-sponsors to include state education authorities on planning councils.

State, and where appropriate, local education agencies should be represented on Private Industry Councils.

School boards should include representation from local industry and labour unions.

Local firms should be encouraged to arrange for young executives to spend regular periods in high schools, and this should be co-ordinated with work experience for pupils. Similar steps should be taken to encourage teachers to become familiar with the world of industry and commerce.

A more structured approach to careers teaching and "career tasting" is required. The Employment Service could play a useful role, given the resources. Wherever possible, careers teaching should be linked to work experience and vocational education.

Targeting of compensatory and CETA programmes on individual children should be replaced by targeting on school districts and individual schools.

The Office of Education should consider indicating a range of course content and an appropriate level of achievement for the granting of credit. Professional evaluators could play a useful role.

Joint monitoring of education and training courses at local level between school boards and prime-sponsors would be valuable.

There should be closer co-operation between CETA prime-sponsors and CETA contractors with local welfare services.

Young mothers at school or on CETA programmes should have some priority for day-care facilities.

We doubt the wisdom of the requirement in the WIN programme that mothers of young children in elementary school must register for work. Training or remedial education on a part-time basis might be a valuable alternative to full-time work.

Annex I

THE COMPREHENSIVE EMPLOYMENT AND TRAINING ACT

The Comprehensive Employment and Training Act, as enacted in 1973, authorised four major programme efforts:

1) A nationwide programme of local services, including training, employment, counselling, and testing (Title I);
2) A programme of transitional public service employment and other services in areas with a 6.5 per cent or higher unemployment rate for three consecutive months (Title II);
3) Nationally sponsored and supervised training, employment, and job placement programmes for special groups with particular labour market disadvantages (Title III); and
4) The Job Corps, a programme of intensive education, training and counselling for disadvantaged youth, primarily in a residential setting, previously funded under the Economic Opportunity Act of 1964 (Title IV).

In addition, Title V of CETA established a National Commission for Manpower Policy, an advisory group with responsibility for examining the nation's manpower needs and goals.

Title VI, a countercyclical programme of public service employment, was authorised by the Emergency Jobs and Unemployment Assistance Act of 1974 and continued under the Emergency Jobs Programme Extension Act of 1976. A Young Adult Conservation Corps (Title VIII) was added to the array of CETA services by the Youth Employment and Demonstration Projects Act of 1977, which authorised three other demonstration programmes for youth now included under Title IV.

Originally enacted for a four-year period in 1973 and extended for an additional year in 1977, CETA was reauthorised on 27 October 1978 by Public Law 95-524. The major features of the reauthorisation are as follows:

Title I, Administrative Provisions, contains the general provisions governing the Act, including the designation of state and local prime-sponsors to administer the programme, the planning and plan approval process, and special responsibilities of the Governor and state and local advisory councils. The Title also establishes an Office of Management Assistance to provide support to prime-sponsors and contains strengthened provisions relating to programme audits and investigation and compliance activities. In addition, it contains time limitations for participation in programmes authorised by the Act, as well as new provisions for public service employment wages.

Title II, Comprehensive Employment and Training Services, combines the comprehensive manpower services previously authorised under Title I and the public employment programmes previously authorised under Title II. Allowable programme activities include training, work experience, upgrading, retraining, education, and other services (Parts A, B and C) and counterstructural public service employment (Part D) needed to enable participants to obtain unsubsidized employment. Participants enrolled in training programmes and services (except upgrading and retraining) must be economically disadvantaged and either unemployed, underemployed, or in school. Participants in public service employment must be on welfare or economically disadvantaged and unemployed 15 or more weeks.

Title III, Special Federal Responsibilities, authorises the Secretary of Labor to provide services to segments of the population which experience particular disadvantages in the labour market. Added to the original list of persons with such disadvantages are women, single parents, displaced homemakers, individuals who lack educational credentials, and public assistance recipients.

The title continues authorisation of programmes of research, training and technical assistance, evaluation, labour market information, and computerised job placement. In addition, it authorises welfare demonstration projects, projects for middle-aged and older workers, and a programme for the co-ordination and partnership between prime-sponsors and state employment security agencies. Voucher demonstration projects are also mandated.

Title IV, Youth Programs, provides for particular youth programmes, including those enacted in the Youth Employment and Demonstration Projects Act of 1977 (except for the Young Adult Conservation Corps, which is still in Title VIII), Job Corps, and the Summer Youth Programme.

Title V, National Commission for Employment Policy, renames and reconstitutes the National Commission for Manpower Policy, with Cabinet participation reduced and increased independence from the Department of Labour provided for.

Title VI, Countercyclical Public Service Employment Program, provides for a countercyclical public service employment programme, authorising the funding of sufficient jobs to employ 20 per cent of the number unemployed in excess of a 4 per cent rate of unemployment. Jobs are authorised for 25 per cent of the number of unemployed in excess of a 4 per cent rate of unemployment when national unemployment is 7 per cent or higher. Half of the funds may be used only for the employment of persons in projects of limited duration, and all persons not working in projects must be employed at entry-level positions.

Title VII, Private Sector Opportunities for the Economically-Disadvantaged, provides for a demonstration programme to test the effectiveness of a variety of approaches to increase the involvement of the business community in employment and training activities supported under the Act and to increase the private sector employment opportunities for economically disadvantaged persons. The title provides funds to prime-sponsors for the establishment of private industry councils, a majority of whose members shall be from the business community. The councils will participate with the prime-sponsor in the development of private sector opportunities for economically disadvantaged persons.

Annex II

THE YEDPA PROGRAMMES

The Young Adult Conservation Corps (YACC)

This is a fairly small, three-year programme providing around 25,000 openings for unemployed young people (aged 16-23) to get "work experience" through job-creation-type work on conservation and other similar projects. Enrollees normally receive the federal minimum wage, and preference is given to youth in high unemployment areas. Only limited training is given - the main emphasis being on supervised work experience. YACC is operated under a tripartite agreement between three Federal Government Departments: Labor, Agriculture and Interior. A limited number of projects are residential.

The Youth Employment and Training Programs (YETP)

The programmes should provide around 150,000 openings mainly through giving practical experience of a job in a supervised work setting. The objective is to enhance the job prospects and career preparation of low-income youth (aged 14-21) who have the severest problems in entering the labour market. Emphasis is also placed on improving the quality of jobs, counselling, and placement services and co-ordinating these services both in school and out of school. About one-quarter of funds must go to projects for young people still at school. This is the largest and most wide-ranging of the YEDPA pro-grammes: it aims to improve the quality and co-ordination of ser-vices - through annual plans, "prime-sponsor planning councils", and the involvement of youth councils, labour organisations and community groups and close liaison (for related training and education) with education agencies and institutions.

The Youth Community Conservation and Improvement Projects (YCIPP)

Designed to develop the vocational potential of unemployed young people (aged 16-19) by providing work in well-supervised community improvement projects. The emphasis is on producing tangible results of community benefit. Projects are planned and organised by community-based organisations. Participants work under skilled supervisors, with no more than 12 young people assigned to each supervisor.

237

Participants can remain in a programme for twelve months and where appropriate can earn academic credit for their work. The capacity of this programme is around 22,000. 75 per cent of the total funds available is allocated among the states, based on the number of unemployed. The states have then to allocate the funds to prime-sponsor units in the same way. Sponsors of the schemes may use up to 5 per cent of their funds for administration, and of the remaining 95 per cent, 65 per cent must be used for wages for participants, 10 per cent for project administration and the rest for materials, supervisors' wages, etc.

The Youth Incentive Entitlement Pilot Projects (YIEPP)

The object is to get information about ways in which high school age youth from poor backgrounds can be provided with opportunities to earn and learn that will encourage them to return or stay in school. This is being attempted by seeing if part-time jobs during the school year or summer full-time jobs can be feasibly guaranteed for 16-19-year-olds. Because of the high costs of the experiments, only a limited number of demonstrations are being undertaken, totalling around 20,000 jobs.

The Job Corps

The object of the Job Corps is to take young people between 14-21 years of age from economically disadvantaged families who require additional education and training and intensive counselling for a (mainly) residential course lasting up to two years. This highly intensive programme working with the highly disadvantaged currently serves over 30,000 young people and is planned to expand to 44,000 places. The programme is administered on a contract basis which allows private companies to bid in order to run a Job Corps Center. The majority of Job Corps Centers are run by private companies. The average cost per place is $15,000 per year.

The Summer Youth Program

The Summer Jobs Program provides summer work, mainly for youth, from economically disadvantaged households, at the federal minimum wage of $2.90 per hour. The programme provided summer-time employment for 943,972 young people in 1979. It is mainly focused on 14-19-year-olds, with 93.5 per cent of enrollees coming from economically disadvantaged families.

Part Five

PROCEEDINGS OF THE MEETING ON YOUTH EMPLOYMENT POLICIES
IN DENMARK, GERMANY AND THE UNITED STATES

Paris, 4-5 December 1980

On behalf of the OECD, <u>M. Paul Lermerle</u>, Deputy Secretary-General, opened the meeting. He stressed the importance attached by the OECD to the problem of youth unemployment and in particular its composition, falling so heavily on certain disadvantaged groups within the youth population. He said the OECD regarded high youth unemployment as posing a potential threat to the nature of democratic industrial societies. It was therefore particularly important that this meeting should be taking place, and on behalf of the Organisation he thanked the participating countries and the examiners, under the chairmanship of Mrs. Shirley Williams, for the work they had put into this exercise. He invited Mr. Gene Fitzgerald, the Irish Minister of Labour and the Public Service, to accept the role of President for the duration of the proceedings.

On behalf of the Secretariat, <u>Mr. James R. Gass</u>, Director for Social Affairs, Manpower and Education, drew attention to the sombre outlook for youth unemployment over the next two years. The most recent Secretariat forecasts pointed to a youth unemployment rate in the OECD area as a whole of almost 16 per cent by mid-1982. Explaining the selection of the three countries which had participated in this first series of examinations, he instanced the remarkable system of vocational education and training which existed in Germany and parallel to this the consistently strong performance of the German economy. The relationship between the two would clearly be important to consider. In regard to the United States, he underlined the importance of the net employment growth which had occurred in recent years and the favourable effect this had had on youth employment rates. There remained, however, something of a paradox in that youth had not benefited as much as might have been hoped from the many millions of additional jobs which had been created. Turning to Denmark, he laid stress on the extent and importance of its highly developed welfare state and on the positive influence of social policies on youth unemployment. Further, the many imaginative and creative measures to tackle labour market segmentation as it affected young females in Denmark warranted a wider international discussion.

On behalf of the examiners, <u>Mrs. Shirley Williams</u>, former Secretary of State for Education and Science in the United Kingdom, emphasized that the problem of youth unemployment was not only individually and socially painful but also carried with it substantial political dangers. In the three countries that had been reviewed the examiners found that questions of attitude were often as important as questions of resources. It was essential to encourage governments, employers,

trade unions and education authorities to take a fresh look at and
adopt fresh approaches to youth unemployment.

She underlined one problem which the examiners had consistently
encountered - the nature of the double disadvantage facing some young
people: the educationally disadvantaged, ethnic minorities and certain groups of young women. Understanding their problems was as
important as understanding the reasons which led to disproportionate
levels of unemployment experienced by young people. Mrs. Williams
then introduced her fellow examiners;(1) Monsieur Jacques Legendre,
Secrétaire d'Etat à la Formation professionnelle, France; Mr. Sar
Levitan, Director of the Center for Social Policies Studies, Washington,
D.C., United States; Professor Robert Leroy, Professor of Economics
at the Catholic University of Louvain, Belgium; Professor Fritz
Scharpf, Director, International Institute of Management, Wissenschaftszentrum, Berlin.

The format of the meeting was as follows. The reviews were focused around three general themes: 1) the transition from school to
work: the links between education and training; 2) youth's disproportionate share of unemployment and 3) the special social and
economic problems of young women, ethnic minorities and second generation migrants. Under each theme one specific question was addressed
by the examiners to each of the reviewed countries. After a brief
reply by the countries concerned, there was a plenary discussion on
each of the three themes.

---

1) Two of the examiners - Mr. Allan Larsson and the Hon. Robert
   Andras, P.C. - were unable to be present at the meeting.

Theme I

THE TRANSITION FROM SCHOOL TO WORK:
THE LINKS BETWEEN EDUCATION AND TRAINING

Mr. Legendre introduced the first questions to the German authorities: "How far is the dual system of training a transition rather than a training system for skilled workers? Is this the most effective approach to the transition and the reduction of youth unemployment?"

The leader of the German Delegation, Mr. Buschfort, Parliamentary Secretary of State, Federal Ministry of Labour and Social Affairs, stressed that the German dual system is primarily a training system which gradually introduces young people to the world of work. The system also has other advantages since it involves practical training in the workplace and the involvement of young people in the responsibilities of the enterprise.

These aspects of young people's development are less provided for in school-based vocational education. The dual system provides young people with a favourable environment for making the transition into regular employment and gives them the chance to participate in, and succeed at, real jobs. This was important in encouraging a positive attitude towards skilled employment.

Nevertheless, the practical element as such did not determine the nature of education and training in the dual system, the principal features of which are:

- a well-defined training content for recognised occupations;
- systematic education and training based on compulsory curricula;
- emphasis on the relevance of practical issues and of recent technical developments;
- the acquisition and application of cognitive and practical occupational abilities.

The dual system was therefore more than just an efficient method to organise the transition from school to work. However, its success did not imply that improvements were not possible or necessary. The following strategies were applied in order to maintain and improve the quality of the system:

- permanent updating of training regulations;
- upgrading of training personnel;
- extension of training facilities for smaller enterprises through inter-enterprise training centres;

- development of broad initial programmes at the beginning
  of the training period, for instance during the "basic
  vocational education year";
- improvement of the co-ordination between training in
  schools and training in the enterprise.

The federal government rejected the idea of shortening the duration of training for recognised occupations. There would be no
short-cycle training programmes which would produce semi-skilled
workers, even if that might temporarily help to reduce the size of
youth unemployment. Each training programme had to ensure a genuine
qualification which would not only enable the trainee to take up a
qualified skilled job but also provide a solid basis for further education and training in the future.

Mrs. Williams asked two supplementary questions: "Will the
introduction of a tenth school year, which was now under way in
Germany, reduce the length of apprenticeship training?"; "Were the
German authorities not concerned with the fact that enterprise training might be too firm-specific and insufficiently broad?"

Mrs. Williams then introduced the second question to the Danish
authorities: "Is there a need to bring together provisions for the
16-19-year-old age group into a combined system and what part could
a youth guarantee play in this process?"

Mr. Westergaard, Director-General, Directorate of Labour who
led the Danish Delegation on the morning of the first day, saw the
question as central to the debate then taking place in Denmark. The
debate has focused on the general objectives behind the education and
labour market policy measures directed at unemployed young people and
young employed persons with no vocational training.

Danish educationalists argued that such young people should, as
far as possible, be directed towards some form of education. The
main objectives would therefore be to develop sufficient educational
facilities, to improve the vocational guidance given to young people
and to adjust the curricula of various educational courses to the
needs of the young persons concerned. The different forms of financial assistance and temporary places offered to young people in the
context of various labour market measures would need to be adjusted
to favour these objectives.

Labour market interests had gradually accepted that the main
objective ought to be to integrate 16-19-year-olds into the education
system. However, the labour market sector was unwilling to cut back
on the offers given to this age group within the framework of labour
market measures until the education system could make new "realistic"
offers to young persons who are tired of the traditional forms of
education. There was also some hesitation at the idea of taking
away offers (e.g. courses of short duration, employment projects, etc.)

which may give those in the weakest group a useful preparation for joining the labour market.

Since the OECD review team visited Denmark the first steps had been taken towards solving these problems. In the first half of 1980 the Danish Parliament, the Folketing, decided that all young people in this age group unable to find work should be offered some form of education. Special measures would be taken in favour of young people who were not motivated to continue with some form of education when they left school. Among the many initiatives which were being taken in this connection two deserved special attention.

The first was the so-called youth guarantee. The youth guarantee aimed at giving all unemployed young people an offer of education or employment. The experiment was a conscious attempt to improve the co-ordination between education and labour market policy. The objectives were as follows:

- to target the measures more specifically towards the weakest groups of young persons;
- to make the measures more orientated towards the various types of education, and
- to co-ordinate and intensify vocational guidance, placement of young persons and the efforts to reach all groups.

Extensive follow-up measures had been planned to ensure a thorough evaluation of the experiment.

The other initiative concerned the schemes of financial assistance to young persons. In Denmark, as in other countries, various types of financial assistance to young people had been introduced. These schemes were the responsibility of the Ministries of Labour, of Education, and of Social Affairs, varied as regards benefit rates and eligibility criteria. Individual schemes may seem fair and justified but taken together they formed an intricate and complicated system. Moreover, the system provided little incentive to young people to engage in some form of education. A committee of government officials were presently examining all these schemes of financial support, with the objective of proposing a new coherent system which would make it more attractive to start on some form of education and relatively less attractive to be without employment.

Mr. Westergaard concluded that the Danish government believed a better co-ordination between the education and labour market policies was clearly needed. The youth guarantee was a central element in the initiatives which have been taken to improve this co-ordination.

Mrs. Williams also introduced the third question to the United States authorities: "Is encouraging young people to stay in, or return to, school and lengthening the amount of time they spend in full-time schooling the best response to dealing with the transition? Why is there so little provision for the industrial training of young people?"

Mr. Bert Carp, Deputy Assistant to the President for Domestic Affairs and Policy, underlined that both anecdotal and research evidence showed that a high school diploma in the United States was essential for achieving success in the workplace. Graduation from high school conferred labour market benefits on youth in terms of earnings, occupational status and employability. These findings had been thoroughly tested as part of the review undertaken by Vice-President Mondale's task force on youth unemployment. Most importantly, employers had reported that what they looked for in potential entry-level employees was the ability to read, write and do basic arithmetic as well as the belief that these young people would show up for work. American employers regarded the underlying credential which provided proof of these skills as being a high school graduation certificate. Accordingly, a central platform of the United States' policy was to make young people competitive with other labour force groups by helping them to achieve a high school diploma or its equivalent.

The Youth Incentive Entitlement Pilot Projects appeared to be successful in meeting this policy goal. This programme guaranteed young people aged 16-19 from low income families who lived in certain low income areas part-time jobs in the school year and a full-time job during their summer vacation which were paid at federal minimum wages. To qualify for these jobs the young people were required to remain in, or return to, school. The results of evaluations of these programmes had shown that the dropout rate in schools in these areas had decreased dramatically. Also this programme had significantly increased the rate of school enrolments for those young people who had previously dropped out of school: more than 36 per cent of former school dropouts returned to school, a figure some 62 per cent higher than the national average. Mr. Carp recognised that the relationship between education and work in the United States was an area of policy in need of improvement and placed special emphasis on the need to expand work experience provision for the most disadvantaged.

As part of recent youth employment legislation, Private Industry Councils had been established (with a budget of some $400 million) which would bring together industrialists, trade unionists and educationalists in order to gear manpower programmes to the future employment demands of specific local labour markets and also to encourage experimentation and innovation in the school curriculum with regard to the world of work. However, he emphasized that most employers still regarded specific skill training for entry-level jobs as being the responsibility of employers and not of public education authorities.

Theme II

YOUTH'S DISPROPORTIONATE SHARE OF UNEMPLOYMENT

Mrs. Williams introduced the first question to the German authorities: "How far do certain once-and-for-all factors, e.g. the emigration of foreign workers, lower rates of female participation, reduction in working hours and improved holiday provisions, give a false impression of the underlying development of employment and unemployment in Germany? What are the prospects for the next few years, given the coming of new technologies and demographic movements?"

The German Delegation agreed that the reduction in the number of foreign workers, the relatively low labour force participation of women and the reduction in working hours had produced an important reduction in labour supply. They disagreed, however, with the suggestion that these factors may have led to an overly-optimistic appreciation of the employment situation in Germany.

The reduction in the number of foreign workers had been achieved by halting immigration after 1973 as well as through the voluntary repatriation of foreign workers to their home countries. However, since 1978, as a result of the entry of young second generation immigrants onto the labour market, the total number of foreign workers had started to increase and was expected to increase further during the coming years.

While female participation was lower than in some other OECD countries, the authorities did not believe that any significant increases above recent trends were to be expected in coming years.

The reduction of working hours had not had a major effect on the labour market. This had been facilitated through collective agreements.

Turning to the second part of the examiners' question, the German Delegation expected that technical innovation would develop at approximately the same speed and in the same direction as in recent years. Eventual changes in the economic structure, caused through technological change, were not expected to lead to major employment dislocations. The potential for the decentralisation of production and administration brought about by micro-electronics could have a positive impact on employment. The development of energy resources and investment in energy conservation were also expected to generate employment.

Largely as a consequence of the world-wide economic recession, Germany expected to face increasing unemployment in the near future.

In addition, up to 1985, 80,000 young Germans and 50,000 young
foreigners would enter the labour market (including the dual system)
every year. However, they were confident that economic and employment policies, as well as educational policies would be able to cope
with these increases in the youth labour force. After 1985 the
situation would rapidly improve. Large enterprises were already increasing their training efforts in view of an eventual shortage of
trainees and qualified workers after 1985.

The federal government therefore did not expect that youth unemployment would increase more than total unemployment. On the contrary, the major burden of increasing unemployment was expected to
fall on older workers, workers with health problems and the unqualified.

Professor Scharpf then introduced the second question to the
United States authorities: "Why does the United States have disproportionately high levels of unemployment for young people under
24 years of age given the very substantial net job creation which
they have recorded in recent years? How do the United States authorities intend to involve the private sector in CETA activities and how
could these be more orientated to private sector demand for labour?"

Professor Scharpf supplemented this question by comparing the
recent employment records of Germany and the United States. Employment in the Federal Republic had remained relatively stable whereas
youth unemployment had almost disappeared. In the United States
employment had increased very rapidly: between 1975 and 1979 over
12 million new jobs had been created. In spite of all this job
creation the fight against youth unemployment was relatively unsuccessful. This raised major questions such as: "Where have the new
jobs been created? What persons have profited?" etc. Professor
Scharpf suggested that, given the relative lack of competitiveness
of young people in the labour market, vocational training directed
towards private sector employment openings might be the only decisive
way to cope with the disproportionately high level of youth unemployment in the United States.

Mr. Carp, for the United States Delegation, underlined that in
the previous four years (1976-1980) a net job creation of 7 million
full-time jobs had been achieved despite the recent recession. This
was unprecedented both as an absolute and a percentage increase.
Most of these jobs had, however, been filled by middle-aged women
returning to the labour market; for example in 1979 two-thirds of
all new jobs created had been taken by women returning to employment.
This was something which the Administration regarded as a healthy
phenemenon, but it further complicated the youth employment problem
especially for the disadvantaged groups and for children who lived
in economically depressed areas.

Undoubtedly racial discrimination was an important factor in the explanation of why young people had not benefited more from the growth in employment. Further there were young people who lacked educational credentials and certificates. Their disadvantage was compounded by the fact that they lived in distressed inner city areas. The problem of youth unemployment was however not generic, but limited to certain disadvantaged groups and to a lesser extent to young women. Minority youth were at the heart of the youth unemployment question and therefore federal efforts had been directed towards this group. Their disadvantage in the labour market was a lack of basic skills, not a lack of specific vocational skills. The United States did not believe that employers could be convinced by public efforts to give specific vocational skills to young people. However, as he had previously mentioned, private sector initiatives were taking place at the local level to involve employers with labour and local government interests in order to improve the transition into the labour market through work experience in schools, innovation in the curriculum and a stronger employment focus in CETA programmes.

Professor Leroy then introduced the third question to the Danish authorities: "Does a guaranteed minimum wage for workers over 18 years of age, reinforced by employment protection, compound the labour market problems of less qualified young workers, or strengthen the segmentation? Do the special youth employment policies reduce their unemployment?"

Mr. Auken, Minister of Labour, who was now leading the Danish Delegation, replied that the issue raised by the examiners was one currently under very intensive discussion in Denmark. In its report the review team highlighted the fact that the rate of registered unemployment among young persons of more than 18 years of age was much higher than that of the group below the age of 18, both in relative and absolute terms. Several factors were responsible for this age differential. First there had been a steady increase in recent years in the proportion of young people between the ages of 15 and 17 who remained in the schooling system; this had resulted in a fall in the number of young job-seekers in this age group. Thus, relatively more young persons joined the labour market after the age of 18 years. Another factor which undoubtedly contributed to this age differential in unemployment rates was the existence of the guaranteed minimum wage for workers over 18 years of age. This guaranteed minimum wage was rather high compared with the average wage for young persons under the age of 18, which was only about 55 per cent of the guaranteed wage for "adult" workers.

A third explanation was the apparent development in Denmark of a so-called secondary labour market for very young persons with poorly-paid jobs of short duration and with very limited future prospects. Such dead-end jobs tended to attract early school-leavers

with a weak educational background who sometimes found it difficult
to meet the necessary productivity requirements which were demanded
of them when they received the guaranteed minimum wage. In Denmark
wages paid to adult workers and, thus, the amount of the guaranteed
minimum wage at the age of 18 were matters dealt with by collective
agreements entered into by the social partners.

Originally this age limit was laid down on the basis of the
assumption that young workers would have acquired sufficient work
experience by the age of 18 to entitle them to "adult wages". As
more and more young people entered the labour market at a more advanced age, it had become increasingly difficult to use age as an
indicator of work experience. One proposal which had been suggested
was to introduce a service-related wage which would be adjusted - not
on the basis of age but on the basis of actual work experience.
However, there were many practical difficulties in calculating the
service of individual workers. The examiners suggested a solution
of introducing a gradual adjustment of the wage over a longer period
of, say two or three years, so that the full guaranteed minimum wage
would not be payable until the age of 21 years, which might solve
part of the problem. However, there was a risk that this solution
would just concentrate unemployment even more on the oldest group of
young people, thus creating three groups: the very young under the
age of 18 with a relatively low rate of unemployment, those between
18 and 20 years with a slightly higher rate of unemployment (but
lower than with the present age limit for entitlement to the guaranteed minimum wage), and those between 20 and 24 years with a very
high rate of unemployment (and higher than with the present 18-year-
old guaranteed minimum wage limit).

Although the guaranteed minimum wage was not the sole factor in
explaining the steep increase in unemployment at the age of 18, it
did play a major part. However, the Danish government believed that
this was a matter which should be dealt with by the social partners
alone and that any changes depended on agreement between them.

In an attempt to reduce that part of the youth unemployment attributable to the guaranteed minimum wage, a special scheme of subsidies to private firms which hire young people who had been unemployed for at least three months had been introduced. The subsidy
could amount to almost one-third of the wage during the first six
months of employment. However, very few employers had made use of
this scheme. This suggested that the guaranteed minimum wage was not
the only factor which made employers reluctant to have young unemployed persons over 18 years old. However, several institutional
factors of the wage subsidy scheme had hindered many employers from
using this scheme.

Theme III

THE SPECIAL SOCIAL AND ECONOMIC PROBLEMS
OF YOUNG WOMEN, ETHNIC MINORITIES
AND SECOND GENERATION MIGRANTS

Professor Scharpf introduced the first question to the United
States authorities: "With unemployment rates in inner cities so
alarmingly high, especially for ethnic minorities, why does it appear
that CETA programmes are not effectively reaching these groups? In
particular do the United States authorities see their renewed emphasis
on categorical appropriations and programmes managed centrally from
Washington as a response to this problem, and if so, it is a successful approach?"

Professor Scharpf followed up this question by underlining the
problem of structural unemployment in the United States. In particular, he asked whether the institutional structure of CETA was not
biased towards measures for the easiest to be reached and therefore
bound to fail to reach the most difficult groups in the labour market.

Professor Levitan agreed with these latter observations and
asked whether the policy efforts should not go even further back to
the family in order to tackle the underlying cause of the problem.

Mr. Carp, for the United States Delegation, stated that the
dilemma posed by Professor Scharpf was one inherent in all areas of
domestic policy undertaken by the federal authorities in the United
States. This was because central government was considerably less
powerful than in most European countries. In co-ordinating youth
employment policies one had to bear in mind the many units of government who shared the responsibility; county and state governments,
school board districts, the federal government and in some cases state
college systems or community college systems. On top of this there
were the private not-for-profit organisations formed especially to
run youth employment programmes. In consequence at the federal level
it was necessary to take a somewhat pragmatic view. Historically the
CETA system had been run on a basis of "dynamic tensions" between
federal and other levels of government. When the local or state
authorities failed to maintain a minimum level of provision there was
an increase in federal regulations and in the categorical nature of
federal funding. Where federal regulation and categorisation con-
strained programme goals, it was somewhat lessened.

Given the size of the CETA budget it would not be possible in
the United States to operate this programme solely at a federal level.

The size of the bureaucracy required would not be tolerated by the electorate. Further, the CETA target population was some 4 million young people in need and their very diverse problems required a localised diagnosis. The thrust of a recent federal initiative had been to concentrate additional manpower expenditures under CETA on young people rather than on other groups in the labour market.

Similarly, within existing programmes the concentration on youth had been focused on disadvantaged groups within this population although the extent to which targeting could be precisely directed towards the most disadvantaged was a question of political power as well as one of policy desirability.

He could only but agree with Professor Levitan that the role of the family was a crucial influence in determining the nature and extent of problems experienced by the most disadvantaged group. However, federal ability to intervene in the family was limited. The federal government had preferred to extend its efforts of compensatory education under the Head Start Programme and the Youth Incentive Entitlement Pilot Projects. He regarded this as an important step forward and he hoped that a consistent policy in this direction would produce marked improvements in the employment and income histories of young people so helped.

Mrs. Williams then introduced the second question to the Danish authorities: "Why are the rate and average duration of unemployment for young women in Denmark so much worse than that for young men? Do the training and education systems tend to reinforce rather than reduce the problem?"

Mrs. Williams added that, in her judgement, Denmark had gone a long way in introducing equal pay but was still far from providing equal opportunities.

Minister Auken replied that activity rates in the 15-24 age group have been falling until recently; during the last few years this fall appeared to have stabilised possibly because many young people were taking part-time jobs as well as continuing with their studies. Further, there had also been some increase in the number of apprenticeships and training places. For 15-19-year-olds the trend in activity rates were identical for males and females. However, for the 20-24-year-olds, female activity rates had increased sharply over the last decade and in the present recession this group faced considerable problems, whereas the male activity rate declined for many years up to 1975 but since then had increased slightly.

Growth of the female labour force over the past few years was attributable not so much to an increase in the number of women entering the labour market, but rather reflected a fall in the numbers leaving the labour market – compared with 1972-73 the number of women leaving the labour force had fallen by one-third in 1977-78.

251

This new pattern of stronger female attachment to the labour force produced an increase in the supply of female labour and, thus, keener competition on the female labour market. Most of the growth in female employment had occurred in the public sector, especially in part-time jobs. The manufacturing sector had experienced the most marked fall in the level of female employment; this factor clearly contributed towards the labour market problems that young women were currently experiencing.

Several factors affected the unemployment level of young men and women with varying intensity. Segregation in the labour market between males and females was only slowly being eroded. Part of cyclical unemployment occurred in sectors with the lowest wages which were at the same time traditionally dominated by females. Contrary to male employment, female employment was influenced to a very limited extent by seasonal fluctuations. Thus, at certain periods of the year there was a large supply of jobs for men and many men obtained seasonal employment, whereas women tended more easily to end up as long-term unemployed.

Turning to the second part of the question, Mr. Auken drew attention to the fact that youth unemployment was increasingly concentrated among those with no vocational training. Although young women as a rule had a higher level of general education, there were between 50 and 100 per cent more women than men without any form of vocational training. There were relatively fewer training places available within the traditionally female occupations than in occupations traditionally attracting men. The development of what might be described as typical "female" types of education and training had been concentrated on the basic year of the commercial and clerical course offered within the context of the general basic vocational education. However, this development had not been followed up by a similar increase in the number of practical training places, so that many of those who started on the basic vocational education courses were prevented from obtaining the practical experience which was necessary in order to complete the course.

The system of financial support or remuneration in connection with most schemes of education and training and the various forms of social assistance were on the whole not designed to suit the needs of female students with family responsibilities. There had not as yet been major co-ordinated measures to try to get more women into the labour market, and it was only in connection with the measures to deal with youth unemployment that women who had chosen non-traditional types of education or employment had benefited from special measures to support them. Efforts in this field would be intensified in the future.

Professor Levitan then introduced the third question to the German authorities: "German policy has not yet come to grips with the education, training or employment of second generation migrants. What has to be done if they are to have a fair share of economic and educational opportunities? Similarly, what steps have been taken to offer women equal opportunities in training and placement?"

He followed up the question by expressing the opinion that without major efforts to integrate foreign workers, the German authorities might soon face the same kind of problems of minority groups which were typical in his own country, the United States. The American experience clearly showed that the social costs of discrimination were very high and that every effort should be made to achieve a timely integration of these workers into the social fabric.

Replying, the German Delegation stated that the population of young foreigners under 18 years of age was around 1.2 million, of which some 552,000 were enrolled in general education. Approximately 50,000 joined the labour force each year. Problems of integration arose not only because of their numbers but also because they were a heterogeneous population coming from different countries, with varying levels of education, duration of residence in the Federal Republic, and knowledge of the German language.

The federal and Laender governments had jointly developed multiple initiatives in order to help the educational and occupational integration of these children. Important decisions in this respect were taken in 1980. Special efforts were now made in schools to provide small classes, training of specialist teachers and intensive teaching of the German language. Many experiments were jointly financed by the federal and Laender governments in order to improve the efficiency of these measures.

The federal government was particularly involved in improving the access of young foreigners to vocational training and employment. Special one-year preparatory courses had been developed in order to prepare young foreigners for training in the dual system. For those young people who could not obtain training in the dual system the Federal Ministry of Education and Science had, in 1980, started a special programme, offering general and vocational training to prepare participants for training in recognised training enterprises.

The German Delegation recognised that the problems of young women in training and the labour market were more serious than those of young men. More than 50 per cent of all available training places were effectively only open to men. The federal government had made great efforts to ensure equal access to training in craft and technical occupations. One important experiment providing such training for young women already showed encouraging results. Legislation which excluded women from certain activities was being re-examined and 30 regulations had already been abolished.

Many of the Laender governments now paid subsidies to training enterprises which accepted young women for training in certain occupations. These efforts were supported through intensive counselling and complemented by efforts to educate the general public about these questions.

In concluding the discussion on the three country reviews, the President, Mr. Gene Fitzgerald, the Irish Minister of Labour and the Public Service, said that while the causes of youth employment problems were many, the major one was the recent low rate of economic growth experienced by most of our countries.

OECD economies were experiencing a second major recession triggered by a sharp rise in oil prices and the outlook for employment over the foreseeable future was not good. Previous experience indicated that the increase in unemployment would be borne disproportionately by young people, and rates of youth unemployment of up to 16 per cent by 1982 had been quoted.

With regard to the selective approaches and measures adopted to deal with the particular problems of youth and the labour market, he commended the reports of the first three reviews of Denmark, Germany and the United States as proof of the value of international co-operation and consultation. He complimented the examining teams on the thoroughness of their work and on the excellence of their report.

He pointed to a number of important conclusions from the meeting:

   i) the importance of having effective structures and programmes to manage the transition from school to work;
  ii) the social problem posed by youth unemployment, and in particular the need to come to grips with the problems of the most disadvantaged groups; and
 iii) the need to look afresh for new policy ideas and initiatives which might help in resolving the problems of youth in the labour market.

On the first of these points it seemed clear that action was needed on the education front. This would require at a minimum that the perspective of the world of work and the post-school world be integrated into compulsory schooling. Renewed emphasis on work experience and careers education were important as were measures to broaden and increase the awareness of teachers in schools. Measures to bring about changes in the content of, and approach to, education also required structural and institutional changes, including effective co-operation between manpower and education authorities at all levels.

Unemployment was a social and personal tragedy, especially for the most disadvantaged young people. This was perhaps the most serious, and most difficult, problem to solve. It seemed that no Member country had yet fully come to grips with the vicious cycle of social disadvantage, followed by educational failure compounded by labour market failure. This problem was wider than a question of manpower policy and required action on both social and educational policy fronts as well.

Mr. Fitzgerald underlined the need to sustain and perhaps extend selective measures to help young people. But he also stressed the need to look for new measures which might produce better results than those tried to date. The broad range of measures indicated by the three country reviews showed that there was room for much experimentation, for improvement and for a pooling of collective experiences. One area that needed attention was how to strengthen the instincts of young people for self-help, entrepreneurial activities and interest in neighbourhood problems.

In concluding, he said that, given the worsening employment situation, it was timely that the meeting had taken place. It had provided an opportunity for drawing to the attention of Ministers responsible for economic policy and government the potential harm of persistent high levels of youth unemployment.

OECD SALES AGENTS
DÉPOSITAIRES DES PUBLICATIONS DE L'OCDE

ARGENTINA – ARGENTINE
Carlos Hirsch S.R.L., Florida 165, 4° Piso (Galería Guemes)
1333 BUENOS AIRES, Tel. 33.1787.2391 y 30.7122

AUSTRALIA – AUSTRALIE
Australia and New Zealand Book Company Pty, Ltd.,
10 Aquatic Drive, Frenchs Forest, N.S.W. 2086
P.O. Box 459, BROOKVALE, N.S.W. 2100

AUSTRIA – AUTRICHE
OECD Publications and Information Center
4 Simrockstrasse 5300 BONN. Tel. (0228) 21.60.45
Local Agent/Agent local :
Gerold and Co., Graben 31, WIEN 1. Tel. 52.22.35

BELGIUM – BELGIQUE
LCLS
35, avenue de Stalingrad, 1000 BRUXELLES. Tel. 02.512.89.74

BRAZIL – BRÉSIL
Mestre Jou S.A., Rua Guaipa 518,
Caixa Postal 24090, 05089 SAO PAULO 10. Tel. 261.1920
Rua Senador Dantas 19 s/205-6, RIO DE JANEIRO GB.
Tel. 232.07.32

CANADA
Renouf Publishing Company Limited,
2182 St. Catherine Street West,
MONTRÉAL, Quebec H3H 1M7. Tel. (514)937.3519
522 West Hasting,
VANCOUVER, B.C. V6B 1L6. Tel. (604) 687.3320

DENMARK – DANEMARK
Munksgaard Export and Subscription Service
35, Nørre Søgade
DK 1370 KØBENHAVN K. Tel. +45.1.12.85.70

FINLAND – FINLANDE
Akateeminen Kirjakauppa
Keskuskatu 1, 00100 HELSINKI 10. Tel. 65.11.22

FRANCE
Bureau des Publications de l'OCDE,
2 rue André-Pascal, 75775 PARIS CEDEX 16. Tel. (1) 524.81.67
Principal correspondant :
13602 AIX-EN-PROVENCE : Librairie de l'Université.
Tel. 26.18.08

GERMANY – ALLEMAGNE
OECD Publications and Information Center
4 Simrockstrasse 5300 BONN Tel. (0228) 21.60.45

GREECE – GRÈCE
Librairie Kauffmann, 28 rue du Stade,
ATHÈNES 132. Tel. 322.21.60

HONG-KONG
Government Information Services,
Sales and Publications Office, Baskerville House, 2nd floor,
13 Duddell Street, Central. Tel. 5.214375

ICELAND – ISLANDE
Snaebjörn Jönsson and Co., h.f.,
Hafnarstraeti 4 and 9, P.O.B. 1131, REYKJAVIK.
Tel. 13133/14281/11936

INDIA – INDE
Oxford Book and Stationery Co. :
NEW DELHI, Scindia House. Tel. 45896
CALCUTTA, 17 Park Street. Tel. 240832

INDONESIA – INDONÉSIE
PDIN-LIPI, P.O. Box 3065/JKT., JAKARTA, Tel. 583467

IRELAND – IRLANDE
TDC Publishers – Library Suppliers
12 North Frederick Street, DUBLIN 1 Tel. 744835-749677

ITALY – ITALIE
Libreria Commissionaria Sansoni :
Via Lamarmora 45, 50121 FIRENZE. Tel. 579751
Via Bartolini 29, 20155 MILANO. Tel. 365083
Sub-depositari :
Editrice e Libreria Herder,
Piazza Montecitorio 120, 00 186 ROMA. Tel. 6794628
Libreria Hoepli, Via Hoepli 5, 20121 MILANO. Tel. 865446
Libreria Lattes, Via Garibaldi 3, 10122 TORINO. Tel. 519274
La diffusione delle edizioni OCSE è inoltre assicurata dalle migliori
librerie nelle città più importanti.

JAPAN – JAPON
OECD Publications and Information Center,
Landic Akasaka Bldg., 2-3-4 Akasaka,
Minato-ku, TOKYO 107 Tel. 586.2016

KOREA – CORÉE
Pan Korea Book Corporation,
P.O. Box n° 101 Kwangwhamun, SÉOUL. Tel. 72.7369

LEBANON – LIBAN
Documenta Scientifica/Redico,
Edison Building, Bliss Street, P.O. Box 5641, BEIRUT.
Tel. 354429 – 344425

MALAYSIA – MALAISIE
and/et SINGAPORE - SINGAPOUR
University of Malaysia Co-operative Bookshop Ltd.
P.O. Box 1127, Jalan Pantai Baru
KUALA LUMPUR. Tel. 51425, 54058, 54361

THE NETHERLANDS – PAYS-BAS
Staatsuitgeverij
Verzendboekhandel Chr. Plantijnnstraat
S-GRAVENAGE. Tel. nr. 070.789911
Voor bestellingen: Tel. 070.789208

NEW ZEALAND – NOUVELLE-ZÉLANDE
Publications Section,
Government Printing Office,
WELLINGTON: Walter Street. Tel. 847.679
Mulgrave Street, Private Bag. Tel. 737.320
World Trade Building, Cubacade, Cuba Street. Tel. 849.572
AUCKLAND: Hannaford Burton Building,
Rutland Street, Private Bag. Tel. 32.919
CHRISTCHURCH: 159 Hereford Street, Private Bag. Tel. 797.142
HAMILTON: Alexandra Street, P.O. Box 857. Tel. 80.103
DUNEDIN: T & G Building, Princes Street, P.O. Box 1104.
Tel. 778.294

NORWAY – NORVÈGE
J.G. TANUM A/S Karl Johansgate 43
P.O. Box 1177 Sentrum OSLO 1. Tel. (02) 80.12.60

PAKISTAN
Mirza Book Agency, 65 Shahrah Quaid-E-Azam, LAHORE 3.
Tel. 66839

PHILIPPINES
National Book Store, Inc.
Library Services Division, P.O. Box 1934, MANILA.
Tel. Nos. 49.43.06 to 09, 40.53.45, 49.45.12

PORTUGAL
Livraria Portugal, Rua do Carmo 70-74,
1117 LISBOA CODEX. Tel. 360582/3

SPAIN – ESPAGNE
Mundi-Prensa Libros, S.A.
Castello 37, Apartado 1223, MADRID-1. Tel. 275.46.55
Libreria Bastinos, Pelayo 52, BARCELONA 1. Tel. 222.06.00

SWEDEN – SUÈDE
AB CE Fritzes Kungl Hovbokhandel,
Box 16 356, S 103 27 STH, Regeringsgatan 12,
DS STOCKHOLM. Tel. 08/23.89.00

SWITZERLAND – SUISSE
OECD Publications and Information Center
4 Simrockstrasse 5300 BONN. Tel. (0228) 21.60.45
Local Agents/Agents locaux
Librairie Payot, 6 rue Grenus, 1211 GENÈVE 11. Tel. 022.31.89.50
Freihofer A.G., Weinbergstr. 109, CH-8006 ZÜRICH.
Tel. 01.3634282

TAIWAN – FORMOSE
National Book Company,
84-5 Sing Sung South Rd, Sec. 3, TAIPEI 107. Tel. 321.0698

THAILAND – THAILANDE
Suksit Siam Co., Ltd., 1715 Rama IV Rd,
Samyan, BANGKOK 5. Tel. 2511630

UNITED KINGDOM – ROYAUME-UNI
H.M. Stationery Office, P.O.B. 569,
LONDON SEI 9NH. Tel. 01.928.6977, Ext. 410 or
49 High Holborn, LONDON WC1V 6 HB (personal callers)
Branches at: EDINBURGH, BIRMINGHAM, BRISTOL,
MANCHESTER, CARDIFF, BELFAST.

UNITED STATES OF AMERICA – ÉTATS-UNIS
OECD Publications and Information Center, Suite 1207,
1750 Pennsylvania Ave., N.W. WASHINGTON D.C.20006.
Tel. (202) 724.1857

VENEZUELA
Libreria del Este, Avda. F. Miranda 52, Edificio Galipan,
CARACAS 106. Tel. 32.23.01/33.26.04/33.24.73

YUGOSLAVIA – YOUGOSLAVIE
Jugoslovenska Knjiga, Terazije 27, P.O.B. 36, BEOGRAD.
Tel. 621.992

Les commandes provenant de pays où l'OCDE n'a pas encore désigné de dépositaire peuvent être adressées à :
OCDE, Bureau des Publications, 2, rue André-Pascal, 75775 PARIS CEDEX 16.

Orders and inquiries from countries where sales agents have not yet been appointed may be sent to:
OECD, Publications Office, 2 rue André-Pascal, 75775 PARIS CEDEX 16.

OECD PUBLICATIONS, 2, rue André-Pascal, 75775 PARIS CEDEX 16 - No. 41931 1981
PRINTED IN FRANCE
1500/SH (81 81 02 1) ISBN 92-64-12240-0